NEW STUDIES IN BIBLICAL THEOLOGY 60

THE ROYAL PRIEST

NEW STUDIES IN BIBLICAL THEOLOGY 60

Series editor: D. A. Carson

THE ROYAL PRIEST

Psalm 110 in biblical theology

Matthew H. Emadi

APOLLOS

Academic
An imprint of InterVarsity Press
Downers Grove, Illinois

APOLLOS (an imprint of Inter-Varsity Press, England)
36 Causton Street, London SW1P 4ST, England
Website: www.ivpbooks.com
Email: ivp@ivpbooks.com

InterVarsity Press, USA
P.O. Box 1400, Downers Grove, IL 60515, USA
Website: www.ivpress.com
Email: email@ivpress.com

Inter-Varsity Press, England, publishes Christian books that are true to the Bible and that
communicate the gospel, develop discipleship and strengthen the church for its mission in the world.

IVP originated within the Inter-Varsity Fellowship, now the Universities and Colleges Christian
Fellowship, a student movement connecting Christian Unions in universities and colleges
throughout Great Britain, and a member movement of the International Fellowship of Evangelical
Students. That historic association is maintained, and all senior IVP staff and committee members
subscribe to the UCCF Basis of Faith. Website: www.uccf.org.uk.

InterVarsity Press®, USA, is the book-publishing division of InterVarsity Christian Fellowship/USA®
and a member movement of the International Fellowship of Evangelical Students.
Website: www.intervarsity.org.

Unless otherwise noted, Scripture quotations are the author's own translation.

Scripture quotations marked ESV are from the ESV Bible (The Holy Bible, English Standard Version,
Anglicized Edition), copyright © 2001 by Crossway, a publishing ministry of Good News Publishers.
Used by permission. All rights reserved.

First published 2022

Set in 10/13.25pt Minion Pro and Gill Sans Nova
Typeset in Great Britain by CRB Associates, Potterhanworth, Lincolnshire
Printed and bound in Great Britain by Ashford Colour Press Ltd, Gosport, Hampshire

Printed on paper from sustainable sources.

UK ISBN: 978-1-78974-414-9 (print)
UK ISBN: 978-1-78974-415-6 (digital)

US ISBN: 978-1-5140-0739-6 (print)
US ISBN: 978-1-5140-0740-2 (digital)

British Library Cataloguing-in-Publication Data
A catalogue record for this book is available from the British Library.

Library of Congress Cataloging-in-Publication Data
A catalog record for this book is available from the Library of Congress.

To my wife, Brittany, who is wonderfully patient,
encouraging, faithful and loving

To our children, Elijah, Jeremiah, Aliyah, Josiah, Judah and Isaiah,
may you be a kingdom and priests
to our God (Rev. 5:10)

Contents

Tables

Series preface

New Studies in Biblical Theology is a series of monographs that address key issues in the discipline of biblical theology. Contributions to the series focus on one or more of three areas: (1) the nature and status of biblical theology, including its relations with other disciplines (e.g. historical theology, exegesis, systematic theology, historical criticism, narrative theology); (2) the articulation and exposition of the structure of thought of a particular biblical writer or corpus; and (3) the delineation of a biblical theme across all or part of the biblical corpora.

Above all, these monographs are creative attempts to help thinking Christians understand their Bibles better. The series aims simultaneously to instruct and to edify, to interact with the current literature and to point the way ahead. In God's universe, mind and heart should not be divorced: in this series we will try not to separate what God has joined together. While the notes interact with the best of scholarly literature, the text is uncluttered with untransliterated Greek and Hebrew, and tries to avoid too much technical jargon. The volumes are written within the framework of confessional evangelicalism, but there is always an attempt at thoughtful engagement with the sweep of the relevant literature.

Depending on exactly how one counts the occurrences, Psalm 110 is the Old Testament chapter quoted or alluded to most frequently in the New Testament. More striking yet is the way in which it combines Davidic royalty and priestly service in one person. When King Saul attempted a similar gambit, it cost him his throne, his family and his life: the disjunction must be observed. Of course, one remembers that Melchizedek is both king and priest (Gen. 14), and Psalm 110 anticipates a messianic figure who embodies the same linkage. But why? And why do Psalm 110 and the royal Melchizedekian priesthood become so controlling in Hebrews? Is this merely a minority report, easily parked to one side of the road while we get on with more central themes? In this book, Matthew Emadi shows us a better way: Melchizedek may be named in only three biblical books, but he is part of a multifaceted biblical-theological structure that runs from Eden to the new covenant and its culmination in the supreme Priest-King. Dr Emadi's work will not only stimulate fresh levels of biblical-theological integration but will also enliven and enrich the sermons of pastors who plumb this book with the care it deserves.

D. A. Carson
Trinity Evangelical Divinity School

Author's preface

I am confident that the publication of this book is the Lord's gracious answer to the simple prayer of its author: 'Lord, may this book be of some usefulness and encouragement to your church.' I thank God for the strength he has given me to complete this project and for the opportunity in his providence to publish it.

This book is an edited version of the dissertation I completed in 2016 as a student at the Southern Baptist Theological Seminary (SBTS) in Louisville, Kentucky. My time at SBTS was a taste of heaven on earth. Studying the Bible and theology with world-class teachers was a gift of God's undeserved kindness. My professors Tom Schreiner, Brian Vickers, Steve Wellum, Peter Gentry and Jim Hamilton deserve a special word of appreciation. Tom Schreiner is a model of academic excellence, pastoral wisdom and genuine humility. I am thankful for his influence and continual guidance. Brian Vickers first taught me hermeneutics and then modelled it in his preaching when we preached through Mark's Gospel together to a handful of people each week. Dr Vickers read every page of the original manuscript and offered insightful and constructive feedback.

I tried to take every course Steve Wellum offered because I wanted to think about theology like him. Dr Wellum's covenantal approach to Scripture's metanarrative gave me a framework for building the argument of this book. Peter Gentry inspired in me a love for the biblical languages. Dr Gentry's classes pushed me beyond my self-imposed limitations and gave me the tools for a lifelong study of the Bible. He is a giant among scholars and a master teacher. Dr Gentry's feedback on this project sharpened the exegesis and prompted new lines of argumentation.

Jim Hamilton is a gifted scholar, a faithful pastor, a mentor and a friend. Dr Hamilton's passion for the Bible is contagious. Sitting under his teaching and preaching made me want to know the Bible and the God of the Bible more deeply. Dr Hamilton helped me with this project every step of the way. He patiently worked through my questions; he took a genuine interest in my work; and he encouraged me when I needed it most. I am thankful for his continuing friendship.

Don Carson, Tom Creedy and Mollie Barker also deserve my gratitude. Dr Carson's kind words of appreciation for my work make me want to labour on in writing books and articles in the service of Christ's church. Thank you, Dr Carson, for the opportunity to publish in NSBT – my favourite biblical theology series. Tom Creedy has been a delight to work with. I am thankful for his editorial expertise and perceptive suggestions. Mollie Barker meticulously edited this manuscript, improving its clarity and saving me from numerous blunders. I am thankful for her skilful attention to detail.

Many friends had a hand in supporting this project. Bryan Magaña is a lifelong friend. He used his writing expertise to carefully read every sentence of my first draft. He sharpened, clarified and improved the style and structure of this project. My friends Josh Philpot, Dave Schrock, Brock Bittner, Bobby Jamieson and Matthew Albanese enriched my writing and my thinking. Josh Philpot lent his expertise to the chapter on intertestamental literature. Dave Schrock has thought about priesthood more than most. He took an interest in my work, pointed me to sources, and offered exegetical and theological insights from his vast study on the topic. Brock Bittner spent hours reading the manuscript to transliterate the Greek and Hebrew script. Bobby Jamieson helped me think about the letter to the Hebrews in the early stages of my work. He also carefully read multiple drafts of my chapter on Hebrews, offering swift feedback and needed encouragement. Matthew Albanese (my brother-in-law) has spent innumerable hours discussing biblical theology with me. His thinking has influenced my own work. I must also thank Laura Strickland. She went above and beyond the call of duty to track down sources at the SBTS library when I was scrambling to get final edits done.

I began this manuscript while serving as a member and elder of New Heights Baptist Church (now Antioch Church) in Louisville. I am grateful to Pastor Cody McNutt for investing in me and giving a young, inexperienced seminarian an opportunity to serve alongside him. I finished the writing process during my first eighteen months as the senior pastor of Crossroads Church in Sandy, Utah. The members of Crossroads Church make pastoring a joy and a delight.

My family deserves more words of appreciation than I can ever write. The impact my parents have had on my life is simply incalculable. Their sincere faith and love for Christ and his people made me want to be a

Christian. My father, Saeed Emadi, is a man of courage, conviction, sacrifice and integrity. He is the Abraham of the Emadi family, a servant of Christ's church, and fiercely and lovingly devoted to his family. My mother, Theresa Emadi, is full of wisdom and a model of godliness and Christian maturity. Her love for the Bible is second to none. She exudes generosity, kindness and patience in exemplary ways. I never once doubted the truthfulness of Scripture as a kid because my mom and dad sincerely loved God and his Word. This book would not have been possible without their investment in my life. I also want to thank both of my parents, especially my mother, for the numerous hours they spent compiling information for the indexes.

My brothers, Sam and Michael, generously read my work and dialogued at length about it. I am forever thankful for the opportunity to go to seminary with my brother Sam. He far outdid me in every way! His keen theological mind and ability to comprehend difficult topics enriched my theological education and influenced my life in countless ways. I hope to write as well as him some day. My older brother, Michael Emadi, is my go-to source for my linguistic and exegetical questions. He brought his expertise to bear on this work and steered my thinking in a different direction on multiple occasions. I am grateful for Michael and Sam, for their steadfastness, for their families and for their example.

My wife's parents, Dwight and Sheryl Franzen, served my family and me during the writing process. Thank you, Dwight and Sheryl, for letting us retreat to the Franzen farm to find refreshment. Your generosity towards us is inspiring.

What can I say to express my appreciation to my wonderful wife Brittany? She is my most precious gift. She loves our children tirelessly and sacrificially. She serves others quietly behind the scenes and desires not a fraction of the spotlight. Brittany, the best decision I ever made was marrying you! Thank you for spending your life on the things that really matter. Thank you for your support, sacrifice and prayer, which enabled me to finish this book. Your children call you blessed, and your husband praises you. You are a woman who fears the Lord.

To our children, Elijah, Jeremiah, Aliyah, Josiah, Judah and Isaiah, I love you more than life itself. The highlight of my day is not writing books; it's spending time with all of you. I wish I had a hundred lifetimes to be your father. I would spend each one of them doing the same things: driveway basketball, never-ending games of tag, epic wrestling matches, trampoline fun, reading stories, riding bikes, and anything else that is ultimately just an expression of my love for you. I hope that some day this book will encourage you to love Jesus more. Let's press on towards the heavenly city together.

Finally, what do I have that I did not receive from the hand of God? I thank God for the privilege of studying his Word and the opportunity to help others understand it a little better. I don't deserve any of the good gifts he has given me. Jesus Christ is my king and my great high priest. I pray that these pages will help others to glory in Christ and his great salvation.

Matthew Emadi

Abbreviations

1QapGen	*Genesis Apocryphon*
11QMelch	*11QMelchizedek*
AB	Anchor Bible
AnBib	Analecta biblica
ANE	ancient Near East(ern)
As. Mos.	*Assumption of Moses*
ATR	*Anglican Theological Review*
BBR	*Bulletin for Biblical Research*
BBRSup	Bulletin for Biblical Research, Supplements
BDB	Brown, F., S. R. Driver and C. A. Briggs, *A Hebrew and English Lexicon of the Old Testament*, Peabody: Hendrickson, 1996
BETL	Bibliotheca ephemeridum theologicarum lovaniensium
Bib	*Biblica*
BibInt	*Biblical Interpretation*
BJRL	*Bulletin of the John Rylands University Library*
BKAT	Biblischer Kommentar Altes Testament
BSac	*Bibliotheca sacra*
BZAW	Beihefte zur Zeitschrift für die alttestamentliche Wissenschaft
CTJ	*Calvin Theological Journal*
DBSJ	*Detroit Baptist Seminary Journal*
DOTP	*Dictionary of the Old Testament: Pentateuch*
EBC	Expositor's Bible Commentary
1 En.	*1 Enoch*
2 En.	*2 Enoch*
ESV	English Standard Version
ExpTim	*Expository Times*
JBL	*Journal of Biblical Literature*
JBQ	*Jewish Bible Quarterly*
JETS	*Journal of the Evangelical Theological Society*
JNSL	*Journal of Northwest Semitic Languages*

JSHJ	*Journal for the Study of the Historical Jesus*
JSJSup	Supplements to the Journal for the Study of Judaism
JSNT	*Journal for the Study of the New Testament*
JSNTSup	Journal for the Study of the New Testament: Supplement Series
JSOT	*Journal for the Study of the Old Testament*
JSOTSup	Journal for the Study of the Old Testament: Supplement Series
JSS	*Journal of Semitic Studies*
JTI	*Journal of Theological Interpretation*
JTISup	Journal of Theological Interpretation Supplements
JTS	*Journal of Theological Studies*
Jub.	*Jubilees*
LDS	Church of Jesus Christ of Latter-day Saints
LHBOTS	Library of Hebrew Bible/Old Testament Studies
LNTS	Library of New Testament Studies
LXX	Septuagint
MS	manuscript
MT	Masoretic Text
NAC	New American Commentary
NASB	New American Standard Bible
NDBT	*New Dictionary of Biblical Theology*, ed. T. D. Alexander, B. Rosner, D. A. Carson and G. Goldsworthy, Leicester: Inter-Varsity Press; Downers Grove: InterVarsity Press, 2000
NICNT	New International Commentary on the New Testament
NIDOTTE	*New International Dictionary of Old Testament Theology and Exegesis*, ed. W. VanGemeren, 5 vols., Grand Rapids: Zondervan, 1997
NIGTC	New International Greek Testament Commentary
NIV	New International Version
NIVAC	NIV Application Commentary
NovTSup	Novum Testamentum Supplements
NRSV	New Revised Standard Version
NSBT	New Studies in Biblical Theology
NT	New Testament
NTS	*New Testament Studies*
OBO	Orbis Biblicus et Orientalis

Abbreviations

OT	Old Testament
REB	Revised English Bible
ResQ	*Restoration Quarterly*
SBJT	*Southern Baptist Journal of Theology*
SBLSP	*Society of Biblical Literature Seminar Papers*
SBTS	Southern Baptist Theological Seminary
SJT	*Scottish Journal of Theology*
SNTSMS	Society for New Testament Studies Monograph Series
STDJ	Studies on the Texts of the Desert of Judah
T. Levi	*Testament of Levi*
T. Reub.	*Testament of Reuben*
TJ	*Trinity Journal*
TNTC	Tyndale New Testament Commentaries
TOTC	Tyndale Old Testament Commentaries
TynBul	*Tyndale Bulletin*
VT	*Vetus Testamentum*
WBC	Word Biblical Commentary
WTJ	*Westminster Theological Journal*
WUNT	Wissenschaftliche Untersuchungen zum Neuen Testament

1

Introduction

In a sermon on Psalm 110 titled 'Getting Excited about Melchizedek', D. A. Carson commented:

> Most of the controlling themes in the Bible do not resonate very well with the dominant secular culture of the West – and for that matter with many other cultures as well. Think through many of the controlling categories: Covenant, Priest, Sacrifice, Blood offering, Passover, Messiah, King, Day of Atonement, Year of Jubilee. I guarantee you that there are not a lot of people on the streets of Chicago asking, 'I wonder when the Year of Jubilee is coming.'[1]

As Carson explains, priesthood and kingship are among Scripture's many controlling themes that 'do not resonate' with Western culture. Priesthood is a strange notion to secular sensibilities. Moreover, kingship, particularly Scripture's notion of kingship, is mostly a foreign concept in a postmodern, anti-institutional, autonomy-loving society.

So what do we do with Melchizedek, a figure who is both a priest and a king? He remains a mystery to many students of the Bible. After all, his name appears only twice in the entire Old Testament. His emergence in Genesis 14 is significant enough to need the space of three whole verses to describe his contribution to redemptive history (Gen. 14:18–20)! His name never appears again in the Old Testament except in Psalm 110:4, which describes the messianic king as a priest 'after the order of Melchizedek'. Nevertheless, the Melchizedekian priesthood, not the Aaronic, is central to David's messianic hope and essential to the saving work of Christ.

---

[1] This quotation is taken from the published manuscript of Carson's sermon (Carson 2013: 146).

With such meagre time on the stage of the drama of redemption, how did Melchizedek rise to prominence in David's messianic expectation (Ps. 110:4)? Furthermore, what warrant did David have for combining the offices of kingship and priesthood in a single individual? From a historical standpoint, there is no evidence that any of Israel's kings also held the office of the priesthood. The Mosaic and Davidic covenants separated the offices of priesthood and kingship, not allowing the king and the priests to encroach upon each other's jurisdiction (2 Chr. 16:16–23). The union of these offices in Psalm 110 appears to be a novelty in the biblical record, leading some scholars to conclude that David received this information as a new special revelation from God.

Other scholars have tried to explain away the priestly role of the monarch in Psalm 110. For example, Gerleman's solution to the perceived dilemma was to assign Psalm 110 to the Maccabean period.[2] H. H. Rowley took a different approach, arguing that the psalm addressed two separate people: the king in verses 1–3 and the priest in verse 4.[3] Still others, such as F. L. Horton, claimed that the term 'priest' (*kōhēn*) in 110:4 referred to an administrative official.[4] Perhaps the confusion is best captured by A. H. Edelkoort's proposal that the poet's belief that the Messiah would also be a priest for ever (Ps. 110:4) was simply an enthusiastic mistake.[5]

Many modern explanations of Psalm 110 give us the impression that David's hope for a priestly messiah is an anomaly in the biblical record – one that defies any biblical-theological rationale. And yet, Carson contends, '[p]recisely because he is both king and priest, the figure Melchizedek turns out to be one of the most instructive figures in the Bible for helping us put our Bibles together'.[6] Overstatement? Is this sermonic hyperbole meant for rhetorical punch? Or, as this book will argue, is the union of priesthood and kingship in Melchizedek precisely the clue that uncovers the larger biblical-theological foundation on which Psalm 110 is built?

For now, the question remains: why has the messianic portrait of a royal priest in Psalm 110 proven so problematic in the history of

---

[2] Gerleman 1981.
[3] Rowley 1950.
[4] Horton 1976: 47–48.
[5] This observation from Edelkoort is taken from Paul 1987: 200. He cites Edelkoort 1941: 330–340.
[6] Carson 2013: 147.

interpretation? The answer, in part, relates to the confusion surrounding the concept of priesthood in modern biblical studies.

Priesthood in crisis

Crispin Fletcher-Louis says, 'Priesthood has been marginalized in modern biblical studies.'[7] Such marginalization may correspond, in Peter Leithart's words, to the 'severe beating' priests took in twentieth-century philosophy, sociology and theology.[8] For the modern age of Kantian rationalism, the cultic affairs of priestcraft were nothing more than an ancient fiction.[9] In a world of electric light and radios (still more, mobile phones and the internet), an office that claims access to the divine realm had to be the product of an unenlightened age or the attempt of power-hungry individuals using religious affairs to gain power in society. The modern period's disinterest in priesthood reflects, according to Fletcher-Louis, 'a deeply felt antipathy to anything that smacks of high church spirituality'.[10]

It is no surprise, then, that modern Old Testament studies has taken a history-of-religions approach to formulating a theology of Israel's priesthood. According to Fletcher-Louis, Old Testament scholarship has judged the descriptions of the priesthood (e.g. in Exodus–Numbers, Ezekiel, Joel, Zechariah 3 – 6, Malachi) as showing 'a lamentable decline in Israelite religion from the pure faith of the prophets and the Deuteronomist into a post-exilic obsession with cultic order and institutional religiosity'.[11] Julius Wellhausen's source-critical programme lifted 'priestly texts' (labelled as 'P') from their canonical context and laid them in the hands of post-exilic redactors in the business of producing pieces of political propaganda on behalf of power-hungry priestly sects.[12] As a result, the task of arriving at a coherent theology of the priesthood gave way to historical reconstructions of the cult in Israel's history. Hence Richard

---

7 Fletcher-Louis 2006: 156.
8 Leithart 1999: 3.
9 Ibid. 1–7.
10 Fletcher-Louis 2006: 156.
11 Ibid.
12 The hypothesis known as the JEDP theory is most often associated with Julius Wellhausen. The JEDP theory asserts that the Pentateuch is a compilation of four different sources. The 'Yahwist' source (J for 'Jehovah') uses the name Yahweh for God. The 'Elohist' source (E) refers to God as Elohim. The 'Deuteronomist' (D) would have been responsible for Deuteronomy (and possibly Joshua–Kings). The 'Priestly' source (P) is post-exilic and concerned with Israel's priesthood.

Nelson's criticism: 'Scholarly literature in this century [twentieth] has focused almost entirely on the problems of historical reconstruction. The theology of priesthood in the Bible has taken a backseat to its history.'[13] New Testament scholarship has suffered from the effects of modernist assumptions about the nature of Old Testament priesthood. Alex Cheung identifies the lack of reflection on Christ's priesthood in conservative circles as an 'irony of modern evangelical scholarship'.[14] Some scholars deny that the historical Jesus had any priestly self-consciousness. Commenting on the Gospels, Jürgen Becker writes, 'If anything is incontrovertible from the Jesus material, it is that there is not the slightest connection between Jesus and the theological self-understanding of the Jerusalem priesthood.'[15] What about Hebrews, where Psalm 110 and its Melchizedekian priesthood are central to the Christological argument? Eric Mason observed in 2008 that despite renewed interest in the epistle to the Hebrews, 'relatively little has been written in recent years about its key motif, Jesus as high priest, but this was not the case in previous decades'.[16]

Happily, biblical scholarship has experienced a resurgence in literary, theological and canonical readings of Scripture.[17] Andrew Malone's 2017 NSBT volume, *God's Mediators*, is worth highlighting as a recent attempt at a comprehensive biblical theology of priesthood.[18] The time is ripe for fresh examinations of Scripture's priestly theology in biblical-theological perspective.

The goal of this book is not to develop a biblical theology of the priesthood but to consider how the union of priesthood and kingship in Psalm 110 fits in the canonical context of the Bible. Nevertheless, this study should help answer important big-picture questions such as: What constitutes a priest in the biblical narrative? What is the relationship between the Melchizedekian priesthood and Aaronic priesthood? Is Aaron's priesthood in some sense a 'royal priesthood'? Is Israel's identity

---

[13] Nelson 1993: ix.
[14] Cheung 1986: 265.
[15] Becker 1998: 215.
[16] Mason 2008: 7.
[17] Since writing the original manuscript of this book, a handful of books on priesthood have been published. See e.g. Malone 2017; Perrin 2019; Schrock 2022.
[18] In the preface to *God's Mediators* (published 2017), Carson remarked, 'There is, as far as I know, no previous book-length *canonical* study of priesthood' (Malone 2017: ix; emphasis original).

as a 'royal priesthood' (Exod. 19:6) or Adam's role as priest-king typologically connected to the royal-priestly messianism of Psalm 110? How do we explain the fact that Hebrews can speak of Jesus as the fulfilment of the Melchizedekian priesthood and simultaneously describe his atoning work according to the duties of the Aaronic priesthood? Is Jesus a priest during his earthly career? Answers to such questions will surface by situating Psalm 110 in biblical-theological and canonical context in order to harmonize Psalm 110 with the rest of the biblical data.

The argument

The aim of this book is to develop a biblical-theological case for how David came to the conclusion that the Messiah would be a royal priest after the order of Melchizedek. These pages will argue that the Melchizedekian priesthood of Psalm 110 builds on the meaning and purpose of Adam's royal priesthood in establishing God's kingdom at creation and captures the order of priesthood associated with the Abrahamic covenant and redemption. In other words, Melchizedek is the type of servant-king Adam was supposed to be, and his priesthood, unlike the temporal Levitical priesthood, can mediate the promises of the Abrahamic covenant to the nations.[19] Melchizedek's close association with the Abrahamic covenant in the literary context of Genesis is an essential clue in deciphering the biblical logic that informed David's messianic convictions (cf. Ps. 110:4). Psalm 110:4 is evidence that David came to the realization that God's promises concerning his heir (2 Sam. 7:8–16) were tied to God's commitment to bless the nations through Abraham and his seed (cf. Gen. 12:1–3).

This argument depends in large part on the close relationship between kingdom and covenant in the structure of the Bible's metanarrative. Peter Gentry and Stephen Wellum have persuasively demonstrated that the relationship between God's kingdom and humanity's role in establishing that kingdom come together in the concept of covenant.[20] God's kingdom comes through God's covenants with human beings. These covenants begin with God's covenant with creation (Adam), where God created

---

[19] This argument will build on the fundamental components of what constitutes or defines a priest, namely covenant mediation (acting as an intermediary) and access to the presence of God. See Gentry and Wellum 2012: 318–324. For a fuller development of the meaning and design of priesthood in the Bible, see Wellum 2013.

[20] Gentry and Wellum 2012.

humans in his own image and commissioned them to rule the earth, perpetuate the divine image and worship in the garden of Eden (Gen. 1:26–28; cf. Gen. 2:15). The success of this mission hinged upon Adam's obedience as God's covenantal son and his faithfulness to carry out the obligations of his office of royal priesthood. Ultimately, his failure marred the image of God in humankind and revoked his priestly access to the presence of God when exiled from Eden. But Adam's role and his status as a priestly ruler continued to find expression in various covenantal figures in redemptive history (i.e. Noah, Abraham, Melchizedek, Moses, Israel, David), reaching its climactic fulfilment in Jesus Christ. Unlike Adam, Jesus is the obedient Son of God who faithfully carries out the obligations of his office. Jesus exemplifies his obedient sonship by establishing God's reign (as king) through his covenant self-sacrifice and covenant mediation from God's heavenly tabernacle (as priest) (Luke 22:20; Heb. 1:5–13; 8:1–2; 9:11–17). He obtained the right to remake a new class of priest-kings with authority to extend God's kingdom throughout the world (cf. Matt. 28:18–20; 1 Pet. 2:9; Rev. 1:6; 5:10).

The union of priesthood and kingship in individuals (or a corporate people) is, therefore, fundamental to the covenantal storyline of Scripture. God's 'creation project' and later 'redemption project' must come to pass through a son of God who perfectly fulfils the job description of the royal priest.[21] Adam's priestly rule in Genesis 1 – 2 sets the trajectory for the purpose of royal priesthood in redemptive history. This book will argue that the union of priesthood and kingship in Psalm 110 fits perfectly into this larger storyline.

As an exercise in biblical theology, there are two ways to look at the purpose of this investigation. First, from a hermeneutical perspective, the objective is to demonstrate that a canonical interpretation of Psalm 110 fits with the metanarrative of Scripture. In other words, the goal is to prove that the psalm's conception of the Melchizedekian priest is part of a developing and unified story across the canon that would have been accessible and recognizable to David during his lifetime. Second, from the perspective of the storyline itself, the aim is to arrive at a clear understanding of exactly what part the Melchizedekian priesthood of Psalm 110 plays in the story of the Bible. Though these two purposes are related,

---

[21] The phrase 'creation project' is taken from Alexander 2009: 76–97. I borrow this phrase from Alexander at several points in this book.

we could say that the difference between them boils down to the nature of their respective tasks. In the former, the task is methodological. In the latter, it is descriptive. For this project, my argument focuses on the descriptive task. The chapters that follow will make the case not for *why* we should read Psalm 110 canonically but *how* we should read Psalm 110 canonically. While I hope to demonstrate that the text itself confirms my presuppositions, I have defined my argument in terms of the descriptive outcome. This approach tightly fits the second and third objectives of the NSBT series, which are to articulate the structure of thought of a particular biblical writer and to articulate a biblical theme across the biblical corpora.

Surveying the landscape

To survey the literature on Psalm 110 would require a book-length treatment of the subject. Indeed, whole books have been written on the history of interpretation of this particular psalm.[22] The voluminous literature on Psalm 110 exists not only because the psalm occupies a pivotal role in New Testament Christology but also because the psalm in its Old Testament context has produced more interpretative conjectures and hypotheses than any other psalm. A summary of the enormous literature is not necessary for the purpose of this study. Instead, this section will survey the modern literature to summarize how scholars have handled the psalm's explicit union of the offices of king and priest in one figure. By canvassing the literature, my goal is not to affirm or deny the validity of each proposal. Instead, this survey should reveal how the nature of the investigation – historical or canonical – has controlled the interpretative task and shaped the interpretative results.[23] The fruit of such a survey will demonstrate the need for an investigation into Psalm 110 that situates it in a biblical-theological and canonical context.

---

[22] See e.g. Hay 1973.
[23] Waltke offers a helpful summary of modern scholarship's interpretative approach to Ps. 110: 'Modern scholarship . . . does not give primacy . . . to its predictions as understood in the New Testament. Rather, these scholars give primacy to its inferential historical use as part of the coronation ritual for David's non-supernatural sons or for a post-exilic priest. For most scholars . . . the New Testament re-interprets the original intention of the psalm. According to them, an exclusively human son of David during Israel's pre-exilic monarchy is the lord and priest-king celebrated in the psalm, and it uses courtly hyperbole, not necessarily substantial prophecy. Most deny Davidic authorship, and some deny the psalm's unity' (Waltke 2008: 63).

Royal priesthood: historical reconstructions of Israelite kingship

Bernard Duhm argued in his book *Die Psalmen: Erklärt* (1899) that Psalm 110 is the product of the Maccabean era (141 BC). According to Duhm, Psalm 110:1–4 is an acrostic on the name 'Simon', referring to Simon Maccabeus, the Hasmonean ruler of priestly descent.[24] The Hasmoneans' leadership skills and success on the field of battle made them king-like in their rise to power. For Duhm and others, Psalm 110 is part of a Maccabean agenda supporting the legitimacy of Hasmonean priest-kings.

In his essay 'Melchizedek and Zadok (Gen 14 and Ps 110)' (1950), H. H. Rowley argued that Psalm 110 was written to legitimize the Zadokite priesthood in Jerusalem. He proposed that the story of Melchizedek in Genesis 14 was redacted during the Davidic age in order to link the ancestor of Israel, Abraham, to the priesthood of Melchizedek, 'whose successor in the Jebusite priesthood Zadok was'.[25] According to Rowley:

> It is understandable that in the age of David, if the Israelite Ark were brought into Zadok's shrine until an Israelite shrine could be built, Zadok's position should be legitimated for Israel by an etiological story in which the authority of the example of the first father of Israel, Abraham, was invoked.[26]

Rowley maintained a strict separation between kingship and priesthood. David should not be thought of as a priest-king; nor, for that matter, should Melchizedek. The combined result of these assumptions led Rowley to assign two different authors to Psalm 110: 'In the first three verses the king is addressed by Zadok; in the fourth Zadok is addressed by the king, who confirms Zadok in the priesthood.'[27]

For some scholars, the priestly function of Israel's king is purely the result of Israel's actions in borrowing its monarchical identity from its

---

[24] Cited in Davidson 1900: 447–448. For a similar argument, see Treves 1965. Treves also suggests that the person addressed in Ps. 110 is not a king: 'If our warrior had been a king, the poet would have found an opportunity to say so' (ibid. 86). For a refutation of Treves' article, see Bowker 1967.

[25] Rowley 1950: 470. For a similar argument, see Johnson 1955: 43.

[26] Rowley 1950: 468.

[27] Ibid. 470.

ancient Near Eastern neighbours to solve political dilemmas.[28] Fundamental to this line of interpretation is the belief that the people of Israel developed a critical posture towards the monarchy. Sigmund Mowinckel, in his book *The Psalms in Israel's Worship* (first translated into English in 1962), suggested that this hostility 'arose from religious motives and finally led to the kingship being regarded as contrary to Yahweh's sovereignty'.[29] Only a new ideal for kingship, combining royal and religious practice, would win back the support of the people. According to Mowinckel, the union of royal and priestly power was characteristic of the El Elyon kings in ancient Jerusalem (cf. Gen. 14:18). The Davidic kingship rested on Jerusalem as its foundation for power. Yahweh's promise of the 'old right' was necessary to offset the priests' threat to the ecclesiastical power of the king.[30] John Emerton drew a similar conclusion about the union of royal and priestly prerogatives in his essay 'The Riddle of Genesis XIV' (1971):

> The Melchizedek passage in verses 18–20 was added, probably in the reign of David. It was hoped to encourage Israelites to accept the fusion of the worship of Yahweh with the cult of El Elyon, to recognize the position of Jerusalem as the religious and political capital of Israel, and to acknowledge that the status of David as king had behind it the ancient royal and priestly status of Melchizedek.[31]

Walter Eichrodt employed a comparable interpretative framework, relying on ancient Near Eastern custom to understand Israel's national political climate. In his *Theology of the Old Testament* (1961), Eichrodt concluded that 'royal psalms such as Pss. 2; 45; 72; 110 present features of the court-style and the king-mythology of the ancient Near East which could only have percolated into Israel from her heathen environment'.[32] The king's priestly quality in Psalm 110:4 was the result of 'the temptation to use cultic apotheosis to enlarge the royal power and authority to disarm popular criticism'.[33]

---

[28] See Mowinckel 2004: 50.
[29] Ibid. 58–59.
[30] Ibid. 64.
[31] Emerton 1971: 437. For a similar interpretation, see Day 1985: 130–131.
[32] Eichrodt 1961: 125.
[33] Ibid.

Similarly, John Day filtered his understanding of the Davidic dynasty through Canaanite culture in his essay, 'The Canaanite Inheritance of the Israelite Monarchy' (1998). He suggests that Psalm 110 is the 'clearest evidence of Canaanite . . . influence on Israel's monarchy'.[34] Psalm 110:4 demonstrates, according to Day, that David's conquest of Jerusalem led to syncretism with the Jebusite cult of Elyon. The Davidic royal priesthood in Psalm 110 thus finds its origin in the Jebusite cult of El Elyon, of which Melchizedek, the Jebusite priest-king, was a pre-Israelite prototype.

Relying heavily on form-critical assumptions, H.-J. Kraus, in his *Theology of the Psalms* (first published in German in 1979), argued that Psalm 110 was part of the liturgy of an enthronement festival that brought together Israelite traditions and the traditions of Jerusalem – the Jebusite royal city-state.[35] According to Kraus, '[t]he ruler enthroned in Jerusalem united several offices in his person and, therefore, . . . in the act of enthronement several assumptions and traditions concerning his office had to be taken into account and their authority conferred on the ruler'.[36] These offices included a blend of Davidic kingship traditions (2 Sam. 7; Ps. 132) and the royal-priestly traditions of Jerusalem, which found their origin in Melchizedek (Gen. 14:18; Ps. 110:4). Kraus makes explicit that the installation of the ruler as a priest after the order of Melchizedek 'was not a genuine and primary tradition of Israel'.[37] Instead, it came from the cultic traditions of Jerusalem.

Lester Grabbe similarly attached a political agenda to the meaning of Psalm 110 and its description of a priestly monarch. In his book *Priests, Prophets, Diviners, Sages: A Socio-Historical Study of Religious Specialists in Ancient Israel* (1995), Grabbe proposes that the development of sacral kingship in the Old Testament is due to priestly redactors 'who would want any future monarch to be subordinate to them in cultic matters'.[38] Grabbe attempts to reconstruct the cultic functions of Israel's kings. He concludes that the king was ultimately responsible for the cult.[39]

[34] Day 1998: 73.
[35] Kraus 1986: 111–116.
[36] Ibid. 112.
[37] Ibid. 115.
[38] Grabbe 1995: 39.
[39] Ibid. 35–40.

Michael Goulder takes a more novel approach to the historical setting of Psalm 110 in his book, *The Psalms of the Return (Book V, Psalms 107–150)* (1998). Goulder argues that Psalm 110 is post-exilic and is probably the work of a poet within the community of the Asaphites, who were the only singers at the time of the return from exile (Ezra 2:41).[40] In this context, Zechariah 6:9–14 is the key to interpreting the psalm's priestly messianism. According to Goulder, David's Lord is the priest Joshua (Zech. 6:9–14). If Psalm 110 was written during the time of the return, then, as Goulder argues, David's Lord should not primarily be thought of as a king, but first and foremost as a priest. He writes, 'The "lord" is in fact a priest, who is being called to a special vocation as secular leader of the nation.'[41] Psalm 110:1, therefore, refers to Joshua who is 'installed in an office which has all the trappings of Davidic kingship, but to which it would be impolitic to give the name of king (cf. Neh. 6.6)'.[42]

From another perspective, Deborah Rooke, in her essay 'Kingship as Priesthood: The Relationship between the High Priesthood and the Monarchy' (1998), attempts to elucidate the difference between the royal priesthood and the 'ordinary' priesthood.[43] She presupposes a priestly redactor (P) as she tries to define the nature of the priesthood and the monarchy at various points in Israel's history. Her investigation leads her to the conclusion that the 'monarch can fulfill priestly duties because of the nature of his kingship, but equally because of the nature of his priesthood the high priest cannot be a king, nor should he ever be confused with a messianic figure'.[44]

In Rooke's later article, 'Jesus as Royal Priest: Reflections on the Interpretation of the Melchizedek Tradition in Heb 7' (2000), she summarizes her findings on the relationship between the king's priesthood and the ordinary priesthood. She describes the monarch's priesthood as 'ontological'. In other words, the monarch's priesthood was inherent in his identity as the son of God. She states:

> The monarch had no choice as to whether or not to fulfill the priestly responsibility of mediation laid upon him; he was a priest forever . . .

---

[40] Goulder 1998: 146.
[41] Ibid. 145.
[42] Ibid. 148.
[43] Rooke 1998: 187.
[44] Ibid. 208.

because of the sonship granted to him by the deity ... His priest-hood was part of his identity as son of God; it was 'ontological', part of his very being.[45]

Her analysis gives historical credence to the view that the king could have a priestly function without actually holding the office reserved for the Levites.

Israel Knohl contends in his article 'Melchizedek: A Model for the Union of Kingship and Priesthood in the Hebrew Bible, 11QMelchizedek, and the Epistle to the Hebrews' (2009) that the Torah depicts a 'total separation' between priesthood and kingship, while in the rest of the biblical tradition the king has royal and priestly functions.[46] According to Knohl, Melchizedek, a non-Israelite king, is not 'restrained by the limitations that the Torah puts on Israelite kings' and thus serves as a model for the union of kingship and priesthood.[47]

Hossfeld and Zenger, in their commentary on the Psalms published in 2011, assert that the priestly role of the king (Ps. 110:4) appears to be a public relations move on behalf of a redactor. They write, 'The priestly dimension of the kingship is meant to relativize or correct the dominant military dimension of the rest of the psalm.'[48] Psalm 110:4 is a redactional comment that confers a kind of dignity on the 'new' kingship.

Even when scholars do not adopt higher-critical assumptions, they tend to formulate their investigation into the union of kingship and priesthood in Psalm 110 primarily through a historical reconstructive lens. M. J. Paul investigated the union of priesthood and kingship in Psalm 110 in his essay 'The Order of Melchizedek (Ps 110:4 and Heb 7:3)' (1987). His historical enquiry led him to the conclusion that the separation of kingship and priesthood in Israel fundamentally distinguished that nation from the surrounding nations. While Israel retained the memory of Melchiz-edek, who was king and priest in the far past, Psalm 110 cannot address one of the kings of Israel. The psalm had to speak of a future messiah.[49] Finding no historical precedent for a priest-king in the life of Israel, Paul

---

concludes that David's insight into the Messiah's priesthood was a special revelation from God. He writes, 'At a moment the Lord revealed to David – how we do not know – that one of the descendants of David should be a priest.'[50] The implication of such a statement is that Psalm 110:4 is devoid of any biblical data or typological structures outside the Melchizedek narrative in Genesis 14.

David Anderson's work *The King-Priest of Psalm 110 in Hebrews* (2001) endeavours to settle a theological debate between dispensational and covenant theologians concerning the nature of the present ministry of Christ.[51] In his chapter on Psalm 110, Anderson analyses the king's priestly role. The focus of his investigation with respect to the priestly function of the king is a historical one. He concludes:

> Lacking more objective evidence of an early king-priest office in the monarchy of Israel, the traditional understanding of a priesthood completely limited to the Aaronic line is preferred. The king of Israel may have been the head of the Yahweh cult, but that does not mean he had the office of a priest.[52]

Daniel Block makes a similar argument in his essay 'My Servant David: Ancient Israel's Vision of the Messiah' (2003), published in *Israel's Messiah in the Bible and the Dead Sea Scrolls*. Block argues for a strict separation between the royal and priestly offices in Israel's history. He states, 'Although the Deuteronomic History and the chronicler recount cultic actions performed by Davidic kings, the narratives never confuse or conflate priestly and royal offices.'[53] Block's insistence on this point is meant to strengthen his argument that the Old Testament distinguishes the priesthood from the Messiah. Psalm 110 is no exception. According to Block, 'Psalm 110 attaches priestly prerogatives to the monarchy . . . without compromising the Aaronide-Davide distinction'.[54] Psalm 110 appeals to a type of kingship that existed in the time of Abraham and thus maintains the Old Testament's consistent distinction between the

---

[50] Ibid. 209.
[51] Anderson 2001: 3.
[52] Ibid. 57–58. I do not disagree with Anderson's historical analysis here. I am simply emphasizing the fact that a historical approach to Ps. 110 has dominated modern scholarship.
[53] Block 2003: 34.
[54] Ibid. 43.

Aaronic–Zadokite priesthood and the Davidic Messiah.[55] What, then, is the priestly role of the king in Psalm 110:4? The priestly prerogative of the king, according to Block, is mediatorial. The king stands in the gap between God and the people – mediating God's rule and blessing to the people of Israel.[56]

Biblical-theological literature

A body of literature relevant to this study includes works of biblical theology that attempt to explain the metanarrative of Scripture or controlling themes within Scripture's metanarrative. Some of the most notable biblical-theological studies informing the shape of my investigation are the works of Dempster,[57] Beale,[58] Alexander,[59] Hamilton[60] and Schreiner.[61] These books unfold Scripture's metanarrative by highlighting major themes in the storyline, such as kingdom, covenant, temple, kingship and priesthood. They all agree that God's mandate to Adam at creation functions as the pattern for redemption in the storyline. Adam is the Bible's prototypical priest-king, and his assignment was to mediate the rule of heaven on earth. His pre-fall responsibility for establishing God's rule over the earth sets the stage for the goal of redemption, which culminates in humanity's final restoration – reigning with Christ as a kingdom and priests to God (Rev. 5:10; cf. Rev. 1:6). Interestingly, only Dempster mentions a connection between the messianic priest-king of Psalm 110 and Adam's assignment in Genesis 1 – 2.[62]

Peter Gentry and Steve Wellum's Old Testament biblical theology, *Kingdom through Covenant: A Biblical-Theological Understanding of the Covenants* (2012), provides one of the most thorough treatments of the royal priesthood in the metanarrative of the Old Testament. Gentry and

---

[55] Ibid. 42. In the same book, J. Daniel Hays contributes a chapter responding to Block. Hays argues that Block overstates his case when arguing that the biblical narratives never confuse or conflate the royal and priestly offices. He suggests that David's priestly activities are not entirely different from those of the Aaronic priesthood and 'mirror instead the old priest-king pattern of patriarchal Israel' (Hays 2003: 66–69).

[56] Block appeals to Rooke's essay 'Kingship as Priesthood' on this point (Block 2003: 43 n. 94).

[57] Dempster 2003.

[58] Beale 2004.

[59] Alexander 2009.

[60] Hamilton 2010.

[61] Schreiner 2013. I submitted this manuscript prior to the publication of Dave Schrock's book *The Royal Priesthood and the Glory of God* (2022).

[62] Dempster 2003: 200.

Wellum show how the concept of royal priesthood is tied to major covenantal figures: Adam, Noah, Abraham, Israel, David and Jesus. They argue for the existence of a creation covenant, which defines the responsibilities that Adam must fulfil as a son of God, servant-king of creation and temple-priest. Adam's covenantal assignment becomes the pattern for the covenantal responsibilities given to Noah, Abraham, Israel and Jesus. Though Psalm 110 is not part of the scope of their project, they suggest that the messianic texts that combine the offices of priest and king indicate 'that the coming figure fulfills an Adamic role planned by God from the beginning for a man over his creation'.[63] They also link the king's priestly role to the identity of Israel, suggesting that 'the king will accomplish in his person the purpose that God had for the nation of Israel as a whole, to be a kingdom of priests'.[64]

Eugene Merrill's essay 'Royal Priesthood: An Old Testament Messianic Motif' (1993) represents a classic typological approach to Psalm 110. Merrill argues from 2 Samuel 6, Psalm 110 and the epistle to the Hebrews that David was the prototypical royal priest, and thus functioned as a type of Jesus' superior royal priesthood.[65] The reason Psalm 110:4 identifies David's Lord as a priest after the order of Melchizedek is to establish a link between the Davidic and Abrahamic covenants. Melchizedek's connection to Abraham, a pre-Mosaic patriarch (Gen. 14), substantiates the superiority of the Melchizedekian priesthood over Aaron's priesthood. 'The Melchizedek-David-Jesus priesthood is a straight-line extension that operates outside of and superior to that of Aaron and the nation of Israel.'[66] What, then, is the relationship between the Sinaitic and Davidic covenants? Merrill writes, 'Israel was the kingdom of priests called to mediate Yahweh's saving grace to the world, and David was the priestly king whose task was to lead them to the full accomplishment of its high and holy calling.'[67]

Similarly to Merrill, Robin Routledge interpreted Psalm 110 and the union of priesthood and kingship against the backdrop of the Genesis 14 narrative in his article 'Psalm 110, Melchizedek and David: Blessing (the

---

[63] Gentry and Wellum 2012: 515.
[64] Ibid. 422.
[65] Merrill argues that 'my lord' in Ps. 110:1 is an honorific title referring to David (Merrill 1993: 55–57).
[66] Ibid. 59.
[67] Ibid. 61.

Descendants of) Abraham' (2009). His analysis focused on the meaning of Psalm 110:4 – 'You are a priest for ever after the order of Melchizedek' – in the light of the prevalence of the concept of 'blessing' in Genesis 14:18–20. He concludes, 'The Davidic king functions as a priest in the way we see Melchizedek functioning as a priest in Genesis 14:18–20, that is, as a means of blessings (the descendants of) Abraham.'[68] Bruce Waltke offered a canonical interpretation of Psalm 110 in his essay 'Psalm 110: An Exegetical and Canonical Approach' (2008). Waltke's reading of royal priesthood in Psalm 110 moves in a straight-line typological approach from Melchizedek to David's Lord to Jesus Christ. Thus, his interpretation of Psalm 110 traverses the canon, but he limits his analysis primarily to Melchizedek–Jesus typology.

One of the most developed canonical readings of Psalm 110 is found in Scott Hahn's *Kinship by Covenant: A Canonical Approach to the Fulfillment of God's Saving Promises* (2009). Hahn's primary objective in this book is to 'construct a covenantal interpretation of the Christ event as it is presented in Luke 22, Galatians 3–4 and Hebrews 1–9, the three loci of the New Testament that correlate the terminology of kinship with that of covenant'.[69] Hahn's work is significant for the purpose of this project because he develops the concept of royal priesthood as it relates to the issue of covenantal sonship. Concerning Psalm 110, Hahn's exegesis focuses on the content of the divine oath in Psalm 110:4. Hahn evaluates this oath in the light of Genesis 14, 2 Samuel 6 – 7, Psalm 89 and Psalm 132. He concludes that the 'content of the oath points to God's dynastic establishment of David's line through a son who is divinely adopted. The son is thereby authorized to build the Temple and rule as priest-king in Jerusalem.'[70] Similarly to Merrill, and Gentry and Wellum, Hahn suggests that the 'royal priestly primogeniture' of David's greater son echoes Israel's calling to be a kingdom of priests.[71] Hahn develops the logic of Psalm 110 in the argument of Hebrews, concluding that royal-priestly primogeniture is fundamental to the author's Christology.[72] Jesus' exaltation as the first-born son and royal priest was prefigured by Melchizedek and thus

---

[68] Routledge 2009: 14.
[69] Hahn 2009: 22.
[70] Ibid. 193.
[71] Ibid. 213. Surprisingly, Hahn offers no treatment of the controversial Adamic–creation covenant. He mentions it only in passing. Adam's role as priest-king in Gen. 1 – 2 is therefore not tied to Hahn's discussion of royal-priestly primogeniture in later biblical texts.
[72] Ibid. 278–331.

'represents the restoration of a more perfect form of covenant mediation originally intended for Adam and Israel and practiced to some extent prior to the Sinai rebellion'.[73]

Summary and observations

Within the field of biblical studies, scholars tend to take one of two trajectories when describing the union of kingship and priesthood in a single figure. They either focus on the union of priesthood and kingship in Psalm 110 from a primarily historical reconstructive perspective or they unpack the Torah's development of Adam's office of priest-king and its fulfilment in Jesus and the church (1 Pet. 2:9). In other words, the Melchizedek–David–Jesus typology is rarely ever harmonized with the development of royal priesthood traced through Adam, Israel, Jesus and the church.[74] Biblical-theological studies examine royal priesthood through the rubric of creation–fall–redemption–consummation, highlighting major points of development in Adam, Israel, Jesus and the church. Historical studies attempt to reconstruct Israelite history by searching for evidence of an Israelite sacral kingship that makes sense out of David's depiction of the Messiah as a priest for ever. Table 1.1 captures the general methodological trend in how modern scholarship has approached the concept of regal priesthood in the Torah and Psalm 110.

Table 1.1 Methodological approaches to royal priesthood (the priest-king)

Canonical section	Primary methodology employed	Redemptive-historical development
Torah	Biblical theology	Adam, Israel, Jesus, church
Psalm 110	Historical reconstruction	Melchizedek, David (Messiah), Jesus

---

[73] Ibid. 280. I must also note Joshua G. Mathews' (2013) work on Melchizedek, which is a thorough analysis of Gen. 14:18–20 in Genesis and the rest of the Hebrew Bible. Though I discovered Mathews' work after completing this book, we both adopt similar lines of argumentation at various points in our respective books. Specifically, we both see Gen. 14:18–20 as original to the Genesis narrative, and we both understand Melchizedek's importance as a function of his association with Abraham and the Abrahamic covenant.

[74] For two recent works that do not bifurcate these two biblical-theological trajectories, see Hahn 2009; Gentry and Wellum 2012.

The chart demonstrates how the different methodological approaches applied to the Torah and Psalm 110 have created a disconnect between the Torah's development of royal priesthood and the regal priesthood of the Messiah found in Psalm 110. Works of biblical theology tend to develop royal priesthood in the Torah and jump over the messianic texts, while historical studies attempt to explain the Messiah's priestly function (i.e. Ps. 110:4) apart from the foundation of the Torah. Critical assumptions combined with the lack of biblical-theological and canonical reflection on Psalm 110 have been so pervasive in much of modern scholarship that, for many interpreters, Melchizedek had to be a later insertion into the Genesis narrative implemented during the rise of Israel's monarchy. Psalm 110 has suffered relentless scrutiny from the historical-critical and form-critical methods of modern scholarship, and though conservative scholarship has opted for a typological and theological interpretation of Psalm 110, more work needs to be done to unpack the meaning of Psalm 110 in biblical-theological context.

This book will argue that the Torah – beyond Genesis 14 alone – provides the theological foundation for David's understanding of the Messiah in Psalm 110. My argument will build on typological and canonical approaches to Psalm 110 to demonstrate how David's messianic expectation is the outworking of earlier biblical literature.[75]

Method

As an exercise in biblical theology, this book will investigate the inner-biblical logic of the union of priesthood and kingship in a single figure in Psalm 110.[76] A biblical-theological approach is not primarily concerned

---

[75] Perhaps the interpretative discrepancies in biblical studies over the relationship between kingship and priesthood in Ps. 110 relate to what Jeremy Treat (2014: 28) laments as the 'oversytematization of certain doctrines, such as the states and offices of Christ' in the field of systematic theology. He writes, 'If Christ's work is divided neatly into the two categories of humiliation and exaltation, with the cross being only in the state of humiliation, it is difficult to see how it could relate to the kingdom at all. If Christ's death is interpreted only in terms of his priestly office then it will be difficult to connect the cross to the kingdom. Although the doctrines of the states and offices themselves are not to blame, they have often been used in a way that draws a thick doctrinal line between Christ's royal and Christ's atoning work.' That 'thick doctrinal line' between Christ's royal and atoning work in systematic theology is probably the cause (or result?) of the lack of biblical-theological reflection on the important place of a priest-king in the Bible's storyline (i.e. in Ps. 110).

[76] By 'inner-biblical logic', I mean the process by which the biblical authors interpreted and applied earlier biblical texts to their own context. In this regard, inner-biblical logic is

with defending issues of authorship or the historicity of the psalm. The final form of the text will control the interpretation. My selection of relevant passages in the Torah and other sections of the Bible will not rely on a word-study approach. The phrase 'royal priesthood' occurs only twice in Scripture (Exod. 19:6; 1 Pet. 2:9) and any attempt to find the specific titles of 'priest-king' or 'royal priest' will prove vain. Even a search for the individual words 'king' and 'priest' used in reference to the same person or entity will prove fruitless. Instead, I am using the phrases 'royal priesthood' and 'priest-king' in the sense that they thematically capture an important biblical-theological theme related to humanity's role in God's plan of redemption.[77]

Presuppositions

I affirm the Scripture's own testimony concerning itself as the Word of God. God moved human beings by his Spirit to author the very words of Scripture so that every word of the Bible is divinely intended and without error. Scripture's divine origin necessitates an essential unity across the canon. Even though Scripture consists of individual books of diverse genres written by various authors, it comes to us as a unified revelation from a single divine author.[78] Amid Scripture's diversity, it is possible to speak of the Bible's own 'meta-story'. T. D. Alexander says it this way:

> The anthology itself, which abounds in intertextual references, pro-
> vides most of the literary context within which its contents may be
> understood. There is not a book within the whole collection that
> can be interpreted satisfactorily in isolation from the rest. Each
> book contributes something special to the meta-story and, in turn,
> the meta-story offers a framework within which each book may
> be best interpreted. In this regard, the long-standing principle of

---

synonymous with what Beale describes as 'inner-biblical exegesis'. Critiquing the use of the term 'intertextuality' in biblical studies, Beale writes, 'In biblical studies . . . "intertextuality" is sometimes used merely to refer to the procedure by which a later biblical text refers to an earlier text, how that earlier text enhances the meaning of the later one, and how the later one creatively develops the earlier meaning. In this respect, "intertextuality" may be seen as a procedure of inner-biblical or intrabiblical exegesis, which is crucial to doing biblical theology' (Beale 2012: 40).

[77] This line of argumentation is taken from Thomas Schreiner's rationale for how the 'kingdom of God' is a central message of Scripture even though the phrase itself and related words are rare in Scripture (Schreiner 2013: xiii). See also Wright 1997: 225.

[78] Gentry and Wellum 2012: 84.

interpreting Scripture by Scripture makes considerable practical sense.[79]

The numerous intertextual references within the anthology imply that the biblical authors themselves relied on earlier biblical texts as they interpreted and applied those texts to their context. Thus, my interpretation of any given passage of Scripture will be an attempt to discover the author's intended meaning in the light of the meta-story of the Bible. Furthermore, this project will try to adopt the interpretative positions of the biblical authors themselves. While modern scholarship may deny Mosaic authorship of the Torah or Davidic authorship of Psalm 110, the New Testament indicates that Jesus, the apostles and the early church did nothing of the sort (Mark 12:35–37; Acts 2:34). The New Testament authors interpret the Old Testament texts on their own terms. Similarly, the canon of Scripture will dictate my interpretative assumptions about issues of authorship and salvation-historical setting. These hermeneutical assumptions are foundational for any biblical-theological investigation. For an interpretation to be truly biblical, it must operate on Scripture's own terms and grow out of Scripture's own world view.

Biblical theology

In his book *What Is Biblical Theology? A Guide to the Bible's Story, Symbolism, and Patterns* (2014), James Hamilton defines biblical theology as the attempt to understand 'the interpretive perspective of the biblical authors'.[80] This 'interpretive perspective', according to Hamilton, is the 'framework of assumptions and presuppositions, associations and identifications, truths and symbols that are taken for granted as an author or speaker describes the world and the events that take place in it'.[81] Hamilton's definition of biblical theology is most helpful because, as he notes elsewhere, '[f]ocusing biblical theology on the *interpretive perspective of the biblical authors* moors it to authorial intent'.[82] Following Hamilton's definition, my investigation will analyse the historical and literary features of particular texts and synthesize their relationship to the

---

[79] Alexander 2009: 10.

[80] Hamilton 2014a: 15.

[81] Ibid. For other helpful discussions on the subject of biblical theology, see Balla 2000; Rosner 2000; Scobie 2000; Klink and Lockett 2006.

[82] Hamilton 2014b: 26; emphasis original.

Bible's overarching narrative in order to arrive at the interpretative perspective of the biblical authors.[83] This process of analysis and synthesis is what Steve Wellum identifies as a 'grammatical/linguistic-historical-canonical' methodology.[84] According to Wellum, '[t]he best way to read Scripture and to draw theological conclusions is to interpret a given text of Scripture in its linguistic-historical, literary, redemptive-historical, and canonical context'.[85] The goal of this kind of theological reading is to extract the theological intent of the biblical authors and situate their individual theology in the context of the canon. The canon of Scripture by its very nature provides the theological boundaries that control the interpretative task.[86] The 'canonical context' will guide my investigation of Psalm 110.[87] Furthermore, the following chapters will operate on the assumption that the biblical authors utilized a typological framework to develop the concept of royal priesthood in Scripture. Typology posits that God intended certain persons, events and institutions in redemptive history to prefigure and correspond to their antitypical fulfilment(s). These typological structures – generally speaking – find their ultimate end in Jesus Christ.[88]

Lastly, the argument developed here will depend heavily on the covenantal structure of Scripture. I am indebted to Peter Gentry and Stephen Wellum and their book *Kingdom through Covenant*. They demonstrate how the concept of covenant is central to the 'narrative plot structure' of the Bible.[89] In their words, 'We assert that the covenants form the backbone of the metanarrative of Scripture and thus it is essential to "put them together" correctly in order to discern accurately the "whole counsel of

---

[83] This statement is also influenced by Brian Rosner's definition of biblical theology: 'Biblical theology may be defined as theological interpretation of Scripture in and for the church. It proceeds with historical and literary sensitivity and seeks to analyze and synthesize the Bible's own teaching about God and his relations to the world on its own terms, maintaining sight of the Bible's overarching narrative and Christocentric focus' (Rosner 2000: 10).

[84] Gentry and Wellum 2012: 100.

[85] Ibid.

[86] See Childs 1979: 83.

[87] The canonical context is a given text's relationship to the entire canon of Scripture.

[88] Clearly, there are biblical types that do not culminate in Christ. For example, Balaam is presented as a type of false teacher in 2 Pet. 2:15, Jude 11 and Rev. 2:14. It is unnecessary here to develop the nature of biblical typology. Instead, I point the reader to Steve Wellum's excellent discussion of typology in Gentry and Wellum 2012: 101–108, 121–126. I will be adopting Wellum's understanding of typology. For other discussions of biblical typology and typological interpretations of Scripture, see Fairbairn 1852; Stek 1970; Baker 1976; Davidson 1981; Ribbens 2011.

[89] Gentry and Wellum 2012: 21.

God" (Acts 20:27).'[90] By situating Psalm 110 in Scripture's larger covenantal framework, the apparent novelty of the union of priesthood and kingship in David's messianic expectation will prove itself to be an essential part of a unified story held together by God's covenants in human history.

Preview

Looking ahead, chapter 2 will analyse the development of royal priesthood in Genesis. This chapter will argue that Adam functions as Scripture's prototypical priest-king, and demonstrate how key figures such as Noah, Melchizedek and Abraham reflect the Adamic prototype. Significant attention will be given to Melchizedek and his purpose in the Genesis narrative as he relates to Abraham and the Abrahamic covenant. Chapter 3 will consider the meaning of Israel's calling as a royal priesthood and the need for a distinct lineage of Aaronic priests within Israel. This chapter will also address the question of how the Melchizedekian priesthood relates to the Aaronic priesthood.

Chapter 4 will investigate Psalm 110 in Old Testament context by evaluating the psalm's immediate context, literary structure, and relationship to the Davidic and Abrahamic covenants. Chapter 5 will focus on the exegesis of each verse of Psalm 110 while keeping the canonical context in mind. An often neglected but important question is how Psalm 110 relates to other Davidic psalms in the Psalter. I will explore verbal and thematic connections between Psalm 110, Psalms 1 – 2 and Psalm 8 in order to understand how Psalm 110 fits with the Psalter's messianic expectations.[91] Chapter 5 will also give attention to 1–2 Samuel to determine how the patterns of David's own life and the content of the Davidic covenant led David to the realization that the Messiah would be a priest and king after the order of Melchizedek.

Chapter 6 will turn to the influence of Psalm 110 on the intertestamental Jewish literature. The majority of this chapter will focus on an ancient fragmentary manuscript found in the mid twentieth century at Qumran

---

[90] Ibid.

[91] This type of canonical reading of the Psalter has precedent in the NT. In 1 Cor. 15:25–28 the apostle Paul juxtaposes Ps. 110 and Ps. 8 as mutually interpretative texts concerning the resurrection of Jesus. Likewise, the author of Hebrews juxtaposes Ps. 2 and Ps. 110 to substantiate the priesthood of Jesus.

near the Dead Sea. Named by modern scholars as *11QMelchizedek* (11Q13), this document presents a saviour who brings redemption on the eschatological Day of Atonement.[92] He is a messianic figure who combines kingship and priesthood within a single personality.[93] This chapter will also examine the Enochic literature and the *Testament of Levi*.[94] A brief survey of the intertestamental literature should suffice to demonstrate how Psalm 110 shaped the messianic hope of the various Jewish communities associated with these writings.

Chapters 7 and 8 move into the New Testament's use of Psalm 110. Since this psalm is the most frequently quoted Old Testament passage in the New Testament, it is beyond the scope of this project to examine every use of it in the New Testament. Instead, these chapters will focus on the New Testament documents that appeal to Psalm 110 to develop both a royal and priestly Christology. In this regard, chapter 7 will consider the Gospel of Mark, while chapter 8 will turn to the epistle to the Hebrews. The author of Hebrews, more than any other New Testament author, utilized Psalm 110 to shape his Christological argument.[95] Chapter 9 will summarize the contents of the book and draw some theological conclusions for the church today.

---

[92] Ancient manuscripts were discovered in eleven caves at Qumran in 1947. '11Q' is a reference to the cave number at Qumran. *11QMelchizedek* is a fragmentary manuscript dating to approximately 100 BC.

[93] Knohl 2009: 263.

[94] Levi is consecrated as a priest of El Elyon. The El Elyon reference associates Levi with the priest-king Melchizedek (Gen. 14:18; Ps. 110:4). See Collins 2010: 97.

[95] Ps. 110 is cited or alluded to in Heb. 1:3, 14; 5:6–9; 6:19 – 7:28; 8:1 – 10:13; 12:3.

2
Royal priesthood in Genesis

Exodus 19:6 describes Israel as a 'kingdom of priests' in a covenant relationship with Yahweh.[1] The Israelites' corporate identification becomes
the basis for the Aaronic priesthood after the covenant at Sinai and makes
possible the rise of the monarchy in Israel's history.[2] Yet David appeals
neither to Israel's corporate priesthood nor to the Aaronic priesthood
as the basis for the Messiah's priesthood in Psalm 110. Instead, a priest
'after the order of Melchizedek' will usher in God's kingdom and execute
judgment over the nations (Ps. 110:4, 6). Why Melchizedek? This chapter
will begin to answer this question by situating the Melchizedek episode
within the literary context of Genesis.

We must start at the very beginning. Genesis begins with God and his
vicegerent Adam. He is the Bible's archetypal priest-king in God's
kingdom. After Adam's failure, Genesis recapitulates his role in Noah and
Abraham, two major covenantal figures. Melchizedek appears in the narrative in close connection with the Abrahamic covenant, and his twofold
office of kingship and priesthood finds its origin in the structure of God's
covenant with creation. By following the covenantal contours of Genesis,
we will discover how the union of priesthood and kingship in a single
individual is an integral part of redemptive history. The conclusions
reached here will lay the groundwork for understanding David's theology
of the Messiah in Psalm 110.

Adam

In the world of the ancient Near East, a man who simultaneously held
the offices of king and priest was more than a mere man; he was a god – a

---

[1] In chapter 3, I point out that Davies (2004) has convincingly argued that 'royal priesthood'
is a better translation of the Hebrew text than 'kingdom of priests'.
[2] Though given distinct jurisdictions, the high priest and the king of Israel together
represent the nation and its regal priesthood.

son of the gods, to be more precise. The ancient Near Eastern kings were regarded as sons of the gods, called to fulfil a divine purpose by representing the gods in temple-palaces.[3] In the Torah, the office of king and priest originally belonged not to a deified man but to a man who bore the divine image. God created Adam, the ideal man, to rule the earth as a servant-king and to fulfil the responsibilities of priesthood in the sanctuary. His calling was to establish God's kingdom by turning the garden-temple into a global estate. Adam is the Bible's archetypal royal priest, even though he failed to fulfil the obligations of his two-fold office.[4]

By focusing on Adam in what follows, I do not intend to imply that the office of priest-king was for Adam alone. Genesis 1 instals every human 'in this office of priest-king and is therefore universally normative'.[5] The creation mandate to rule the earth in Genesis 1:26–28 belongs to human beings (men and women) as bearers of God's image. Nevertheless, Adam is the federal head of humankind in the Bible's storyline. What is universally normative for human beings in Genesis 1 is specifically embodied in Adam as the covenant representative of humanity.

Adam as king

Fundamental to the storyline of Scripture is the concept of the kingdom of God.[6] In the twentieth century, studies on the nature of God's kingdom focused on the 'reign versus realm' debate.[7] But Jeremy Treat rightly observes that there is now a scholarly consensus that the phrase 'the kingdom of God' refers primarily to God's dynamic reign.[8] God is king over his creation, and his plan of redemption culminates in his undisputed rule over the cosmos.

The remarkable truth of Genesis 1 – 2 is that God chooses to mediate his divine reign over the world through human beings. They are the pinnacle of God's creative work since they alone bear his image. Genesis

---

[3] Hallo and Younger 1997: 417–443; Averbeck 2002.

[4] Smith (2011: 102) says, 'The origins of kingship and priesthood are to be found in the Genesis story of God's creation of Adam.'

[5] Leeman 2016a: 37.

[6] Graeme Goldsworthy says that the concept of the kingdom of God 'dominates the whole biblical story' (Goldsworthy 2000: 60). See also Schreiner 2013: xiii.

[7] For a balanced discussion of the meaning of βασιλεία as denoting both reign and realm, see Pennington 2007: 279–300.

[8] Treat 2014: 41.

1:26–28 portrays the significance of humans and the impact they will have on the created order:

> Then God said, 'Let us make man in our image according to our likeness so that they may rule over the fish of the sea and over the birds of the heavens and over the livestock and over all the earth and over every creeping thing that creeps on the earth.' So God created man in his own image, in the image of God he created him; male and female he created them. And God blessed them. And God said to them, 'Be fruitful and multiply and fill the earth and subdue it and rule over the fish of the sea and over the birds of the heavens and over every living thing that moves on the earth.'[9]

These few verses capture God's intention to establish a universal kingdom through human viceroys. They will mediate God's rule over the world as they perpetuate the divine image through procreation. Their task is a function of a royal office. Three concepts deserve further attention if we are to understand how Genesis 1 – 2 develops and interprets Adam's kingship: (1) the 'image of God'; (2) the role of a gardener in the ancient Near East; and (3) covenantal sonship.

Image of God

The noun *selem* ('image') appears three times in Genesis 1:26–27 to describe the creation of man and woman. The meaning of *selem* in Genesis 1 has received much attention in scholarly literature.[10] The objective here is only to point out the royal and filial connotations of the term. Both are evident in the ancient Near Eastern and literary context of Genesis 1:26–27.

The Hebrew word *selem* is related to the Akkadian *slmu* meaning 'statue'.[11] In Egyptian and Mesopotamian literature, the king alone possessed the privilege of bearing the image of the gods. The king, as a living statue, was the visible representation of the gods on earth. The Egyptian deity Amon Re identified King Amenophis III as his human

---

[9] Unless otherwise indicated, all translations of biblical texts are my own.

[10] A few examples include Barr 1968; Garr 2003; Gentry and Wellum 2012: 181–208; Kilner 2015. It is not my intention to rehearse an exhaustive study of the term *selem*, but simply to highlight its royal connotations.

[11] Wildberger 1997: 1080.

counterpart: '[You are] my living image, the creation of my limbs', and 'my beloved son, coming from my limbs, my image which I have put upon the earth. I have let you govern the earth in peace.'[12] The pharaoh was 'bodily (son of Re) . . . the good god, image of Re, son of Amun, who tramples down foreigners'.[13] He possessed dominion over the world and everything in it: 'the earth is subject to you because of your prowess.'[14] These ancient Near Eastern texts associate the concept of 'image' with sonship and dominion (kingship).[15] Both themes (sonship and kingship) are apparent in the biblical usage of *ṣelem* in Genesis 1:26–28.

In Genesis 1:26–28, God gave Adam and Eve the commission to 'rule' (*rādâ*) and 'subdue' (*kābaš*) the earth (Gen. 1:28). The verb *rādâ* occurs twenty-five times in the Hebrew Bible and means 'to tread' or 'to trample' (cf. Joel 3:13 [MT 4:13]). Most of the occurrences of *rādâ* appear in relational contexts and are immediately followed by the *bet* preposition. This syntactical construction (*rādâ* followed by *bet*) communicates the idea of one person *ruling over* someone or something else.[16] In Psalm 72:8 and Psalm 110:2 the verb appears in the context of kingly rule or dominion.

The verb *kābaš* has a similar connotation in Genesis 1, meaning 'to subdue'. In later biblical literature, *kābaš* describes the conquest of the king over foreign nations (cf. 2 Sam. 8:11) and the subjugation of Israel's enemies (Zech. 9:15). Commenting on the Bible's own perspective of Genesis 1, Dempster writes, 'The rest of the canon assumes the royal overtones of Genesis 1, indicating the unique authority assigned to the primal couple, and thus to all humanity.'[17] The repetition of *rādâ* in the volitional mood (Gen. 1:26, 28) together with the imperative *wěkibšuhâ* (i.e. 'and subdue it') expresses God's intent for humanity to exercise kingly dominion over the rest of creation. Adam and Eve possessed a regal authority unique to human beings as bearers of the divine image.

Psalm 8 interprets Genesis 1:26–28 in the same way. Here David reflects on Genesis 1:26–28 and marvels at God's design for humanity – 'the son

---

[12] Schmidt 1983: 195.

[13] Wildberger 1997: 1083. See also Helck 1961: 176.

[14] Wildberger 1997: 1083.

[15] According to Gentry (Gentry and Wellum 2012: 192), '[t]he term "image of god" in the culture and language of the ancient Near East in the fifteenth century B.C. would have communicated two main ideas: 1) rulership and 2) sonship'.

[16] See Gen. 1:26, 28; Lev. 25:43, 46; 1 Kgs 5:4, 30; 9:23; 2 Chr. 8:10; Neh. 9:28; Pss 49:15; 110:2; Isa. 14:2, 6; Ezek. 29:15.

[17] Dempster 2003: 60.

of man' (*ben-'ādām*) (Ps. 8:4–5 [MT 8:5–6]).[18] David uses royal imagery to describe God's creative purpose for human beings. Humanity is thus 'crowned' ('*āṭar*) with 'glory' (*kābôd*) and 'honour' (*hādār*) (Ps. 8:5 [MT 8:6]), exercising dominion (*māšal*) over the works of God's hands (Ps. 8:6 [MT 8:7]). God places all things, including the created animals (cf. Gen. 1:28), under humanity's feet (Ps. 8:6–8 [MT 8:7–9]; cf. 1 Kgs 5:3 [MT 5:17]). The syntax of Genesis 1:26 corroborates the evidence that bearing God's image establishes the right to rule. The first-person plural cohortative *na'ăśeh* is followed by a jussive with a conjunctive *waw* (*wěyirdû*). The *waw* in this arrangement always communicates the purpose or result of the volitional antecedent.[19] A more accurate translation of Genesis 1:26a than the common 'Let us make man . . . and let them rule' would therefore be 'Let us make man in our image according to our likeness *so that* they may rule'.[20] Ontological status results in functional purpose. In other words, to be made in God's image brings with it the responsibility of kingship.[21]

The gardener of Eden

Gardening does not carry any special significance to the modern reader of the Bible, but in the ancient Near East the king was a gardener who brought agricultural prosperity to the land.[22] Catherine Beckerleg explains:

> In Mesopotamian royal ideology the king, who could be referred to specifically as 'gardener' . . . and 'farmer, cultivator' . . ., was responsible for tending the royal and sacred gardens and for harvesting rare trees and plants from conquered countries and cultivating them within his own kingdom.[23]

---

[18] It is possible that the author uses both '*ĕnôš* (man) and *ben-'ādām* (son of man) in Ps. 8:4 in order that the latter might evoke Adam and his role in God's creation project.

[19] Waltke and O'Connor 1990: sec. 34.6.

[20] For supporters of this syntactical argument, see Alexander 2009: 77 n. 3; Gentry and Wellum 2012: 188.

[21] Alexander makes a similar statement: 'To be made in the "image of God" is to be given regal status' (Alexander 2009: 77). Leeman says it this way: 'To be born as a human is to step into a royal office' (Leeman 2016a: 38).

[22] This is not to say that commoners were not gardeners in the ANE as well. See Gentry's discussion of this point in Gentry and Wellum 2012: 210.

[23] Beckerleg 2009: 190.

Later biblical literature poetically captures King Solomon's role as a gardener:

> I magnified my works. I built houses for myself and I planted vineyards (*kerem*) for myself. I made gardens (*gan*) and orchards for myself, and I planted in them all kinds of fruit trees. I made for myself pools of water from which to water the forest of growing trees.
> (Eccl. 2:4–6)

Similarly, in Song of Songs 4:12 – 5:1 the king compares his bride to his bountiful gardens. She is like the king's very own garden – 'my garden' (*lĕgannî* [5:1]), a 'garden spring' (*ma'yan gannîm* [4:15]) – and an orchard of pomegranates with the choicest fruit (4:13). Both the ancient Near Eastern context and biblical associations between kingship and gardening suggest that Adam's vocation as a gardener was part of his kingly office.[24]

Covenant and sonship

One final observation on the image of God in Genesis 1 is necessary at this point. The terms *ṣelem* and *dĕmût* (likeness) in Genesis 1 indicate that humanity's relationship to God is covenantal.[25] Genesis 5:1–3 employs the terms *ṣelem* and *dĕmût* to describe Seth's relationship to Adam. The terms 'image' and 'likeness' therefore denote a filial relationship between father and son.[26] Commenting on the relationship between image and sonship in Genesis 5:1–2, Meredith Kline has written:

> Since the Spirit's act of creating man is thus presented as the fathering of a son and that man-son is identified as the image-likeness of

---

[24] Commenting on Mary's mistake of believing the resurrected Jesus to be the gardener (John 20:11–16), N. T. Wright (1995: 59) has written, 'It wasn't, after all, such a silly mistake for Mary to think that Jesus, the true Adam, was the gardener.'

[25] Though a debated point in scholarship, the existence of a covenant in Gen. 1 – 3 has received much support from scholars associated with various theological traditions. See Robertson 1981: 67–92; Hafemann 2001; Dumbrell 2009: 11–46; Gentry and Wellum 2012: 177–221. For a recent work arguing against the existence of an Adamic–creation covenant, see Williamson 2007.

[26] Kilner (2015) describes the image of God as having a special connection with God and reflecting God. Sonship is part of that connection. Christ, the Son of God, is the standard and starting point for understanding what it means to bear God's image. Since Christ is the Son of God, one aspect of bearing God's image involves sonship. In redemption, believers are made children of God and conformed to the image of Christ. See Kilner 2015: 77–78.

God, it is evident that image of God and son of God are mutually explanatory concepts. Clearly man's likeness to the Creator-Spirit is to be understood as the likeness which a son bears to his father. And that understanding of the image concept . . . is further and unmistakably corroborated by Genesis 5:1–3 as it brings together God's creation of Adam and Adam's begetting of Seth, expressing the relation of the human father and son in terms of the image-likeness that defines man's relation to the Creator. To be the image of God is to be the son of God.[27]

Adam's filial relation to God moves their relationship beyond merely a formal viceroy agreement. As the son of God, Adam is in covenant with God himself. Through a detailed analysis of the terms 'image' and 'likeness' in both their ancient Near Eastern contexts and the literary context of Genesis, Gentry concludes that *image* is 'consistently used of man representing God in terms of royal rule', while *likeness* is 'closely associated with the creation of the human race, human genealogy, and sonship.'[28] Gentry explains:

Although both terms specify the divine-human relationship, the first focuses on the human in relation to God and the second focuses on the human in relation to the world. These would be understood to be relationships characterized by faithfulness and loyal love, obedience and trust – exactly the character of relationships specified by covenants after the Fall. In this sense the divine image entails a covenant relationship between God and humans on the one hand, and between humans and the world on the other.[29]

Being made in God's image and likeness enables Adam to *image* God in the same way that sons image or represent their fathers. In other words, Adam's monarchic rule over creation represents his heavenly Father's ultimate and sovereign kingship. God ruled as king; so too would his son Adam.

Adam stands between heaven and earth as God's covenantal son and servant-king, mediating God's divine rule and blessing to the rest of

---

27 Kline 2000: 45–46.
28 Gentry and Wellum 2012: 199.
29 Ibid. 195.

creation.[30] Gentry is right to argue that from the very first page of Scripture, the Bible's narrative structure is built on the concept of kingdom through covenant. Perhaps it is also appropriate, in the light of humankind's central role in God's kingdom, to nuance the structuring principle of the Bible as kingdom through covenant *mediator*.[31] Adam's mediatorial role between God and creation hints that he is more than a mere king; he is also a priest of God Most High (see below). Dempster's comment on the relationship between 'image', kingship and priestly mediation is well put:

> Thus, there is a deliberate anthropological climax in Genesis 1 with the creation of humanity as the 'image' and 'likeness' of God. In a deft literary move, with the use of these terms the writer makes the goal of creation anthropological and thus doxological, since to crown the creation with the creation of humanity is firmly to stamp God's own image in the very heart of the created order. It is as if humanity is functioning as a type of priest-king, mediating God to the world and the world to God.[32]

Adam as priest

Dempster is certainly correct to associate Adam's role of mediation with the office of priesthood. Adam exercises a type of *priestly* rule by fulfilling his commission from the garden-temple. The garden of Eden is, in the words of Wenham, 'not viewed by the author of Genesis simply as a piece of Mesopotamian farmland, but as an archetypal sanctuary, that is the place where God dwells and where man should worship him'.[33] Several lines of evidence support this conclusion.[34]

First, Genesis 2:10–14 describes a river that flowed out of Eden to water the garden. The river divides into four rivers as it spreads out into the earth (Gen. 2:10). The description of Eden's four rivers parallels Ezekiel's vision of the eschatological temple in Ezekiel 47:1–12. In Ezekiel's vision,

---

[30] See Middleton 2005: 26.

[31] The accent on mediator gives Gentry and Wellum's excellent thesis more of a Christocentric focus by highlighting the role of the story's protagonist, who establishes God's kingdom by mediating God's covenant.

[32] Dempster 2003: 62.

[33] Wenham 1994: 399.

[34] Biblical scholarship widely regards the garden of Eden as the Bible's first temple. See e.g. Wenham 1994; Dumbrell 2002: 57–61; Walton 2003; Beale 2004: 66–80; Schachter 2013: 73. Daniel Block (2013) does not adopt this popular position. He argues against the notion that the garden of Eden should be understood as a temple-sanctuary.

a river flows from the temple threshold in Jerusalem towards the east (cf. Gen. 3:24). The river is a source of life and blessing to the rest of the world (Ezek. 47:9). Edenic imagery colours the description of the eschatological temple in Ezekiel 47. The river's description as a source of life to every 'living creature which swarms' (*kol-nepeš ḥayyâ 'ăšer-yišrōṣ* [Ezek. 47:9]) echoes the creation of 'swarming creatures' (*šereṣ nepeš ḥayyâ*) in Genesis 1:20–21 and Adam's naming of the 'living creatures' (*nepeš ḥayyâ*) in Genesis 2:19. The banks of the river are lined with 'trees for food' (*'ēṣ-ma'ăkāl*) bearing 'their fruit for food' (*piryô lĕma'ăkāl*) and leaves for healing (Ezek. 47:12; cf. Gen. 1:29; 2:9).

Second, the entrance into the garden was from the east (Gen. 3:24). After Adam and Eve's sin, the cherubim stood guard at this eastern entrance to guard the way to the tree of life. The tabernacle and the temple were both entered from the east and guarded by cherubim (Exod. 25:18–22; 1 Kgs 6:23–29).

Third, Eden was the place of God's presence. Genesis 3:8 describes the Lord God 'walking' (*mithallēk*) in the cool of the day. The same verb (*mithallēk*) in the hithpael stem is used to describe the Lord's presence in the tabernacle (Lev. 26:12; Deut. 23:15; 2 Sam. 7:6).

Fourth, the construction of the tabernacle and priestly garments with 'gold' (*zāhāb*) and 'onyx' (*šōham*) alludes to the Edenic imagery described in Genesis 2:11–12.

Fifth, Genesis 2:15 indicates that God placed Adam in the garden 'to work' (*'ābad*) and 'to keep' (*šāmar*) it. The same two verbs are used together in later passages to describe the responsibilities of priests in the tabernacle and temple (Num. 3:7–8; 8:25–26; 18:5–6; cf. Ezek. 44:14). Adam is like a 'Levite who fulfills his role or task by maintaining the priority of worship'.[35]

Sixth, after Adam and Eve sin, the Lord 'clothes' (*lābēš*) them with 'tunics' (*kuttōnet*) of skin (Gen. 3:21). This act of God parallels the Lord's instruction to Moses to 'clothe' (*lābēš*) the priests with 'tunics' (*kuttōnet*) to prepare them for their priestly duties (Exod. 28:40–41; 29:5, 8).

Seventh, the tree of life in the midst of the garden reflects Israel's understanding that life is found in the sanctuary of God.[36] All of these

---

35 Gentry and Wellum 2012: 12.
36 Wenham 1994: 401. It is also the case that the menorah in Israel's tabernacle symbolized the garden's tree of life (ibid).

observations support the notion that Eden serves as the Bible's first temple.[37]

When God places Adam in the garden 'to work' (*'ābad*) and 'to guard' (*šāmar*) it, he is doing more than simply establishing a primeval landscaping operation (Gen. 2:15). As noted above, the verbs *'ābad* and *šāmar* appear together in passages describing the duties of priests in relation to the tabernacle and temple (cf. Num. 3:7–8; 8:25–26; Ezek. 44:14). God gave Adam access to the divine presence to minister as a royal priest on holy ground. Walton observes that the verbs *'ābad* and *šāmar* refer to Adam's priestly role of caring for sacred space: 'In ancient thinking, caring for sacred space was a way of upholding creation. By preserving order, chaos was held at bay.'[38] Moreover, Mathews notes that *šāmar* describes the duty of the priests to obey God's instructions (Lev. 8:35).[39] Taken together, *'ābad* and *šāmar* anticipate the 'Mosaic context of worship and obedience'.[40]

Worship and obedience are naturally tethered to the keeping of God's law. God gave Adam the command not to eat from the tree of the knowledge of good and evil under the threat of death (Gen. 2:17). The psalmist's description of the law in Psalm 19:7–8 (MT 19:8–9) as 'making wise the simple', 'rejoicing the heart' and 'enlightening the eyes' (ESV) echoes the description of the tree of the knowledge of good and evil as 'good for food and desirable to the eyes, and . . . desired to make one wise' (Gen. 3:6).[41] The law was kept in the holy of holies inside the ark, and touching or seeing the ark resulted in death (Num. 4:20; 2 Sam. 6:7).[42] According to David Schrock, Adam's responsibility for upholding the law parallels the duty of Israel's priests: 'Just as later priests, under the threat of death, guarded the ark of the testimony (Exod 25:16; Deut 31:26), so Adam was commanded to guard God's law.'[43] Leeman similarly concludes, 'Like a priest, Adam was to be utterly consecrated to God (Exod 19:22), which is

---

[37] Sacrifices and altars do not fundamentally define the temple and the priesthood associated with the temple. Alexander rightly states, 'The absence of references to sacrifices and altars should not detract from seeing temple imagery in the opening chapters of Genesis. Since no one had yet sinned, there was no need for atonement sacrifices' (Alexander 2009: 25).

[38] Walton 2003: 206.

[39] Mathews 1996: 210.

[40] Ibid. 209 n. 96.

[41] Gentry and Wellum 2012: 213.

[42] Wenham 1994: 403.

[43] Schrock 2013: 60.

to say, careful to ensure that God's ways were kept and his judgments accepted.'[44]

Lastly, Ezekiel 28:12–19 describes the king of Tyre as a guardian cherub in Eden, the garden of God (Ezek. 28:13–14). His covering is made up of precious stones that adorned the breastplate of Israel's high priest (Exod. 28:17–20). Ezekiel's description of the king of Tyre as a priestly Adamic figure in Eden implies that Adam himself was a priest before God.[45] When God places Adam in the garden, Adam begins his reign as a priestly viceroy in God's royal temple.[46] In Beale's words, 'Adam should always be referred to as a "priest-king", since it is only after the "fall" that priesthood is separated from kingship.'[47] Leeman's summary of the interconnectedness of these two offices – priest and king – in Adam captures the intention of Genesis:

> To be a king whose task is to image, represent, or give witness to the rule of another king requires the under-king to be a priest for the over-king. It requires him to consecrate himself to the law of the over-king, assent to the over-king's judgments, name what is clean and unclean according to the over-king, and guard the over-king's glory or the weightiness of his name. A representing or imaging-king, in other words, must mediate. He must *priest*. And Adam was this priest-king.[48]

Expanding Eden

Finally, a few comments about the eschatological nature of Adam's role as priest-king are in order. Implicit in Genesis 1 – 2 is a relationship between Adam's role as priest-king and his duty to expand God's garden-sanctuary over the earth.[49] Again, the ancient Near Eastern context is instructive on this point. In the ancient Near East, building a temple was the duty of the king.[50] A prime example of this fact is found in the Sumerian Gudea

---

44 Leeman 2016b: 167.
45 Dumbrell 2002: 61. Dumbrell also points to Ezekiel's use of *bārā'* (Ezek. 28:13), the presence of cherub, expulsion from God's presence due to sin, and the phrase 'mountain of God' as evidence that the king of Tyre is an Adamic figure. See also Beale 2004: 75.
46 Beale 2004: 70.
47 Ibid.
48 Leeman 2016a: 39.
49 The argument that Gen. 1 – 2 implies that Adam was to expand the borders of Eden to make the entire earth God's sanctuary has been developed by various scholars. See Beale 2004: 83–121; Alexander 2009: 25–26; Hamilton 2010: 73–74; Alexander 2012: 123–126.
50 See Averbeck 2002.

Cylinders. This ancient text records a temple-building hymn from the Mesopotamian king: 'To build the house for his king he does not sleep by night, he does not slumber at midday.'[51]

Genesis 1 – 2 similarly implies that the first image-bearers were to establish God's kingdom by building God's temple.[52] Adam and Eve, however, were not to build with bricks and mortar but by extending the boundaries of the garden through procreating the divine image. The Hebrew word *gan* (garden) literally refers to an enclosure, usually protected by some type of fence or hedge.[53] The garden of Eden (Gen. 2:8) was a distinct piece of terrain, set apart from the rest of the world.[54]

The world outside Eden needed order. God commanded Adam to take dominion over the entire earth. Beale argues that Adam's task of 'working' and 'guarding' the garden in Genesis 2:15 is an expression of the Genesis 1:28 mandate to 'subdue' and 'rule' the earth.[55] A necessary implication surfaces from the relationship between Adam's localized work in the garden and his commission to be fruitful and take dominion over the earth. The boundaries of the garden would expand to 'inhospitable outer spaces' as Adam and Eve populated the earth with images of God.[56] Just as the kings of the ancient Near East placed their own statues (images) in newly conquered lands as a tangible symbol of their geographical authority, so God's image, and thus his kingdom, was to cover the entire world. Through procreation, Adam and Eve's descendants would build God's garden-temple by extending the borders of Eden into a worldwide sanctuary, filling the earth with the glory of God.[57] By populating the earth with images of God, royal priests would mediate God's rule and

---

[51] Keel 1978: 269.

[52] See Dumbrell 2002: 61–65; Beale 2004: 93–100; Alexander 2009: 76–78.

[53] BDB 171.

[54] Dumbrell 2002: 56. Beale's suggestion that the use of the verb *nûaḥ* in Gen. 2:15 underscores the garden's uniqueness as a place of rest is unwarranted. He argues that the verb *nûaḥ* in the hiphil stem literally means 'to cause to rest'. As such, Beale writes, '[t]he selection of a word with overtones of "rest" may indicate that Adam was to begin to reflect the sovereign rest of God discussed above and that he would achieve a consummate "rest" after he had faithfully performed his task of "taking care of and guarding" the garden' (Beale 2004: 70). The problem with this argument is that the verb *nûaḥ* in the hiphil stem can be vocalized two different ways. According to BDB, the hiphil *hēnîaḥ* means 'to cause to rest'. The problem is, however, that this is not the form used in Gen. 2:15. The hiphil form of *nûaḥ* in Gen. 2:15 is *hinnîaḥ*, which means 'to place' or 'to put'.

[55] Beale 2004: 83–85.

[56] Ibid. 85. See also Walton 2001: 186–187.

[57] Ps. 8, which is a commentary on Gen. 1:26–28, frames the description of humankind's dominion over the earth with statements describing how God's majesty and glory fill the earth.

reign to the far corners of the earth. The entire earth would become God's temple and display his glory for ever.

Summary

All of these facts taken together reveal a teleological or eschatological purpose in the creation account and set the trajectory for the rest of the biblical storyline. Genesis 1 – 2 lays the biblical-theological foundation for the meaning and purpose of royal priesthood (the priest-king), and the necessary framework for understanding the union of priesthood and kingship in Psalm 110. Leeman summarizes the biblical meaning of the office of priest-king this way:

A priest-king . . . is an office with a structural aspect as well as inward and outward activities. Structurally, Adam was to represent, or image, God. Inwardly, he was to watch over the Garden since it was where God dwelled, keeping it consecrated to God and free of serpents. Outwardly, he was to work the Garden and push back the borders of Eden.[58]

Adam's office of royal priesthood was inseparably bound to his covenantal relationship with God as God's own son.[59] Sonship, kingship and priesthood all trace their origins to Adam. These roles will later define the nation of Israel, epitomize the Messiah in Psalm 110 and ultimately find purest expression in Jesus Christ.[60]

As the story continues beyond Eden, Genesis 3 introduces a dramatic intrusion into the narrative that threatens to dissolve the entire created

---

[58] Leeman 2016b: 168.

[59] Ralph Smith comments on the covenantal nature in which Adam was created and the implications for all of humanity. He writes, 'To begin at the beginning, Adam was created into a covenant relationship with God. He was not created into a "natural" situation and then granted a covenant afterwards, as an added feature to his relationship with God. The intratrinitarian counsel of Genesis 1:26 already defines man as God's covenantal representative and ruler of the world before Adam is created. The covenantal meaning of Adam and his race precedes the existence of Adam and already qualifies every cell of his body when God breathes into him the breath of life. His position as king over the world and priestly servant of Yahweh in the Garden is fundamental not only for Adam, but for the whole race descended from him. The Garden is the biblical and theological starting point for royal priesthood' (Smith 2011: 105).

[60] Concerning Jesus' identity as Son of God, priest and king, Hahn writes, 'Christ's threefold role as firstborn son, king, and high priest . . . represents the restoration of an original and superior form of covenant mediation that has been lost since the institution of the Levitical priesthood' (Hahn 2009: 278). See also Rooke 2000: 81–88.

order. Adam and Eve fail to distinguish between clean and unclean when they succumb to the serpent's temptation. God exiles them from Eden and a cherubim takes over Adam's priestly role of guarding the garden (Gen. 3:24). Humanity is now locked in a struggle to take dominion over cursed soil, sin, death, Satan and evil.[61] Nevertheless, God's plan to rule the world through human mediation does not fade away. The promise of Genesis 3:15 that the seed of the woman will crush the serpent's head (*rōʾš*) echoes Adam's role in the garden. Genesis 2:15 implied that part of Adam's *priestly* rule entailed the responsibility to 'guard' (*šāmar*) the garden-sanctuary. When the serpent confronted Adam and Eve in the garden, Adam should have exercised his authority by banishing the serpent for ever. Perhaps the serpent-crushing seed of the woman is a better Adam who faithfully executes the office of royal priesthood. Psalm 110:6 alludes to Genesis 3:15 by describing the messianic priest-king as one who will 'shatter the head (*rōʾš*) over the wide earth'.

From Genesis 3:15 onwards, God's creation project has turned into his 'redemption project'. God's plan to establish his kingdom through human agency unfolds through a series of covenant relationships. Adam's role now finds expression in other covenantal figures. The rest of the biblical narrative describes how God's creational project is going to succeed in a fallen world infested with chaos and sin. Priesthood and kingship are still an integral part of the story.

Noah

Noah appears in the narrative in a world filled with violence and murder (Gen. 4:23–24). Noah's name (*nōaḥ*) is a word play on the verbs *niḥam* meaning 'to comfort' (Gen. 5:29) and *nûaḥ* meaning 'to rest'. His name also recalls Genesis 2:15 where God 'put' (*nûaḥ*) Adam in the garden. Lamech's prophecy over his son Noah implies that Noah will be the one to reverse the curse on creation and bring rest to humanity. He will provide comfort from the 'pain' (*ʿiṣṣābôn* [Gen. 5:29; cf. Gen. 3:16–17]) of a 'cursed' (*ʾārar* [cf. Gen. 3:14, 17]) land. Redemption mirrors creation and Noah is a new Adam in a fallen world. Genesis 6 – 9 depicts Noah as the ancestor of a new humanity and, like Adam, a priestly ruler carrying forth the creation mandate.

---

[61] See Beale 2004: 70.

Noah as a new Adam

Noah's royal function in the narrative of Genesis 6 – 9 must be understood in the light of his status as a new Adam. The parallels between Genesis 1 – 2 and Genesis 8 – 9 indicate that the 'new creation' initiated with Noah replaces the original creation mandate begun with Adam (see Table 2.1).[62] Dempster rightly concludes that the flood represents a return to the 'pre-creation chaos' of Genesis 1:2 before the new creation dawns with the 'presence of the Spirit of God pushing back the primal waters (Gen 8:1)'.[63] Von Rad remarks: 'perhaps the words of Genesis 8:21ff. may actually be called the real conclusion of this history, for at that point the history of mankind begins anew.'[64] Through Noah, then, the world will receive a new beginning.

Table 2.1 Correspondences between the creation narrative and flood narrative

Correspondences	Creation narrative	Flood narrative
The spirit (*rûaḥ*) is active over the waters	Gen. 1:2	Gen. 8:1b–2
Boundaries between sky and earth	Gen. 1:6–8	Gen. 8:2b
Separation of dry ground from waters	Gen. 1:9	Gen. 8:3–5
Birds, animals and creeping things that swarm the earth	Gen. 1:20–25	Gen. 8:17–19
Days and seasons established	Gen. 1:14–18	Gen. 8:22
Humans and animals must be 'fruitful and multiply'	Gen. 1:22, 28	Gen. 8:17; 9:1, 7
Dominion theme	Gen. 1:28	Gen. 9:2
God provides food ('every green plant')	Gen. 1:29–30	Gen. 9:3
Image of God	Gen. 1:26–28	Gen. 9:6

[62] Gary Smith identifies seven parallels between Gen. 1 – 2 and Gen. 8 – 9 (Smith 1977: 310–311). See also Mathews 1996: 383; Waltke and Fredricks 2001: 128–129; Gentry and Wellum 2012: 162–163.

[63] Dempster 2003: 73.

[64] Von Rad 1962: 164. This quote is also cited in Smith 1977: 310.

Noah is, at this point in the narrative, the saviour of the world. Despite the fact that creation will be undone (Gen. 6:7; cf. Gen. 1:25–26), Noah finds favour in the eyes of the Lord. The description of Noah as a man who 'walked (*hithallēk*) with God' is reminiscent of the Lord 'walking' (*mithallēk*) in the garden with Adam and Eve (Gen. 6:9; cf. Gen. 3:8). Noah experiences the life-giving presence of God as opposed to the shadow of death that hovers over those who are blotted out from the cursed ground (Gen. 3:17; 6:7). Unlike Adam, who brought death into the world, Noah will be an agent of life.

After the flood, God gives Noah the same commission originally given to Adam. In Genesis 9:1, God blesses Noah and his sons, commanding them to be fruitful and multiply and fill the earth (Gen. 9:1; cf. Gen. 9:7). The language is almost an exact replica of Genesis 1:28 (see Table 2.2). Noah is to fulfil in a new creation what God had intended for Adam in the original creation. That is, Noah is to be fruitful and multiply images of God across the globe so that God's worldwide kingdom will be secured, and God's glory will be on display from the far corners of the earth.

Table 2.2 Linguistic parallels between Genesis 1:28 and Genesis 9:1

Genesis 1:28	Genesis 9:1
Waybārek 'ōtām 'ĕlōhîm wayyō'mer lāhem 'ĕlōhîm pĕrû ûrĕbû ûmil'û 'et-hā'āreṣ	*Waybārek 'ĕlōhîm 'et-nōaḥ wĕ'et-bānāyw wayyō'mer lāhem pĕrû ûrĕbû ûmil'û 'et-hā'āreṣ*

The original command given to Adam to subdue and rule the earth is absent from God's commission to Noah. Nevertheless, the text hints at Noah's regal authority even if it is less prominent than Adam's clear position of kingship. God puts the fear of humankind into all the animals (Gen. 9:2). Similarly, God gives all the created beings into the hand of Noah and his lineage (Gen. 9:3). Furthermore, Genesis 9:16 indicates that the Noahic covenant pertains to 'every living creature among all flesh that is on the earth'. According to Hahn, the covenant assigns Noah 'a dynastic authority over "all flesh" (9:16, 17)'.[65] Noah occupies a position of servant-rulership over the created order even though he is a not a perfect reflection of the Adamic ideal (Gen. 9:2; cf. Gen. 1:26–28).

---

[65] Hahn 2009: 97.

Noah's priestly worship

Noah's priestly ministry is apparent in Genesis 8:20–22.[66] After the flood subsides, Noah leaves the ark and builds an altar to offer sacrifices to Yahweh (Gen. 8:20). Before the Mosaic era, altars functioned as the place of God's special presence.[67] They were small sanctuaries where God met his people.[68] The restatement of the creation mandate (Gen. 9:1) immediately following the Lord's acceptance of Noah's sacrifice at a localized sanctuary (altar) may also recall Adam's priestly assignment to expand the borders of the garden-sanctuary over the entire earth.[69]

Noah's act of offering 'clean' (*ṭāhôr*) animals as 'burnt offerings' (*'ōlâ*) on an 'altar' (*mizbēaḥ*) anticipates the sacrificial ministry of the Levitical priesthood (cf. Lev. 1:17; 10:10; 20:25). Israel's priests were responsible for separating unclean animals from clean animals for sacrifice. Adam failed in his priestly task by not protecting the garden from the profane serpent, so Noah must now separate the clean from the unclean in order to make an appropriate sacrifice for fallen sons and daughters of Adam.

The smoke rising from Noah's burnt offering becomes a 'soothing aroma' (*rêaḥ hannîḥōaḥ*) to Yahweh (Gen. 8:21). The same phrase regularly appears in Leviticus where the burnt offerings of the priests result in the same 'pleasing aroma' to the Lord (Lev. 1:9, 13; 2:2; 4:31; 6:21; 8:21: 17:6). Upon smelling the pleasing aroma, the Lord promises that he will never again destroy humankind, even though 'the inclination of man's heart is evil from his youth' (Gen. 8:21). The Lord's response to humanity's sinful nature is a powerful contrast to Genesis 6:5–7 where the Lord determines to blot out human beings because 'every inclination of the thoughts of [their] heart is only evil every day' (Gen. 6:5). The difference between the Lord's response to human evil in these two passages – judgment in Genesis 6:5–7 and mercy in Genesis 8:21 – has everything to do with Noah's sacrifice. The 'soothing aroma' appeases God's wrath.

Noah's propitiatory sacrifice is a priestly act on behalf of the entire human race. Wenham concludes that 'we can view Noah's offering of sacrifice as a prototype of the work of later priests, who made atonement

---

66 Before Sinai, the responsibility of priestly ministry belonged to the patriarchal head of any particular family. See Payne 1962: 373.
67 See Longman 2001: 15–23.
68 Ibid. 18.
69 See Beale 2004: 96–97.

for Israel . . . Here, however, Noah's sacrifice is effective for all mankind.'[70] Noah's priestly sacrifice does not only function as a prototype of the work of later priests; its universal character also anticipates the ministry of Israel as a royal priesthood.[71] On account of Noah, the rest of the world will have an opportunity to live under the rule and blessing of God.

Summary

The numerous links between Genesis 6 – 9 and the creation account in Genesis 1 – 2 identify Noah as a new Adam. The Noahic covenant is an expression of the original creation covenant, which means that Noah's authority and priesthood find their origin in the royal priesthood of Adam. Adam and Noah functioned as covenantal mediators on behalf of humanity and as the natural ancestors of the entire human race. The covenant relationships that make up the rest of redemptive history are expressions of the original covenants God made with Adam and Noah. The development of kingship and priesthood in the history of Israel is not the product of borrowing by Israel, whereby the nation allegedly copied the institutions of its ancient Near Eastern neighbours as it progressed from an uncivilized tribe to a sophisticated political entity. Instead, we can conclude from the historical record of Genesis that the development of kingship and priesthood in Israel's history, and later in the messianic vision of Psalm 110, finds its origin in Adam and Noah.[72]

The next major question needing attention, then, is how Melchizedek's royal priesthood fits into the narrative of Adam and Noah. If Adam is creation's archetypal priest-king and Noah inherits the Adamic office in a fallen world, then why does David appeal to a priesthood of the Melchizedekian order in Psalm 110?

Melchizedek

The Melchizedek narrative in Genesis 14 has proven to be a *crux interpretum* for modern scholars. Source critics could not find Genesis

---

70 Wenham 1995: 81.

71 Wenham 1997: 462. Wenham writes elsewhere, 'Noah is portrayed as an exemplary keeper of the covenant law, observing the Sabbath, distinguishing between clean and unclean, and offering a sacrifice effective for all mankind' (Wenham 1994: 403).

72 Smith (2011: 94) says Adam and Noah were 'the two greatest "king-priests" of the ancient world'.

14:18–20 a home in J, E, D or P.[73] Many interpreters concluded that the Melchizedek episode was a redacted story from the time of David's conquest meant to provide theological support for Jerusalem's Jebusite priesthood.[74] For most of the modern period, scholarship simply could not (or *would* not) fit the Melchizedek narrative into the literary and historical context of Genesis.[75] If the text is allowed to stand on its own terms, as part of an intelligently designed narrative, then the reader can arrive at an intelligible interpretation of the pericope within the historical and literary context of Genesis. Only this kind of literary reading can uncover how Melchizedek's priesthood relates to the priesthoods of Adam, Noah, Israel and Aaron, and demonstrate that Melchizedek's importance for biblical theology (i.e. for understanding the interpretative perspective of later biblical authors [Ps. 110]) is bound up with his relationship to the Abrahamic covenant.

Priest after the order of Adam and Noah

Genesis 14:18 identifies Melchizedek as 'king of Salem' and 'priest of God Most High' (*kōhēn lĕ'ēl 'elyôn*). In Genesis 14:22 the title El Elyon (*'ēl 'elyôn*) stands in apposition to Yahweh (*yahweh*).[76] Melchizedek, then, is a royal priest of the one true God, the covenant God of Adam and Noah. But what is the origin of Melchizedek's royal priesthood? On what basis does he claim the offices of *melek* (king) and *kōhēn* (priest)? The answer proposed here is that Melchizedek's royal priesthood is an expression of the office of priest-king held by Adam and Noah.[77] Several literary and thematic connections between Melchizedek, Adam and Noah support this observation.

73 On this point, see Fitzmyer 2000: 64.
74 See e.g. Emerton 1971: 437.
75 P. J. Nel (1996: 7–8) writes, 'I am convinced that Gen 14:18–20 can only make sense when the tradition of Ps 110 is presupposed. Nothing in the narrative flow of Gen 14 anticipates the almost miraculous appearance of the priest-king, Melchizedek.' For a defence of the historical and literary integrity of the Melchizedek incident in the book of Genesis, see McConville 1994.
76 The LXX supplies no translation for *yahweh* in Gen. 14:22. For the sake of argument, if we were to assume that the LXX is the more accurate reading, then we can no longer clearly identify El Elyon with Yahweh. However, to suggest that Abraham has in mind someone other than Yahweh at this point in the Genesis narrative when he refers to the 'God Most High' is difficult to fathom. Abraham's announcement that he will not receive any goods from the king of Sodom is a demonstration of his trust that God will fulfil his promises. Abraham knows this promise-making God as Yahweh.
77 Smith (2011: 94) similarly argues that 'the Melchizedekian priesthood was a particular expression of the priesthood inherited from Noah and Adam'.

First, Melchizedek's name means 'king of righteousness'. Prior to Genesis 14, Noah is the only other person described as 'righteous'. Noah walked with God and was blameless in his generation. After an explicit statement in the narrative about Noah's obedience in following all of God's commands (Gen. 6:22), Yahweh declares, 'I have seen that you are righteous (*ṣaddîq*) in this generation' (Gen. 7:1). Most probably, then, Melchizedek's name, 'king of righteousness', is meant to recall Noah's faithful obedience to God.[78] Like Noah, Melchizedek is an obedient worshipper of the God Most High.

Second, Melchizedek blesses Abraham with bread and wine (Gen. 14:18). Before Genesis 14, the only mention of wine is in Genesis 9:21–24. Here, Noah is portrayed as a gardener planting a vineyard, probably alluding to Adam's regal role as a gardener in Eden (9:20).[79] Just as Adam failed in the garden by disobeying God's law, Noah fails in his garden by becoming intoxicated with wine, leaving him naked and ashamed (Gen. 9:20–23). Melchizedek, however, uses wine to bless victorious Abraham. It is also significant that the only other occurrence of 'bread' (*leḥem*) prior to Genesis 14 is found in Genesis 3:19, where God's curse on Adam means that man will have to eat bread by the sweat of his brow. Thus, the two elements, bread and wine, that were associated with Adam's and Noah's failure and God's curse become elements of blessing to Abraham, perhaps signifying that Melchizedek's royal priesthood is a replacement of the royal priesthood originally belonging to Adam and Noah. Through Abraham, God will reverse the curse and failure of the two previous covenantal heads of humanity.

Third, by submitting to Melchizedek through the giving of the tithe, Abraham acknowledges Melchizedek's authoritative and even superior status (Gen. 14:20). Melchizedek's position of honour implies that his priesthood was rooted in a pre-existing covenant. Smith explains:

> Given Abraham's position as covenant-head of the new era and the one through whom the world would be blessed, it may seem odd that

---

[78] Though his concern is with the book of Hebrews, Andrei Orlov (2007: 63–65) also links Melchizedek to Noah through the use of the term 'righteousness'.

[79] The use of the verb *nāṭaʿ* recalls its only previous occurrence in the narrative found in Gen. 2:8: 'And the LORD God *planted* a garden in Eden . . . and there he put the man whom he had formed' (ESV; emphasis mine).

he would recognize another priest, unless that priest was established under the terms of a superior covenant. Melchizedek's priesthood, therefore, had to be prior to the gift of the covenant to Abraham and based upon the more fundamental Noahic covenant.[80]

Fourth, Melchizedek's blessing on Abraham echoes Noah's blessing on Shem (Gen. 9:26; 14:19).[81] Noah, a priestly ruler, pronounced a blessing on Shem, while the priest-king Melchizedek pronounced a similar blessing on Shem's descendant Abraham, the one through whom the blessing of Shem would come to pass. Perhaps the associations between Melchizedek's blessing on Shem's descendant (Abraham) and Noah's blessing on Shem suggest that Melchizedek's royal priesthood is tied to and in succession with the royal priesthood of Noah.[82]

Fifth, by contrasting Melchizedek with the king of Sodom in the same pericope (more on this contrast below), we discover that Melchizedek's kingship – like Adam's before him – is subservient to God's rule as creator. Unlike Melchizedek, the king of Sodom desires the spoils of victory, namely people to control. His strength is in numbers. His kingship represents corrupt human kingship of a type that clamours for power at the expense of others.[83]

Melchizedek, on the other hand, does not rule with tyranny and oppression. He is, after all, the king of 'peace' (*šālēm* [Gen. 14:18; cf. Heb 7:2]). Melchizedek's confession about God embodies the meaning of his name (king of righteousness) and the nature of his peaceful kingship. He blesses Abraham in the name of 'God Most High, possessor of heaven and earth' (Gen. 14:19). His blessing acknowledges the universal rule of God over all creation. God controls the universe, and God is the one who gives victory in battle (Gen. 14:20). Melchizedek does not seek Abraham's spoils but instead offers Abraham a priestly blessing of bread and wine. In this sense,

---

[80] Smith 2011: 106.

[81] In ancient Jewish and Christian tradition, Melchizedek is Shem. If this were the case, Shem would have inherited his priestly role by virtue of his status as Noah's firstborn son. Abraham's tithe to Melchizedek (Shem) would have been an act of submission to the authority of his greater ancestor. Scott Hahn attempts to make a case that Melchizedek was Noah's firstborn son Shem in Hahn 2009: 130–134. While the notion that Melchizedek is Shem is intriguing, it is impossible to prove or substantiate from the text of Genesis.

[82] Hahn (2009: 130) also observes links between Abraham, Melchizedek, Noah and Shem at a structural level.

[83] Alexander 2009: 82.

Melchizedek is a servant-king of the creator God. His authority flows from God's sovereignty over the created realm.[84]

Melchizedek's confession about the sovereignty of God defines the nature of his kingship. His kingship is characterized by submission to the supreme king, namely Yahweh, the God Most High. Melchizedekian kingship is servant-kingship and representational. It is the type of kingship Adam should have embodied as God's true image and servant-king. Such kingship is 'divinely instituted', according to Alexander, in that it 'seeks to re-establish God's sovereignty on the earth in line with the divine mandate given to human beings when first created'.[85] It, therefore, comes as no surprise that Melchizedek's kingship is a *priestly* kingship. This priest of God Most High is a mediator and representative of God's authority to Abraham.[86]

Finally, Melchizedek's connection to God's creation blueprint surfaces through a comparison of Genesis 14 – 15 with Exodus 17 – 18. Several similarities exist between Abraham's encounter with Melchizedek and Moses' encounter with Jethro.[87] Both narratives follow similar structures (see Table 2.3).[88]

Table 2.3 Sailhamer's compositional similarities: Genesis 14 – 15 and Exodus 17 – 18

The nations	*The seed*
The nations (Gen. 14:1–12)	
Divine victory (Gen. 14:14–17)	
Melchizedek (Gen. 14:18–20)	
	Abraham's covenant (Gen. 15)
War with nations (Exod. 17:8–10)	
Divine victory (Exod. 17:11–13)	
Jethro (Exod. 18:1–12)	
	Moses' covenant (Exod. 19 – 24)

---

[84] It is possible that Melchizedek's blessing of bread and wine also hints at his submission to God as the creator and ruler of the universe. See Wenham 1995: 78.

[85] Alexander 2009: 82.

[86] McConville 1994: 116.

[87] I came to this conclusion through my own study before I found Sailhamer's treatment of the same topic. See Sailhamer 2009: 369–378. For the sake of space, it is not necessary to observe all of the textual and thematic similarities between the two episodes. For a full summary of the narrative similarities see ibid. 370–371.

[88] This table is adapted from ibid. 369.

The general flow of events in both narratives proceeds as follows: war with Gentiles, divine victory, appearance of a royal-priestly figure and establishment of a covenant. Similarly, the actions and identities of Melchizedek and Jethro mirror one another. Melchizedek is 'priest' (*kōhēn*) of Salem (*šālēm*) (Gen. 14:15); Jethro is 'priest' (*kōhēn*) of Midian (Exod. 18:1) who asks for 'peace' (*šālôm*) for Moses (Exod. 18:7). Melchizedek meets Abraham with 'bread' (*leḥem*) and wine (Gen. 14:18) after Abraham returns from battle; Jethro offers sacrifices and eats 'bread' (*leḥem*) with Moses after Moses' victory in battle (Exod. 18:12). Melchizedek pronounces a blessing on Abraham (Gen. 14:20); Jethro pronounces a similar blessing on Moses (Exod. 18:10). (See Table 2.4.)

Table 2.4 Linguistic parallels between Genesis 14:20a and Exodus 18:10

Genesis 14:20a	Exodus 18:10
And blessed (*ûbārûk*) be God Most High who delivered (*miggēn*) your enemies into your hand (*běyādekā*)...	And Jethro said, 'Blessed (*bārûk*) be Yahweh who has delivered (*hiṣṣîl*) you from the hand (*miyyad*) of the Egyptians and from the hand (*miyyad*) of Pharaoh and has delivered (*hiṣṣîl*) the people from under the hand (*yad*) of the Egyptians.'

Furthermore, Abraham submits to Melchizedek by paying him a tithe, while Moses submits to Jethro by bowing down to him (Gen. 14:20; Exod. 18:7). Both narratives take place near a significant mountain: Mount Zion ([Jeru]salem) (Gen. 14:18; cf. Ps. 76:1–2) and Mount Sinai (Exod. 18:5).[89] And lastly, both narratives close with reference to a meal (Gen. 14:24; Exod. 18:12).

The structural and thematic similarities between the two narratives reveal an important connection between the nations and God's chosen people (Abraham and Israel). In both episodes, God's chosen people – represented by Abraham and Moses – experience divine victory in battle with Gentile nations, encounter a Gentile priest-king and enter into a

---

[89] Gen. 14:17 indicates that the king of Sodom and Melchizedek, the king of Salem, met Abraham in the Valley of Shaveh. It is likely that this ancient location was near Salem, which is to be identified with what would later become Jerusalem (cf. Ps. 76:1–2).

covenant with God (Gen. 15; Exod. 19 – 24).[90] John Sailhamer rightly determines the importance of these patterns: 'The author shows that Israel's dealings with these nations tell something about the nature of the covenants that they were to enter and their relationship to the nations.'[91] In other words, Melchizedek and Jethro reveal that God's covenantal purposes with Abraham and Israel have global implications. Melchizedek ties the Abrahamic covenant to creation (Gen. 14:19–20, 22), while Jethro's reference to the exodus (Exod. 18:10) links the Mosaic covenant to redemption. Sailhamer's summary on this point is well put:

> These two important pentateuchal narratives, Genesis 14–15 and Exodus 18–24, link creation and redemption blessings to God's covenants with the 'seed' of Abraham. Genesis 14–15 links the creation blessing (Gen 14) to covenant blessing (Gen 15), and primeval law (Ex 18) to Mosaic law (Ex 19–24). God's work of redemption is grounded in creation and covenant.[92]

Sailhamer's conclusion is accurate, but it is necessary to emphasize the fact that the priests involved in these narratives were also *royal* figures. A Gentile *kingly* priest appears in the narratives immediately before the covenantal episodes with Abraham (Gen. 15) and Israel (Exod. 19). God's covenant with Israel (Abraham's seed) will be the means to establish God's kingdom so that the entire world may experience the blessing of God. In the narrative plot of Scripture, Melchizedek and Jethro remind the reader of God's purpose begun with the primal priest-king Adam at a time when God's redemption plan narrows down to one man (Abraham) and his progeny (Israel). God has not abandoned his purposes for the world. The nations, typified by Melchizedek and Jethro, will experience the overflow of blessing that comes through God's covenant relationships with a particular person (Abraham) and particular nation (Israel). God's covenant

---

[90] Jethro is never explicitly identified as a 'king', yet he appears to possess royal authority. Davies (2004: 152–153) summarizes this point well: 'Rather than being "a priest of Midian" (Exod 2.16 NIV), the construction (construct state followed by proper noun) requires that he be *the* priest of Midian, and he appears to enjoy something like a general authority, civil and religious, in his community that the Israelite patriarchs, as portrayed in Genesis, did in theirs . . . [T]he biblical characterization of the priest-king of Midian does add another facet to the broad portrayal of the status of priests in the world familiar to the Israelites'; emphasis mine.

[91] Sailhamer 2009: 371.

[92] Ibid. 374.

will establish his universal kingdom. Melchizedek and Jethro serve as reminders that all of humanity will be priests and kings (cf. 1 Pet. 2:9; Rev. 5:10) unto God as a result of God's covenant faithfulness.

The observations that link Melchizedek to creation, Adam and Noah imply that Melchizedek's royal priesthood is an expression of the office originally given to Adam and later inherited by Noah. The question remains, then, as to why David would appeal to Melchizedek and not Adam since Adam is Scripture's royal-priestly prototype. If Melchizedek's royal priesthood is an expression of Adam's office, why not cast the Messiah as 'a priest after the order of Adam'? Chapter 3 will address this issue at greater length, but for now the answer, simply put, is that David appeals to Melchizedek in Psalm 110:4 because the text of Genesis uniquely identifies Melchizedek with the Abrahamic covenant – the covenant that will serve as the basis for and find fulfilment (albeit partial) in the Davidic covenant.

Melchizedek and the Abrahamic covenant

How does a figure who appears only once in the biblical narrative become such an integral part of redemptive history? People of importance are not always the ones who perform heroic acts, make spectacular discoveries or distinguish themselves as innovators in their generation. Often, importance is a factor of *who* you know. As the old adage says, 'It's good to know people in high places.' Melchizedek knew people in high places. He knew Abraham and, more importantly, he knew Abraham's God. But the reverse is also true: Abraham knew Melchizedek and recognized Melchizedek's greatness by paying him a tithe.

Melchizedek's significance in redemptive history is a factor of his relationship to Abraham. To understand why the Melchizedekian priesthood became an essential component of David's messianic theology, it is necessary to explore two related issues. First, we must understand Melchizedek's importance in Genesis 14 and later biblical history in relation to the life of Abraham and the Abrahamic covenant.[93] The Abrahamic covenant informs a correct reading of the Melchizedek episode, and the Melchizedek episode informs the nature of the Abrahamic covenant. They are inseparable. Second, the covenant solidarity shared by these two figures supports the evidence that Abraham is himself a

---

[93] See Mathews 2013: 54–70.

royal-priestly figure like Melchizedek. An examination of Genesis 14:18–20 in its literary context will substantiate these assertions and should yield some implications for understanding the logic of Psalm 110 and, later, the theology of Hebrews.

Genesis 14:18–20 in covenantal context

McConville's essay 'Abraham and Melchizedek: Horizons in Genesis 14' examines Genesis 14:18–20 in the literary context of Genesis. Following Wenham, McConville highlights textual evidence that indicates verses 18–20 are not an intrusion into the text without any attachment to the surrounding narrative, but rather an integral part of the broader context:

> Melchizedek knows that Abram has won a victory (v. 20). Abram's refusal to be made rich by the King of Sodom (הֶעֱשַׁרְתִּי, v. 23) entails a play on the word for tithe (מַעֲשֵׂר, v. 20). Melchizedek's bringing out bread (הוֹצִיא לֶחֶם, v. 18) contrasts with the King of Sodom's going out to war (מִלְחָמָה, יָצָא, vv. 2, 8, 17). And finally . . . Abram's ascription of praise to 'Yahweh, El-Elyon, creator of heaven and earth', v. 22, picks up the terms used by Melchizedek, v. 19, with the significant addition of the name Yahweh.[94]

The Melchizedek episode (14:18–20) is at home in the broader context of Genesis 14. But what is Melchizedek's purpose in the narrative?

McConville argues that the function of Genesis 14 is to resolve questions raised by the patriarchal narrative in Genesis 12 – 13, while Genesis 14:18–24 affirms that Abraham will receive God's covenantal promises by faith. McConville situates Genesis 14 in the flow of Genesis 12 – 15 by connecting its contents to the covenantal promises of posterity and land (Gen. 12:1–3). Both themes – posterity and land – appear in Genesis 13. Lot chooses to dwell in a land outside the land of promise, while Abraham occupies the land of Canaan. Lot's prevalent role in the narrative raises the question: is Lot Abraham's heir? Even though Lot chose to dwell outside the land of promise, McConville does not believe this fact settles every suspicion that Lot might be the one to inherit the promises made to Abraham. In Genesis 14, Abraham remains deeply committed to his kinsman Lot. Lot's captivity is, after all, what springs the events of Genesis 14

---

94 McConville 1994: 113.

into action. Is it possible, according to McConville, that Abraham set out to rescue Lot not simply out of loyalty to his kinsman but because Abraham was 'trying to preserve his stake in Lot as heir'?[95] Genesis 14 shuts down any possibility that Lot would be heir to Abraham and, therefore, accentuates the need for an heir in Abraham's direct line.[96] Hence, Abraham laments his childlessness in Genesis 15:2.

Within this covenantal context, the Melchizedek episode of Genesis 14:18–20 finds meaning. Melchizedek arrives at a time when it appears that Abraham might lay claim to wealth, possessions and perhaps even the land by virtue of his strength as a major political leader.[97] McConville asks the question here: 'If he [Abraham] is to receive a land, by what right shall he hold it?'[98] As noted earlier, the king of Sodom and the king of Salem (Melchizedek) represent two possible answers. The king of Sodom operates within the logic of a human kingdom. He wants the people for his own possession. He wants to build his strength by human means because in his world might makes right. McConville observes that the king of Sodom extends an offer to Abraham built on the assumption that Abraham might lay claim to the possessions 'by virtue of his prowess'.[99]

The king of Salem, however, operates within the logic of God's kingdom. Melchizedek acknowledges that Abraham's success in battle was the result of God's goodness. In other words, Abraham's victory was a gift from God (Gen. 14:20). Abraham identifies with Melchizedek by paying him a tithe and rejects the world view of the king of Sodom by refusing his offer. McConville concludes that, at this moment, Abraham demonstrates by what right he will lay claim to the covenant promises: he will possess them by faith:

> In the gift and the polite refusal, therefore, Abram shows how he will possess the land; he will receive it as a gift . . . Perhaps we can say that Abram learns this, or relearns it, in the encounter with Melchizedek, for this is implied in the suggestion that the one encounter bears upon the other. Yet he is not a bland receiver of the doctrine, for in assimilating it he re-expresses, now for the benefit of the King

---

[95] Ibid.
[96] Ibid.
[97] Ibid. 114.
[98] Ibid.
[99] Ibid. 115.

of Sodom (v. 22), his own faith in the God, Yahweh, who has promised him land and posterity. The priest-king of Salem knows that it is the Most High, the Maker of heaven and earth, who alone can give; but Abram knows that this is none other than Yahweh.[100]

McConville's analysis highlights how integral the Abrahamic covenantal context is to the Melchizedek episode. The literary connections between Genesis 14:18–20 and the Abrahamic covenant, however, do not end with Genesis 14. On the heels of Abraham's interaction with the priest-king of Salem, God appears to Abraham in Genesis 15 to reaffirm his covenant promises. Several literary connections hold the two narratives together.

First, Genesis 15:1 opens with the words 'after these things', a reference to Abraham's military expedition and encounter with Melchizedek in Genesis 14. God's command to Abraham to 'fear not' in Genesis 15:1, and his twofold promise of protection and reward are best understood against the backdrop of Genesis 14. Gentry draws out the significance of the narrative flow:

> Both the command and the promises relate directly to the events of chapter 14. Will the 'Four Big Bad Guys from the East' be back next year to take their vengeance on Abram? Certainly the fear of reprisal is both real and significant. Yahweh will be Abram's shield. He will protect Abram from possible reprisal. Second, at the end of Genesis 14, Abram took none of the spoils of the victory which were his by right. He wanted his sources of wealth to come from the Lord and not from the king of Sodom. So Yahweh promises Abram that he will reward him.[101]

Immediately after Melchizedek's sudden appearance, Yahweh comes to Abraham in a manner that proves Melchizedek's words to be true. Yahweh is Abraham's protector ('shield'), just as Melchizedek indicated by affirming that the Most High gave Abraham victory over his enemies (Gen. 15:1; cf. Gen. 14:20). Moreover, Yahweh's promise of reward to Abraham flows naturally out of Melchizedek's confession that God is the 'possessor of heaven and earth' (Gen. 14:19, 22). Abraham refused the spoils of war from the hand of the king of Sodom, but God will reward Abraham greatly. Kline draws out the covenantal subtext here:

> The imagery of Genesis 15:1 is that of the Great King honoring Abraham's notable exhibition of compliance with covenant duty by the reward of a special grant that would more than make up for whatever enrichment he had foregone at the hands of the king of Sodom for the sake of faithfulness to Yahweh, his Lord.[102]

Second, Melchizedek's blessing acknowledges God as the sovereign Lord who 'delivered' (*miggēn*) Abraham's enemies into his hand (Gen. 14:20b). The verb *māgan* only occurs in the piel stem and it means 'to deliver'.[103] The nominal form of the same word occurs in Genesis 15, where the Lord tells Abraham in 15:1b, 'Do not be afraid. I am your shield (*māgēn*); your reward will be exceedingly great.' The nominal *māgēn*, translated 'shield', links God's covenantal blessing (Gen. 15:1–6) to Melchizedek's blessing of Abraham in Genesis 14:20. Just as God delivered Abraham from the battle against the kings (Gen. 14:20), so too will God protect Abraham and his future descendants so that they may inherit their reward (Gen. 15:1–6).

Third, Melchizedek identifies with the Abrahamic covenant in Genesis 15 through the terms 'righteousness' and 'peace'. As I have already noted, Melchizedek's name means 'king of righteousness'. He is also the king of Salem (*šālēm*), the Hebrew word for peace (cf. Heb. 7:2). In Genesis 15:6, Abraham's faith is counted to him as 'righteousness' (*ṣĕdāqâ*), while in Genesis 15:15 God promises Abraham that he will go to his ancestors in 'peace' (*šālōm*).

The preponderance of evidence situates the Melchizedek episode within the broader context of the Abrahamic covenant. Before drawing any conclusions from this observation, I turn now to the second and related issue concerning Abraham's role as a priest-king like Melchizedek.

Abraham as priest-king

Abraham's story is part of the metanarrative begun with Adam. Like Adam who had three sons (Gen. 5:4) and Noah who had three sons (Gen.

---

102 Kline 2000: 324.
103 BDB 171.

5:32), Abraham is one of Terah's three sons (Gen. 11). Gentry describes this genealogical parallel as 'a literary technique inviting the reader to compare Abram with Noah and Adam'.[104] God's call of Abraham in Genesis begins to hint that, through Abraham, God's purpose for creation will come to pass.[105] Like Adam, Abraham receives God's blessing (*bārak*) (Gen. 12:2; cf. Gen. 1:28), the promise of an Eden-like land (Gen. 12:6–8; cf. Exod. 15:17) and the guarantee that God will make him exceedingly 'fruitful' (*pārâ*) and 'multiply' (*rābâ*) his offspring (Gen. 17:2, 6; 22:17; cf. Gen. 1:28). The hope for God's kingdom will come through Abraham; his offspring will become a nation of royal priests (Exod. 19:6) mediating God's rule and blessing to the rest of the world. Hamilton captures the Abraham–Adam link by connecting Abraham's seed to the land promise. He writes, 'As the story of the Pentateuch unfolds, the Promised Land almost becomes a new Eden. The Lord will walk among his people in the land, just as he walked in the garden.'[106]

If Abraham is a new Adam, then we would expect Abraham to represent God by fulfilling the role of a priest-king. Abraham's actions and behaviour in Genesis 14 support this claim. According to McConville, Genesis 14 presents Abraham as a 'powerful figure' and a 'major player in international affairs'.[107] Alexander moves a step further when he claims that the 'events of Genesis 14 indicate that Abraham is no ordinary semi-nomadic pastoralist. His military exploits place him on a par with kings.'[108] Similarly, Wenham writes, 'In these scenes Abram is portrayed not merely as the archetypal Israelite who has faith in God, but as a conquering king who has been promised victory over his foes and a great territory.'[109]

Abraham's rescue of Lot presents his power in contrast to corrupt human kingship. By delivering Lot, along with a handful of Gentile kings, Abraham uses his strength for service. Abraham's success illustrates, on a small scale, how he will mediate the blessing of God's covenant to others. In other words, Genesis 12:1–3 has already begun to work itself out in the events of Genesis 14.

---

[104] Gentry and Wellum 2012: 224.
[105] Hamilton (2010: 82) has demonstrated that the blessings promised to Abraham match the curses of Gen. 3:14–19 point for point so as to provide a redemptive solution to humanity's plight.
[106] Ibid. 81.
[107] McConville 1994: 111.
[108] Alexander 2009: 82.
[109] Wenham 1987: 335.

According to Sung Jin Park, Abraham's two functions in Genesis 14, deliverer and mediator, 'came from God by the nature of the Abrahamic covenant' and could be regarded as identical to the two offices of kingship and priesthood.[110] By the time Abraham encounters the priest-king Melchizedek, his actions in Genesis 14 have already identified him as a royal-priestly figure in his own right.

The nature of Abraham's interaction with Melchizedek solidifies Abraham's role as a priest-king. Abraham identifies with Melchizedek by accepting Melchizedek's priestly blessing of bread and wine, by offering Melchizedek a tithe and by swearing an oath in language identical to that spoken by Melchizedek: 'God Most High, the possessor of heaven and earth' (Gen. 14:19, 22). Commenting on Abraham's tithe and solemn oath, Hahn writes:

> After the blessing, Abram gives tithes to Melchizedek (v. 20) . . . Abram then swears a solemn oath (vv. 22–23), which entails the renunciation of the benefaction of the King of Sodom. By means of these two acts (paying the tithe and swearing the oath), Abram pledges continued loyalty to El Elyon and to his priest-king, Melchizedek. The mutuality of covenant solidarity is formally acknowledged by Melchizedek through his priestly blessing and the shared meal of bread and wine.[111]

The covenant solidarity between Abraham and Melchizedek supports the notion that Abraham will exercise the type of priestly rule characterized by Melchizedek himself. Alexander has drawn the same conclusion:

> By affirming the truthfulness of what Melchizedek has to say and rejecting the offer of the king of Sodom, Abraham indicates his own commitment to be a righteous priest-king. Abraham will not inherit the earth through the use of aggressive military power, although clearly his defeat of the eastern kings indicates he has the capacity to do so. Rather, he looks to God to provide for his future well-being.[112]

---

110 Park 2011: 3.1.1.
111 Hahn 2009: 131.
112 Alexander 2009: 82.

The biblical data outside the narrative of Genesis 14 also depicts Abraham as a royal-priestly figure. With regard to his royal status, several observations are worth noting. First, the Hittites identify Abraham as a 'prince of God' in Genesis 23:5–6. Second, Abraham's treaty with King Abimelech implies that Abraham was the king's equal. Third, God promises Abraham that kings will come from his line (Gen. 17:6). Fourth, God promises to make Abraham's name great, just as he would later promise to King David.[113]

With respect to his priestly function, Abraham builds altars and offers sacrifices to God. In Genesis 12, Abraham builds an altar in Canaan – the place later described as the mountain sanctuary of God (Exod. 15:11–13, 15–17).[114] Similarly, Abraham offers a ram as a burnt offering instead of Isaac on Mount Moriah, the future site of Israel's temple (2 Chr. 3:1). Moreover, Alexander argues that Abraham's divine encounters and communications with God indicate 'he enjoys a status equivalent to that of a priest, although he is never designated as one'.[115] Furthermore, Abraham's intercessory prayer on behalf of the righteous ones in Sodom portrays him as a kind of priestly mediator (Gen. 18:22–33).[116]

The covenantal ceremonies recorded in Genesis 15 and 17 also highlight Abraham's priestly role as a covenant mediator. Shrock's assessment of Genesis 15 is well put:

> In Genesis 15, Abraham is observed preparing the sacrifices and guarding the holy place of God – the place where God's presence would soon pass. In these twin functions – especially in his driving away the carrion-eating birds of prey – he is acting out the duties that would later be given to the Levitical priests.[117]

Finally, by comparing and contrasting the practice of circumcision in Egypt and Israel, John Meade has demonstrated that circumcision signified the consecration of the priesthood in service to Yahweh.[118] Abraham

---

[113] Arnold 2008: 132.
[114] Gentry (Gentry and Wellum 2012: 235) suggests that here 'we see Abram fulfilling *an Adamic role*: he offers sacrifice as a priest and worships God in this mountain sanctuary'; emphasis original.
[115] Alexander 2009: 83.
[116] Gentry and Wellum 2012: 283.
[117] Schrock 2013: 77–78.
[118] Meade 2008. See also Gentry and Wellum 2012: 275.

and his offspring are set apart through circumcision to become a nation of priests (Gen. 17:12; Exod. 19:6).

Theological implications

Now comes the 'so what?' Why does any of this matter for the larger purpose of this project? If the Melchizedek episode takes place in the broader context of the Abrahamic covenant, and if Abraham is a priest-king like Melchizedek, then where does that lead us? What bearing does this have on redemptive history and the logic of Psalm 110? Here are four answers.

First, by depicting Abraham as a priest-king in his own right, Moses demonstrates to the people of Israel that they are part of God's plan for creation and redemption. Their calling as a 'royal priesthood' (see Exod. 19:6) finds its origin in God's covenant with Abraham and, by extension, God's covenant with creation. Through his covenant mediator, Israel, God will establish his kingdom.

Second, the covenant solidarity between Abraham and Melchizedek implies that Melchizedek himself embodies the universal scope of the Abrahamic covenant. In other words, the blessing of the Abrahamic covenant will have an impact on the Gentiles (typified by Melchizedek), who will themselves become priests and kings unto God (cf. 1 Pet. 2:9; Rev. 1:6; 5:10).

Third, Melchizedek's solidarity with Abraham hints at the type of priesthood that will be capable of mediating the blessings of the Abrahamic covenant to the world. In simpler terms, a Melchizedekian priesthood is necessary to bring the promises of the Abrahamic covenant to fruition. The close association between Melchizedek and Abraham has led Robert Letham to the conclusion that Melchizedek is the priest of the Abrahamic covenant:

> In Genesis chapter 14 Melchizedek functions in a covenantal context. His blessing of Abram is parallel to Yahweh's blessing him in Genesis 12. In that sense, Melchizedek can be seen as the one through whom the promised covenant blessings are channeled, even mediated. Consequently, he is the priest of the Abrahamic covenant, just as Aaron is the priest of the Mosaic covenant.[119]

---

[119] Letham 1993: 109.

Whether or not Melchizedek is the priest of the Abrahamic covenant is up for debate. Nevertheless, we must admit that the Melchizedekian priesthood is uniquely bound to Abraham and the Abrahamic covenant. The author of Hebrews will make it clear that Melchizedek's priesthood is the order of priesthood that qualifies to mediate the Abrahamic covenant in a way that priests under the Mosaic law simply could not do (cf. Heb. 6:14 – 7:28). In chapter 4, I will argue that Psalm 110:4 reveals that David recognized a Melchizedekian priesthood would be necessary to mediate the promises of the Abrahamic covenant and, by necessary extension, the promises of the Davidic covenant.

Fourth, the strong association between Abraham and Melchizedek lays the foundation for the Melchizedekian priesthood to become a vital component of Davidic messiahship. As I demonstrated above, Melchizedek identifies with the Abrahamic covenantal context of Genesis 15 through the terms 'righteousness' and 'peace'. From a canonical perspective, the terms 'righteousness' and 'peace' appear together in both Davidic and Abrahamic covenantal contexts. Concerning the Messiah, Isaiah writes:

> Of the increase of his dominion and of *peace* (*šālōm*)
> there will be no end,
> upon the throne of David and over his kingdom
> to establish it and to support it
> with justice and with *righteousness* (*ṣĕdāqâ*)
> from now unto eternity.
> The zeal of the LORD of hosts will do this.
> (Isa. 9:7 [MT 9:6]; emphasis mine)

In Psalm 72, the Davidic king possesses the righteousness of God and judges with righteousness (Ps. 72:1–2). His reign is described as one of righteousness and peace in verse 7:

> May the *righteous* (*ṣaddîq*) abound in his days,
> and may *peace* (*šālôm*) multiply until the moon expires.
> (Ps. 72:7; emphasis mine)

The terms occur together in Isaiah 48:18, followed immediately by an allusion to the Abrahamic covenant:

Oh that you had paid attention to my commandments!
   Then your *peace* (*šālôm*) would have been like a river,
     and your *righteousness* (*ṣĕdāqâ*) like the waves of the sea;
   your offspring would have been like the sand,
     and your descendants like its grains;
   their name would never be cut off
     or destroyed from before me.
   (Isa. 48:18–19 ESV; emphasis mine)

These verses from Isaiah 9:7 and 48:18–19 demonstrate that later biblical authors characterized the reign of the Davidic king in terms of 'righteousness' and 'peace', qualities that were to be characteristic of the nation of Israel, Abraham's offspring (Isa. 48:18–29; cf. 12:2; 22:17). In the immediate context, then, the terms function to link Melchizedek and Abraham together, while from a canonical perspective, 'righteousness' and 'peace' are defining qualities of the Davidic king.[120]

One final observation is worth noting at this point. Psalm 76:1–2 identifies Salem with Zion, the city of (Jeru)salem:

In Judah God is known;
   his name is great in Israel.
His abode has been established in Salem,
   his dwelling place in Zion.
(Ps. 76:1–2 ESV)

The terms 'Salem' and 'Zion' stand in synonymous parallelism, highlighting their identification with each other. If we understand Salem in Genesis 14 as Jerusalem – the future city of David – then we have in a patriarchal narrative an account of Abraham encountering Jerusalem and its priesthood. Having just established peace by experiencing victory in warfare (Gen. 14:1–16), Abraham immediately arrives near Salem, the city of peace. Abraham's movement from conqueror to fellowship with Melchizedek (the 'king of peace') anticipates David's own peace-producing reign and triumphal entry into Jerusalem (2 Sam. 6) – events that will be important for understanding David's portrait of the Messiah in Psalm 110.

---

120 See Rooke 2000: 85–86.

Conclusion

Through the associations between Abraham and Melchizedek, we begin to understand why David would appeal to Melchizedek in Psalm 110:4. Melchizedek was a priest uniquely associated with Abraham, the Abrahamic covenant and (Jeru)salem. Apart from his desire to see Melchizedek as Shem, Hahn accurately summarizes Melchizedek's canonical importance:

> A canonical interpretation of the Melchizedek narrative generates a series of important connections that will be invaluable for examining the reappearance of these traditions in the Davidic covenant (Ps 110:4), and also in the royal high priestly Christology of Hebrews. By linking Melchizedek with Shem, and Salem with Jerusalem, the canonical narrative underwrites the application of such traditions to David, and the divine covenant sworn to 'the son of David.'[121]

If David recognized that the Davidic covenant would bring to fruition the promises of the Abrahamic covenant, then it would be logical to assume that he also recognized that the priesthood associated with the Abrahamic (Melchizedekian) covenant would play a role in fulfilling the promises of the Davidic covenant.

Furthermore, the Melchizedekian priesthood claims salvation-historical superiority over the Aaronic–Levitical priesthood by virtue of its association with Abraham. Abraham, the ancestor of Israel and chosen by God to bring blessing to the nations, acknowledges Melchizedek's superior status by paying him a tithe. Melchizedek, in turn, blesses the inferior Abraham (cf. Heb. 7:9). These facts imply that the Melchizedekian priesthood is rooted in the terms of a covenant superior to the Abrahamic and Mosaic covenants. This superior covenant is the covenant of creation mediated through Adam and later inherited by Noah.

We, therefore, have a theological rationale for saying that Melchizedek's priesthood is superior to the Levitical priesthood because it is tied to the creation ordinance, not the codification of the law. Hahn is right to suggest that 'the exaltation of Jesus as the firstborn Son and royal high priest – prefigured by Melchizedek – represents the restoration of a more perfect

---

[121] Hahn 2009: 134.

form of covenant mediation originally intended for Adam and Israel'.[122]

Smith similarly says, 'David . . . realized that the Messiah would be a king-priest like Melchizedek because the Messiah would replace Adam as the king of the world, the firstborn son of all mankind.'[123] Thus, David appeals to the Melchizedekian priesthood – not Adam, Noah or the Levitical priesthood – because the Melchizedekian priesthood simultaneously looks back to God's purposes at creation and typologically points forward to the Davidic covenant by linking Jerusalem to the Abrahamic covenant.

To sum up, three important truths surface from Melchizedek's inter-actions with Abraham: (1) the Melchizedekian priesthood maintains salvation-historical superiority over the Levitical priesthood and func-tions as the order of priesthood that mediates the blessings of the Abrahamic covenant to the world; (2) the blessings of the Abrahamic cov-enant will bring about God's creational purpose for human beings (of all nations) to exist as kings and priests unto God; and (3) Melchizedek's connection to Jerusalem and solidarity with the Abrahamic covenant lays the groundwork for David's typological interpretation of the Melchiz-edekian priesthood in Psalm 110.

---

[122] Ibid. 280.
[123] Smith 2011: 108.

3

Israel's royal priesthood and the Aaronic priesthood

In Exodus 19:6, God defined the reason for Israel's existence: 'And you will be to me a royal priesthood and a holy nation.' It is evident by now that Israel's calling to be a royal priesthood does not appear in a vacuum but is part of the story that has been unfolding since creation. Adam's office now resides in a nation of priest-kings. Israel is the nation through which God's rule and blessing will flow to the rest of the world.

Why include a chapter on Israel's corporate priesthood and the Aaronic priesthood in a study focusing on Psalm 110? At the very least, this chapter is necessary because the priest of Psalm 110 is *Israel's* king. Interpreted in the light of Israel's story, the king of Psalm 110 is the embodiment of corporate Israel. Priesthood and kingship may have been separated in Israel's history, but their union in the Messiah represents the continuation of a more fundamental type of covenant mediation originally intended for God's son Adam and later applied to Israel (Exod. 4:22).

As part of the biblical-theological foundation for Psalm 110, this chapter will develop the meaning of Israel's royal priesthood in the light of the metanarrative thus far. My goal is (1) to demonstrate that Israel's identity as a royal priesthood is a function of the nation's role as a new Adam, and (2) to show that Aaron's priesthood represents the corporate royal priesthood of the nation and is itself a symbolic expression of the priesthood originally assigned to primal humanity. Although the offices of king and priest become institutionalized and separated in Israel's history, the Torah's storyline sets a trajectory for a messianic hope contained in a priestly ruler who will execute the kind of covenant mediation that reunites the jurisdictions of priesthood and kingship into one office.

Corporate Adam

Prior to Israel's birth as a nation, God's covenantal dealings with Noah and Abraham were extensions of his covenant with Adam.[1] Noah and Abraham were to mediate God's rule and blessing by filling the earth with descendants (Gen. 9:1; 12:2–3). At the end of Genesis, Abraham's seed is in Egypt, and it remains to be seen how God's purposes will come to pass. Enter Israel. Israel inherits the Adamic role and owns the privilege of being the last Adam in Old Testament history.

Several observations attest to Israel's Adamic role. First, Exodus 1:7 describes the numerical growth of Israel in language reminiscent of Genesis 1:28: the people were 'fruitful' (*pārâ*) and 'multiplied' (*rābâ*) and 'filled' (*mālē'*) the earth.[2] Adam's creation mandate is now coming to pass through Israel. Second, Israel is Yahweh's 'firstborn' son, called out of Egypt to serve the Lord (Exod. 4:22–23).[3] Like Adam, Israel now exists in a covenantal relationship with Yahweh characterized by sonship and faithful service. Third, Exodus 15:17–18 reveals the grand purpose of Israel's redemption:

> You will bring them and plant them on the mountain of your
> inheritance,
> the place you have made for your dwelling, O Yahweh,
> the sanctuary, O Lord, your hands have established.
> Yahweh will reign for ever and ever.

God will restore to Israel the kind of relationship that existed between God and humanity in Eden.[4] Dumbrell helpfully summarizes the relationship between Adam and Israel and their roles in establishing God's kingdom:

> Thus the relationship of Israel to Adam is important for the devel-
> opment of the eschatology of the Bible in that the creation account

---

[1] Smith 2011: 103.

[2] All of these Hebrew terms appear in Gen. 1:28.

[3] The verb *'ābad* appears twice in Gen. 2 to describe humankind's responsibility for maintaining God's garden-sanctuary (Gen. 2:5, 15). Furthermore, priests are identified as 'servants of Yahweh' (*'abdê yahweh*) in Pss 134:1 and 135:1 and 'servants/ministers' (*měšārĕtê*) in several other places (cf. 2 Chr. 13:10; Jer. 33:21; Ezek. 45:4).

[4] Dempster 2003: 100. See also Gentry and Wellum 2012: 227. For a typological reading of the Song of Moses, see Lohfink 1968: 67–86.

indicates the nature and purpose of Israel's special status in its role of exercising dominion in its world, a status that Adam had once exercised. For beginning with the Cain narrative, the movement from Adam to Israel will be accomplished by a series of divine selections that are designed to bring Israel onto the world stage. This series of movements results in God's concluding the Sinai covenant, by which he establishes a special relationship with Israel. In turn the Sinai covenant is designed to bring the world of nations into the sphere of the universal kingdom of God. The final status of the saved will be as kings and priests unto God (Rev 1:5–6; 5:10; 20:4–6), with the fulfillment of this expectation met at Revelation 22:1–5. These texts make it clear that the function of the creation account is to indicate the nature and purpose of Israel's special status as the bearer of the role that Adam once occupied.[5]

A royal priesthood

The purpose of the Sinai covenant is made plain in Exodus 19:5–6: obedience to Yahweh will make Israel Yahweh's own 'treasured possession', 'royal priesthood' and 'holy nation'. God enters into a covenant with Israel so that Israel will become a 'royal priesthood' (*mamleket kōhănîm*) showing the rest of the world what it means to worship the one true and living God. But what exactly is meant by the phrase *mamleket kōhănîm*?

Since its publication in 2004, John Davies' monograph *A Royal Priesthood: Literary and Intertexual Perspectives on an Image of Israel in Exodus 19.6* has become the *locus classicus* on the meaning and function of *mamleket kōhănîm* in Exodus 19:6. Often translated 'kingdom of priests', Davies argues that 'royal priesthood' is a better rendering of *mamleket kōhănîm*. He proposes what he calls an 'active-corporate' interpretation of the phrase *mamleket kōhănîm*.[6] The combination of terms, according to Davies, denotes a 'collective royal company consisting of "priests"'.[7] Their corporate regal priesthood grants Israel a unique and privileged position in the world. Davies concludes:

---

5 Dumbrell 2002: 62.
6 Davies 2004: 76.
7 Ibid. 86.

As a nation, Israel is assured of the privilege of royal status, a royalty characterized by the essence of priesthood, namely, access to the divine presence. Israel's corporate priesthood is pre-eminently that which is exercised towards God, not other nations.[8]

Israel's priestly service to God is part of what it means for that nation to exist as Yahweh's 'personal treasure' and firstborn son (Exod. 19:5; cf. Exod. 4:22).

Israel's royal-priestly prerogative is reminiscent of Adam's privileged position in the garden-sanctuary. The book of Exodus links Israel's role to Adam's role in two more ways: (1) by highlighting parallels between the tabernacle and creation and the garden of Eden, and (2) by demonstrating that the Aaronic priesthood, as a representation of Israel's corporate priesthood, echoes primal humanity's office of priest-king.

An Edenic tabernacle

The tabernacle constructed by the Israelites was their Eden in the wilderness. The description of the tabernacle in Exodus 25 – 31 and 39 – 40 echoes the creation narrative of Genesis 1 – 2.[9] Yahweh's seven speeches to Moses ('The LORD said to Moses . . .') in Exodus 25 – 31 recall the seven days of creation in Genesis 1 and the respective substance of each of those days.[10] Most notable in this regard are the sixth and seventh speeches of Yahweh to Moses. The sixth speech emphasizes the 'installation of two human beings filled with the Spirit of God to implement the making of the structure',[11] while the seventh is a reminder of the importance of sabbath-keeping for the people of Israel. It concludes with a direct reference to creation: 'in six days the LORD made heaven and earth, and on the seventh day he rested and was refreshed' (Exod. 31:17 ESV). Weinfeld has provided a helpful summary of the linguistic parallels between the completion of the tabernacle described in Exodus 39 – 40 and the creation narrative in Genesis 1 – 2 (see Table 3.1).[12]

---

[8] Ibid. 102.
[9] On the relationship between the tabernacle and creation, see Weinfeld 1981; Beale 2004: 66–76; Davies 2004: 145–149; Alexander 2012: 122–124.
[10] Fletcher-Louis 2002: 63, 76.
[11] Dempster 2003: 102.
[12] Table 3.1 is adapted from Weinfeld 1981: 503.

Table 3.1 Linguistic parallels between Genesis 1 – 2 and Exodus 39 – 40

Genesis 1 – 2	Exodus 39 – 40
And God saw all that he had made, (*kol-'ăšer 'āśâ*) and found it (*wĕhinnê*) very good (Gen. 1:31)	And when Moses saw that they had performed all the tasks (*kolhammĕlā'kâ*) as the LORD had commanded, so they had done (*wĕhinnê 'āśû 'ōtāh*)... (Exod. 39:43a)
The heaven and the earth were completed (*waykullû*) and all (*wĕkol*) their array (Gen. 2:1)	Thus was completed all (*wattēkel kol*) the work of the tabernacle of the Tent of Meeting (Exod. 39:32)
God finished the work which he had been doing (*waykal 'ĕlōhîm*... *mĕla'ktô 'ăšer 'āśâ*) (Gen. 2:2)	When Moses had finished the work (*waykal mōšeh 'et-hammĕlā'kâ*) (Exod. 40:33)
And God blessed (*waybārek*)... (Gen. 2:3)	...Moses blessed (*waybārek*) them (Exod. 39:43b)
And sanctified (*wayqaddēš*) it (Gen. 2:3)	...to sanctify (*wĕqiddaštā*) it and all its furnishings (Exod. 40:9)

Commenting on the relationship between the tabernacle, sabbath and creation and its significance in Israel's history, Dempster writes:

> the covenant at Sinai marks a people that manifests God's intentions for creation from the beginning: the rule of God. Just as the Sabbath was a sign of God's rule at creation, so it becomes a sign of his rule in history. There is a significant progression here: the stability of the world order, the blessing of descendants, human activity mirroring divine activity. This is a noteworthy expression of rulership and dominion in history. Created order leads to descendants who exercise dominion. Just as the divine ruler worked and rested, human beings are to work and rest. This kingdom of priests is to manifest God's rule to the world.[13]

---

[13] Dempster 2003: 103.

Once world order is stabilized, represented by the construction and maintenance of the tabernacle, a new humanity (Israel) is to fulfil the Adamic role of mediating God's rule and blessing to the rest of the world.

The people of Israel were a corporate Adam, and the holy of holies was their garden of Eden where their priests would meet God. Beale has demonstrated that the tripartite structure of the tabernacle and temple was a reflection of the tripartite structure of the garden of Eden.[14] Genesis 2:10 indicates that the garden and Eden formed two distinct regions: 'a river flowed *out of* Eden to water the garden' (ESV; emphasis mine). The eschatological temples in Ezekiel 47 and Revelation 22 use similar imagery to describe a river flowing out of the inner sanctuary to water the earth around. If, as Beale argues, the outer court of the temple represented the land and seas outside the garden, then the tripartite structure of the tabernacle-temple is a mirror image of the tripartite structure of Eden, the garden and the world outside:

> Thus, one may be able to perceive an increasing gradation in holiness from outside the garden proceeding inward: the region outside the garden is related to God and is 'very good' (Gen 1:31) in that it is God's creation (= the outer court); the garden itself is a sacred space separate from the outer world (= the holy place), where God's priestly servant worships God by obeying him, by cultivating and guarding; Eden is where God dwells (= the holy of holies) as the source of both physical and spiritual life (symbolized by the waters).[15]

The association between the tabernacle and Eden is strong evidence that Israel has inherited Adam's office as priest. Like Adam, who was placed in the garden to enjoy God's presence and learn God's ways before taking dominion over the earth, the people of Israel – through their priests – enjoy access to God and must make the worship of Yahweh primary if they are to extend God's rule to other nations.

Furthermore, Israel's collective responsibility for building the tabernacle parallels Adam's royal commission to build God's temple by expanding the borders of the garden-sanctuary. Davies explains:

---

[14] Beale 2004: 74–75.
[15] Ibid. 75.

In keeping with the expectation that sanctuary-building is the work of a chosen king, acting on instructions of a god and according to a divinely revealed pattern, it is suggested that Israel corporately functions as a royal sanctuary builder according to Exodus, in keeping with the designation as a 'royal priesthood.'[16]

Israel's calling as a *royal* priesthood implies that the tabernacle (God's dwelling place) was not intended to remain relegated to the people of Israel alone.[17] Their influence was to find expression beyond their own borders. Beale advances this argument by noting a connection between the patriarchs and their altars, and Israel and its tabernacle. The repetition of the Adamic commission to the patriarchs in Genesis often accompanies small sanctuary (altar) construction (Gen. 8:20 – 9:1; 12:1–9; 14:14–18; 26:24–25; 35:1–12). According to Beale, the patriarchs built these 'impermanent, miniature' sanctuaries as symbolic of the fact that their descendants were to spread out 'and subdue the earth from a divine sanctuary in fulfillment of the commission in Genesis 1:26–28'.[18] These sanctuaries anticipate Israel's tabernacle and temple 'from which Israel was to branch out over all the earth'.[19] As a corporate covenant mediator, Israel would bring others into the boundaries of God's dwelling presence.

Finally, it is worth noting that as a microcosm of creation (kingdom) and Edenic sanctuary (priestly tent), the tabernacle functions as a symbolic representation of Israel's identity as a royal priesthood. The likelihood of this claim receives support from the fact that the priest, who embodied Israel's identity as a royal priesthood, wore clothing that was regal in character and displayed imagery, colours and design similar to those of the tabernacle.[20] In the tabernacle, then, we have a picture of the dwelling place of God representing a new humanity – redeemed Israel.

If the tent symbolized Israel's identity as a royal priesthood, and the Messiah would represent the nation as a righteous priest-king (Ps. 110), then it is not a stretch to suggest that the tabernacle typologically pointed

---

[16] Davies 2004: 169.
[17] Blackburn 2012: 150.
[18] Beale 2004: 97.
[19] Ibid. 97–98.
[20] See Davies 2004: 157–161. On the association between the priestly vestments and the tabernacle, see Kline 1977: 46–51; Beale 2004: 39–42.

to an individual embodying God's presence in his own person as the true king and true Israel. God's house – made of wood, stone and fabric – pointed forward to a house that would be made of flesh (John 1:14).

Aaron as *royal* priest

Israel's priesthood raises questions about the existence of the Aaronic priesthood. If Israel's royal priesthood carries the Adamic role forward, then how does the Aaronic priesthood fit into the picture? Why does the Aaronic priesthood even exist? Is there any relationship between the Aaronic priesthood and Adam's role as priest-king or Melchizedek's priesthood? To situate the Aaronic priesthood in redemptive history from Eden to Sinai, it is necessary to develop two main observations: (1) the Aaronic priesthood embodies the corporate priesthood of Israel and thus the nation's role as a new Adam, and (2) the high priest symbolizes God's original design for human beings: regal servants possessing access to God's presence.

Israel's royal priesthood and Aaron's priesthood

If God called Israel to be a royal community of priests, why was there a need for the Aaronic order? Hahn argues that the people of Israel lost their status as royal priests because of their idolatry with the golden calf (Exod. 32). As a result, the rites of the priesthood transferred to the tribe of Levi.[21] Sailhamer offers a more nuanced interpretation of the relationship between Israel's royal priesthood and the Aaronic priesthood. By analysing the compositional strategy of Exodus 19 – 24, Sailhamer argues that the need for a priesthood within the community of Israel arose out of the people's failure to meet God at Mount Sinai (Exod. 19:13, 16–21; 20:18–21). At Sinai, the Israelites were afraid to approach God, so they asked Moses to go before God on their behalf. The people 'appear to be asking for a priesthood to represent them, to teach them, and to stand before God in their place'.[22] Whereas Hahn argued that the failure of the golden calf incident gave rise to the Levitical priesthood, Sailhamer suggests that it is the people's failure to draw near to Yahweh that necessitates a priesthood

---

[21] Hahn 2009: 146–155.
[22] Sailhamer 2009: 390.

in the community of Israel. According to Sailhamer, '[t]he funda-mental failures recorded in Exodus 19:19 and Exodus 20:18–21 thus lead to and give an occasion for the need of a priesthood and a temple (Exod 19:20–25)'.[23] Both Hahn and Sailhamer are less than satisfying on this point.

The texts in question do not demand that we conclude that Israel's priesthood was *replaced* by a 'professional priestly class' after the golden calf incident. Indeed, Aaron was an integral part of the idolatrous affair (Exod. 32:2–6, 35) and his priesthood was later restored after God graciously renewed his covenant with Israel (Exod. 34:10–27). The problem with Sailhamer's argument is that his reconstruction of the events at Sinai contradicts what the text actually says. The people were commanded not to go near the mountain or touch it (Exod. 19:12), but Sailhamer claims they were to do just the opposite. A more satisfying solution is that the events at Sinai show us that while the Israelites maintained their communal identity as a royal priesthood, they needed a representative such as Moses to mediate on their behalf.[24] Within the community of priests, there remained a need for a single covenant mediator to represent the people and order their relationship to God; hence the Aaronic–Levitical priesthood.

Thus, Davies is accurate in concluding that the 'Levitical priesthood as portrayed in Exodus is seen not as diminishing or supplanting the collective royal priesthood, but as providing a visual model of that vocation, and secondly as facilitating it'.[25] There is, according to Davies, a 'deliberate typology' between the priestly activity of Aaron and the communal priestly identity: 'What is declared to be ideally true for all Israel at one level is portrayed stylistically in Aaron and his sons on another level.'[26] Similarly, Smith proposes that the 'Aaronic priesthood supplemented the royal priesthood of the nation and was charged with the responsibilities of priestly service in the tabernacle, but the royal priesthood remained fundamental'.[27] The representative nature of the Aaronic priesthood finds

---

[23] Ibid. 394.
[24] Ibid. 390; Gentry and Wellum 2012: 309.
[25] Davies 2004: 240.
[26] Ibid. 123.
[27] Smith 2011: 107. Davies summarizes the relationship between corporate Israel and the institutional priesthood. He writes, 'The notion of the corporate royal priesthood of Israel is not inherently in tension with the notion of a restricted institutional (Aaronic or Levitical) priesthood any more than it is with the notion of the Davidic monarchy . . . Rather, the Aaronic

support in the symbolism of the priestly garments, since Aaron, when standing before Yahweh, wore an ephod with two stones bearing the names of the twelve tribes of Israel (Exod. 28:6–12). When Aaron entered the most holy place, the twelve tribes entered through him.[28]

As the embodiment of Israel's corporate royal priesthood, the Aaronic priesthood also contains elements of continuity with the priesthood originally assigned to Adam in the garden. Adam was a priest-king, Israel is a new Adam and royal priesthood, and Aaron and his sons embody Israel's communal identity as priests before God. This unity of priestly development in the canon of Scripture does not deny the unique differences that characterize the Aaronic priesthood. Unlike Adam, Noah and Melchizedek, the Aaronic priesthood takes on a new form of cultic and liturgical responsibility due to its position in salvation history. Smith's comment on this matter is well put:

> Though the nature of priestly ministry did not fundamentally change, the service of the Aaronic priests at the tabernacle and temple delineated in the Mosaic covenant constituted the most specialized and refined epitome of priestly service in the entire old covenant era. As an advanced form of the Adamic and Noahic priesthood, the Aaronic ministry provided the most exalted typological depiction of priestly labor and therefore had to be fulfilled by the Messiah, even though His priesthood was not Aaronic.[29]

The establishment of the nation of Israel and the covenant at Sinai required an institutionalized priesthood in relation to the tabernacle. The Mosaic covenant gave priestly labour a formal job description, so to speak. The stipulations of the covenant defined how priests were to minister before God and on behalf of the people within the confines of the central sanctuary. Thus, even though the nature of priestly duties became more

---

(note 27 *cont.*) priesthood is presented as both modeling and facilitating (in the cultic drama) the nearness to God which is the objective of Israel's covenantal relationship to Yhwh . . . Priests share characteristics of royalty in the prevailing ideology of priesthood in the ancient Near East. Israel had a collective memory of ancient priest-kings, and the descriptions of the garb of the Israelite priests preserve something of these royal associations. In their priests, the Israelites had a perpetual reminder of their own royal-priestly standing and privilege' (Davies 2004: 168–169).

[28] Davies 2004: 166.
[29] Smith 2011: 108.

nuanced and detailed with the establishment of the Aaronic priesthood in the Mosaic covenant, there remains an obvious connection between Aaron's priesthood, Israel's status as a royal priesthood and human beings' creational purpose of functioning as priest-kings in the service of God. The Aaronic priesthood does not introduce a radically new kind of priesthood into the narrative but instead represents an institutionalized form of cultic ministry within the confines of a geopolitical nation. The ontology of priesthood in Israel, nevertheless, finds its aetiology in God's original design for humanity. Consequently, we would expect to find some association between the Aaronic priestly ministry and humanity's original royal-priestly role.

The priest as the primal man

Commenting on Israel's high priest, Keil writes, 'The Old Testament knows nothing whatever of a royal dignity as attaching to the office of the high priest.'[30] Is this true? Yes, the offices of priesthood and kingship were institutionalized and separated in Israel's history, but Aaron's priesthood reflects something of the 'royal dignity' given to Adam, the first priest in the Bible's storyline.[31] The priest's vestments had a regal quality. The priest's 'turban' (*miṣnepet* [Exod. 28:4; Lev. 8:9]; *ṣĕnûp* [Isa. 62:3; Zech. 3:5]) was set with a holy 'crown' (*nēzer* [Exod. 29:6; Lev. 8:9]). The *nēzer* symbolized royal power (Pss 89:40; 132:18) and was worn by kings during the period of the monarchy (2 Sam. 1:10; 2 Kgs 11:12).[32]

Moreover, the cosmic symbolism of the priestly garments harks back to Eden.[33] The symbolic colours of 'blue' (*tĕkēlet*), 'purple' (*'argāmān*) and 'scarlet' (*šānî*) appear together twenty-six times in Exodus 25 – 28 and 35 – 39, all describing either the tabernacle or the priest's clothing.[34] The 'onyx' (*šōham*) stones set in 'gold' (*zāhāb*) filigree similarly appear as

---

[30] Keil 1887: 232.

[31] Kline (1977: 46) argues that 'Aaron's priestly investiture corresponds to the original creation of man in the image of God's Glory'.

[32] In Ezek. 21:25–26 (MT 21:30–31) Yahweh orders the 'prince' (*nĕśî'*) of Israel to remove the 'turban' (*miṣnepet*) and take off the 'crown' (*'ăṭārâ*). The imagery conflates the priestly and kingly roles into the single figure of the prince.

[33] Fletcher-Louis (2006: 159 n. 13) has written that 'the making of the priestly garments in Exodus 39 is structured so as to recall the tenfold sequence of creative acts of Genesis 1 . . . This seems to say that the "manufacture" of Aaron's garments by Bezalel, the one who has divine Wisdom and the Spirit of God (Exod 31.1–3), recapitulates God's own creation of the cosmos.'

[34] See Exod. 25:4; 26:1, 31, 36; 27:16; 28:5–6, 8, 15, 33; 35:6, 23, 25, 35; 36:8, 35, 37; 38:18, 23; 39:1–3, 5, 8, 24, 29.

material for both the tabernacle and the priestly ephod and breastplate (Exod. 25:7; 28:9, 20; 35:9, 27; 39:6, 13) and allude to the Edenic world of Genesis 2.[35] Ezekiel 28:13 uses similar terminology to describe the king of Tyre as a priestly Adamic figure in the garden of God.[36]

Other observations connect the Aaronic priesthood to Adam's original glory. Beale has demonstrated that the priest's garment had three primary sections that corresponded to the three segments of the tabernacle and temple.[37] The shared imagery between the tabernacle and priestly vestments may imply that the priest is responsible for keeping order in the microcosm (tabernacle) of creation. Twice in Exodus 28, we read that the priest's garments are 'for glory and for beauty' (lĕkābôd ûlĕtip'āret [Exod. 28:2, 40]). Cheung thinks the description is 'most likely an echo of God's original purpose to crown . . . man "with glory . . . and majesty" (Ps 8:5)'.[38] The garment covered the priest's 'naked flesh' (Exod. 28:42), recalling Genesis 3 where God covered the nakedness of Adam and Eve – a condition now necessary for access to God's presence in a fallen world (Gen. 3:10, 21).[39] Priests were also not allowed to have any bodily imperfections because they represented Adam's pre-fallen condition (Lev. 21:16–23).[40] The cumulative effect of these considerations is 'the prospect of Eden restored, and a restored humanity to dwell in it in security and harmony with God and with the world around them'.[41]

Conclusion

The union of the offices of priest and king in a single figure is an integral part of Scripture's metanarrative. Adam failed to fulfil his God-given

---

[35] The terms šōham and zāhāb both appear in Gen. 2:12.

[36] The precious stones listed in this chapter include šōham and zāhāb.

[37] Beale 2004: 39–40.

[38] Cheung 1986: 268. Isaiah later applies the terms 'glory' and 'beauty' to a redeemed Israel that models for the nations the righteousness that comes from living in covenant relationship with Yahweh (Isa. 62:2–3). Isa. 28:5 appears to ascribe royal and priestly imagery to Yahweh: 'In that day Yahweh of hosts will be a crown of honour (ṣĕbî) and a diadem of beauty (tip'ārâ) to the remnant of his people.' If this is right, then the picture of Yahweh himself as a royal priest would be consistent with the picture of Yahweh in Isa. 6 as a priest-king in the temple (cf. John 12:36–43).

[39] Exod. 20:26 applies a similar concept to the nation as a whole: 'And you shall not go up by steps to my altar, that your nakedness be not exposed on it' (ESV).

[40] Cheung 1986: 267–268. It is also likely that the priest's responsibility for discerning between 'good' and 'evil' recalls Adam's similar responsibility in the garden (Lev. 27:12, 14; cf. Gen. 2:9, 17; 3:5).

[41] Davies 2004: 165.

responsibility. Nevertheless, the biblical narrative recapitulates Adam's assignment in several covenantal figures: Noah, Abraham and Israel. Adam was a priest-king; Noah was a new Adam; Abraham was a priest-king like Melchizedek; Israel was a royal priesthood and firstborn son of Yahweh, and the Aaronic priesthood represented the corporate priesthood of the people of Israel and humanity restored. We might articulate these connections in different ways, but the overall point stands: the concept of royal priesthood is a major biblical-theological theme that begins with Adam in the garden and continues to play a role in each of the major biblical covenants. We would expect, then, that later biblical authors would pick up on the importance of the notion of royal priesthood in biblical history as they formulated their messianic expectations.

Looking ahead to Psalm 110, we understand why David combined the roles of *melek* and *kōhēn* in his messianic expectation. The Messiah would be a new Adam, a priest (like Melchizedek) mediating the blessings of the Abrahamic covenant, and would embody in himself Israel's corporate identity as a royal priesthood.

Dumbrell's comments on Psalm 110:4 serve as a helpful segue into the next chapter:

> In its contemplation of priestly kingship (cf. Ps 110:4), the psalm appears to suggest that in the person of the king, the demand contemplated for all Israel in Exod. 19:3b–6 has been embodied. Only kingship of that character, the Psalm seems to imply in its second half, will guarantee the political extension of the Jerusalem kingdom, which it anticipates (Ps 110:5–7). David's line is thus to reflect, in the person of the occupant of the throne of Israel, the values which the Sinai covenant had required of the nation as a whole. David therefore is operating as Yahweh's vice-regent, operating . . . as the 'divine image.' For . . . the Davidic covenant as the 'charter of humanity' seems to prefigure in political terms the establishment of divine government through a human intermediary, so that the full intentions of the divine purpose for the race, expounded in Gen. 1–2, might be achieved.[42]

---

[42] Dumbrell 2009: 152.

To suggest that David's messianic description in Psalm 110 stems from something other than the biblical storyline is tantamount to straining credulity.

4

The Davidic priest-king: Psalm 110 in Old Testament context

We must now probe more deeply into David's understanding of the Messiah as a priest after the order of Melchizedek (Ps. 110:4). In other words, if we assume that the words of Psalm 110:4[1] were not the product of a divinely dictated inspirational event, how did David interpret the Torah, the patterns of his life and the promises of the Davidic covenant to arrive at a Melchizedekian messianic theology?[2]

Chapters 4 and 5 will answer this question by proceeding along five major lines of development. Chapter 4 will (1) discuss Psalm 110 in the flow of Psalms 108 – 111; (2) consider the literary structure of Psalm 110; (3) highlight the importance of the Davidic covenant for a correct interpretation of Psalm 110; and (4) describe the relationship between the Davidic and Abrahamic covenants. Chapter 5 will (5) comment on the individual verses of Psalm 110.[3] The exegesis will take into account how Psalms 1 – 2 function as the interpretative lens of the entire Psalter, and how 1–2 Samuel shapes our understanding of Psalm 110 and its Melchizedekian messiah.

---

[1] For the sake of clarity, unless otherwise indicated, all Scripture references follow the English Bible chapter and verse system.

[2] I am not denying the Holy Spirit's inspiration of Ps. 110:4 by making this statement. I am simply suggesting (and will argue) that David formulated his messianic convictions by reflecting on earlier biblical texts and by understanding the promises of God's covenant with him.

[3] The majority of my exegesis will focus on Ps. 110:1 and Ps. 110:4. These two verses are the most quoted by NT authors and perhaps most significant for the issue of kingship and priesthood in Ps. 110.

Psalm 110:
translation of the Masoretic Text

1   A psalm of David

The LORD said to my Lord,
'Sit at my right hand
until I make your enemies a footstool for your feet.'

2   The LORD sends the staff of your power from Zion.
Rule in the midst of your enemies.

3   Your people will offer themselves freely on the day of your
power.
In holy garments, from the womb of the dawn, to you belongs
the dew of your youth.

4   The LORD has sworn and will not change his mind,
'You are a priest for ever after the order of Melchizedek.'

5   The Lord is at your right hand;
he will shatter kings on the day of his anger.

6   He will execute judgment among the nations, filling them with
corpses;
he will shatter [the] head over the wide earth.

7   He will drink from the brook by the way;
therefore he will lift the head.

Psalm 110 in immediate context

Contrary to form-critical assumptions, Psalm 110 is part of an intelligently
shaped psalter, and its placement in relation to the adjoining psalms is
interpretatively significant. Psalm 110 is part of Book V of the Psalter,
which begins with Psalm 107 and ends with Psalm 150. Within this
section, John Crutchfield has demonstrated that Psalms 107 – 118 form a

'redactional unit' functioning as the opening section of Book V.[4] Zooming in a little more, we discover that Psalm 110 is part of a 'Davidic triad' beginning with Psalm 108 and ending with Psalm 110.[5]

The theme of impending danger at the hands of violent enemies runs through Psalms 108 – 110. According to Crutchfield, the final verses of Psalm 108 (vv. 12–13)

> *introduce* the concept of enemies; Psalm 109 continues and deals extensively with the concept . . . and the first two verses of Psalm 110 . . . *conclude* the concept of enemies, in both an eschatological and messianic context.[6]

It is also likely that Psalm 108:13 anticipates the victory that God will accomplish through the messianic priest-king of Psalm 110:1:

Psalm 108:13   With God we shall achieve power;
               he will tread down our foes.

Psalm 110:1   The LORD said to my Lord,
               'Sit at my right hand
               until I make your enemies a footstool for your
               feet.'

In Psalm 108:13, the language of 'treading' (*bûs*) pictures God as single-handedly stomping out the Davidic king's enemies. Psalm 110:1 similarly describes the subjection of the Messiah's enemies in terms of a 'footstool for [his] feet'.

At the textual level, the repetition of the word *yāmîn* ('right hand') throughout Psalms 108 – 110 hooks these psalms together. In Psalm 108, David pleads for salvation from the enemies of God's people by referring to the 'right hand' (*yāmîn*) of Yahweh (Ps. 108:6). In Psalm 109, *yāmîn* occurs in verses 6 and 31. David appeals to God for a wicked accuser to

---

[4] Crutchfield (2011: 13–14) argues for 'internal signs' of coherence among Pss 107 – 118, the most obvious being the apparent inclusio between the beginning of Ps. 107 and the end of Ps. 118.

[5] Ibid. 14.

[6] Ibid; emphasis original. Crutchfield is right in his thematic assessment of these psalms. However, I would suggest that the concept of enemies is actually introduced in Ps. 108:6: 'That your beloved ones may be delivered, give salvation by your right hand and answer me!' (ESV).

stand at the 'right hand' (*yāmîn*) of his enemy (Ps. 109:6). In the final verse (Ps. 109:31), David states that Yahweh stands at the 'right hand' (*yāmîn*) of the needy one to save him from his enemies. Psalm 110 then begins with David's Lord at the 'right hand' (*yāmîn*) of Yahweh (Ps. 110:1; see below). Again, in Psalm 110:5 David's Lord is at the 'right hand' of Yahweh, executing judgment on the kings of the earth.

> Psalm 109:31 – 110:1:   For he stands at the right hand (*yāmîn*) of the needy one, to deliver his soul from those who condemn. The LORD said to my Lord, 'Sit at my right hand (*yāmîn*) until I make your enemies a footstool for your feet.'

The proximity between *yāmîn* at the end of Psalm 109 and the beginning of Psalm 110, along with the repeated uses of *yāmîn* in Psalms 108 – 110 binds the interpretation of each psalm together with the others. In other words, Psalms 108 – 110 develop a narrative strategy. Jinkyu Kim asserts that these three psalms 'indicate the stages of the Messiah's eschatological warfare against his enemies'.[7] Psalm 108 introduces the reality of enemy threat against the Davidic king and the people of God (Ps. 108:6, 12–13). Psalm 109 develops the theme of enemy threat through David's petitions for deliverance.[8] In this psalm, David is a righteous sufferer (Ps. 109:1–5) in need of vindication from Yahweh (Ps. 109:26–29). David's word of praise at the end of Psalm 109 coupled with his confidence that Yahweh 'stands at the right hand of the needy one' leaves the reader with an expectation that Yahweh will vindicate the Davidic king. But how will vindication come? Psalm 110 provides the answer. The Lord will station a Davidic priest-king at his right hand until he has removed every enemy threat from the face of the earth (Ps. 110:1, 6).[9]

---

[7] Kim 2003: 160.

[8] Kim (ibid.) suggests that Ps. 109 refers to an individual enemy. He writes, 'This individual enemy seems to occupy a significant position among this group of enemies because the psalmist aims his curses at this particular enemy. If this understanding is correct for the present context, the personal enemy in this psalm may be identified as "the evil leader of the assembled nations" as Mitchell contended . . . This particular enemy in singular corresponds well with the *rō'š* (the chief man) in the singular in the next psalm (Ps 110:6). In this verse, Yahweh is depicted as shattering the chief man over the wider earth.' Kim quotes from Mitchell 1997: 266.

[9] Crutchfield 2011: 32.

Underlying Yahweh's actions on behalf of the king in Psalms 108 – 110 is Yahweh's covenant faithfulness. The covenantal term *ḥesed* appears five times in Psalms 108 – 109.[10] In 109:21 and 109:26, Yahweh's *ḥesed* is the basis for the king's appeal for deliverance. Yahweh's answer to the king's request in Psalm 110 picks up a theme woven into every major biblical covenant thus far: a royal priest will establish God's rule on the earth. God will indeed prove himself faithful to his covenant promises (cf. 2 Sam. 7:11–16). In fact, as Kim has observed, Psalm 111 responds to the priest-king's success by stating that Yahweh remembers his 'covenant for ever' (*lĕ'ôlām bĕrîtô* [Ps. 111:5]) and commanded his 'covenant for ever' (*lĕ'ôlām bĕrîtô* [Ps. 111:9; cf. Ps. 110:4]).[11]

Literary structure

Psalm 110 forms a chiasm consisting of two stanzas (vv. 1–3 and 4–7) with seventy-four syllables each.[12] Hamilton describes the psalm's chiastic structure as follows:[13]

1   A   The king enthroned
2   B   Authority to reign granted
3   C   The day of power
4   D   The priest installed
5   C¹   The day of wrath
6   B¹   Authority to reign executed
7   A¹   Refreshed by the waters and head raised

The chiastic structure highlights the parallels between verses 1–3 and 5–7, and targets verse 4 as the central feature of the psalm. Here, Yahweh swears an oath to the Messiah, promising him an enduring priesthood after the order of Melchizedek. The Lord's oath and the promise of a

---

10 Pss 108:5; 109:12, 16, 21, 26. Robert Wallace (2014: 199–200) thinks the use of *ḥesed* at the end of Ps. 109 could be a plea for Yahweh to remember the Davidic covenant.
11 Kim 2003: 161–162. In Ps. 111, the language of 'for ever' appears five times in the ten verses. In Ps. 111:3, Yahweh's righteousness endures 'for ever' (*lā'ad*). His covenant is 'for ever' (*lĕ'ôlām* [111:5, 9]). His precepts are established 'for ever' (*lĕ'ôlām* [111:8]) and his praise endures 'for ever' (*lā'ad* [111:10]). The repeated use of 'for ever' appears to be an intentional link to the pivotal statement of Ps. 110: 'You are a priest for ever'.
12 This structure with symmetry of syllables is adapted from Hahn 2009: 185 with phrasing from Hamilton 2021: 290. Hahn follows Alden 1978: 204.
13 Hamilton 2021: 290.

priesthood uncover the psalm's covenantal framework. Up until this point in the Bible's metanarrative, the concept of royal priesthood has been connected to each of the biblical covenants. The same is true of the Davidic covenant, as we will see below.

Davidic covenant

God's covenant with David is described in 2 Samuel 7.[14] Prior to that chapter, David defeated the Philistines (2 Sam. 5) and brought the ark to Jerusalem (2 Sam. 6). In 2 Samuel 7:1, David is in his 'house' (*bayit*) enjoying 'rest' (*nûaḥ*) from all of his surrounding enemies. The mention of 'rest' at the outset of this chapter is significant for several reasons. First, the theme of 'rest' recalls Deuteronomy 12:9–11. Here Moses anticipated the rest that Israel would enjoy as a result of the conquest of the Promised Land. Dumbrell notes a contextual parallel between Deuteronomy 12 and 2 Samuel 7:

> We cannot overlook the fact that this verse [Deut. 12:10] refers to the promise of rest to be fulfilled, in a key chapter which is devoted to the establishment of a central sanctuary in Israel, and thus to circumstances remarkably parallel to the sequence of 2 Sam. 6 and 7.[15]

The remainder of 2 Samuel 7 reveals that David's heir will grant Israel rest and build a permanent temple for Yahweh.

Second, the concept of rest recalls the goal of Joshua's conquest: 'Remember the word that Moses the servant of the LORD commanded you, saying, "The LORD your God is providing you a place of rest (*nûaḥ*) and will give you this land"' (Josh. 1:13 ESV). Once the conquest was over, the narrative states three times in the closing chapters that the Lord had given the Israelites rest (*nûaḥ*) from all their enemies (Josh. 21:44; 22:4; 23:1). Joshua succeeded and Israel was at peace, but Israel failed to drive out the remaining foreign nations during the period of the judges – a reality implied by 2 Samuel 7:11. David's attainment of rest suggests that the conquest that began with Joshua has finally come to completion with

---

[14] Though the term 'covenant' (*bĕrît*) never appears in 2 Sam. 7, the term appears in later passages that interpret 2 Sam. 7. See 2 Sam. 23:5; Pss 89:3, 28; 132:12.
[15] Dumbrell 2009: 145–146.

David.[16] The connection between Joshua's conquest and the Davidic covenant will play an important role in understanding the biblical background of Psalm 110.

Finally, the theme of rest connects the Davidic covenant to God's purpose at creation. King David's desire to build Yahweh's temple (house) emerges after a description of David's priestly activity in 2 Samuel 6.[17] David, as priest-king, follows the pattern laid out for Adam at creation. Just as God put Adam in the garden to fulfil the task of building God's garden-temple, David similarly responds to his own God-given 'rest' (*nûaḥ*) by deciding to build God's temple. 'The temple building impulse', writes Hamilton, 'seems to reflect a desire to establish the presence of God among the people of Israel, to recapture a glimmer of Eden's glory.'[18]

Before David attempts to build the temple (*bayit*), the Lord puts an end to it, promising instead, in 2 Samuel 7:11, to build David a house (*bayit*). The house that the Lord builds for David will not be an architectural structure but rather a lineage – a royal dynasty. The terms of the covenant are described in 2 Samuel 7:8–16:

> Now, therefore, thus you shall say to my servant David, 'Thus says the LORD of hosts, I took you from the pasture, from following the sheep, that you should be prince over my people Israel. And I have been with you wherever you went and have cut off all your enemies from before you. And I will make for you a great name, like the name of the great ones of the earth. And I will appoint a place for my people Israel and will plant them, so that they may dwell in their own place and be disturbed no more. And violent men shall afflict them no more, as formerly, from the time that I appointed judges over my people Israel. And I will give you rest from all your enemies. Moreover, the LORD declares to you that the LORD will make you a

---

[16] Ibid. 146. The literary structure of 2 Sam. 7 also implies that there is a rest yet to be achieved by David. In 2 Sam. 7:1 the verb *nûaḥ* appears in the perfect tense, marking past time. In 2 Sam. 7:11, the verb *nûaḥ* appears as a *waw*-consecutive perfect, marking future time. Gentry (Gentry and Wellum 2012: 394) has observed that the shift from past tense to future tense occurs in the middle of v. 9 as a literary device that separates the past blessings and the future promises. The promise of rest given in v. 11 will be achieved during David's lifetime, but the consummate rest that will come about as a result of an eternal kingdom will be an eschatological reality brought about by one of David's offspring.

[17] I will develop the concept of David as priest from 2 Sam. 6 later in this chapter.

[18] Hamilton 2007: 267.

house. When your days are fulfilled and you lie down with your fathers, I will raise up your offspring after you, who shall come from your body, and I will establish his kingdom. He shall build a house for my name, and I will establish the throne of his kingdom for ever. I will be to him a father, and he shall be to me a son. When he commits iniquity, I will discipline him with the rod of men, with the stripes of the sons of men, but my steadfast love will not depart from him, as I took it from Saul, whom I put away from before you. And your house and your kingdom shall be made sure for ever before me. Your throne shall be established for ever.

(ESV)

Four important observations surface from this passage.[19] First, Yahweh's plan for Israel will depend on a Davidic king. The Lord will 'plant' (*nāṭaʿ*) Israel in its own place free from enemy threat (2 Sam. 7:10). The term *nāṭaʿ* echoes Exodus 15:17 where Yahweh promised to 'plant' (*nāṭaʿ*) Israel on a mountain-sanctuary to live under the eternal reign of Yahweh. Now 2 Samuel 7:8–16 reveals that David's greater son will mediate God's reign over his people. The goal of the exodus will come to fruition through the Davidic line.

Second, the Lord promises that one of David's own 'offspring' (*zeraʿ*) will build Yahweh's temple and reign from an eternal throne (2 Sam. 7:12–13). This 'seed' (*zeraʿ*) of David will exist in a father–son relationship to Yahweh: 'I will be to him a father and he shall be to me a son' (2 Sam. 7:14 ESV). The covenantal relationship that defined Adam and Israel will now belong to the Davidic king. He will capture what it means for humanity to be made in God's image: sonship, kingship and covenant mediation.

Third, it is impossible not to see a connection between 2 Samuel 7 and Deuteronomy 17. In Deuteronomy 17:16–20, Moses describes ideal kingship in Israel. Verses 18–20 focus on the king's responsibility as it pertains to the Torah. The king is to copy the Torah, keep the Torah with him and read the Torah so that he can learn to fear Yahweh and thus ensure the continuation of his kingdom (Deut. 17:18–20). The king's responsibility to the Torah is 'exactly the point of the father-son relationship set out in

---

[19] It is beyond the scope of this project to explore all the issues surrounding the Davidic covenant. I will limit my analysis to the issues most relevant to the thesis of this project.

2 Samuel 7'.[20] As God's son, the king represents God by embodying Torah and mediating Torah to the nations, bringing them under God's righteous rule.[21]

Finally, David's response to God's covenant provides the reader with a glimpse into how David himself understood the covenantal promises. The all-important phrase is found in 2 Samuel 7:19: 'this is the instruction for man (*tôrat hā'ādām*), O Lord Yahweh.' David recognized that the covenant would have implications for all of humanity. But what does *tôrat hā'ādām* mean? Walter Kaiser has demonstrated that the phrase *tôrat hā'ādām* means the 'charter for humanity'.[22] Kaiser comments, 'The ancient promise of blessing to all mankind would continue; only now it would involve David's dynasty, throne, and kingdom. Indeed, it was a veritable "charter" granted as God's gift for the future of mankind.'[23] Agreeing with Kaiser, Gentry further develops the logic behind David's statement:

> As the divine son, the Davidic king was to effect the divine instruc-
> tion or torah in the nation as a whole and was, as a result, a mediator
> of the Mosaic Torah. However, since the god whom the Davidic
> king represented was not limited to a local region or territory, but
> was the creator God and Sovereign of the whole world, the rule of
> the Davidic king would have repercussions for *all* the nations, not
> just for Israel . . . Thus, faithfulness on the part of the Davidic Son
> would effect the divine rule in the entire world, much as God
> intended for humanity in the covenant of creation as indicated by
> the divine image in Genesis 1:26ff.[24]

The contents of the Davidic covenant and David's response to the cov-enant provide the backdrop for David's messianic expectation in Psalm 110. The priest-king's ruling of the nations in Psalm 110 is built on the unified and progressive development of the covenants in the canon of Scripture. Below, I will briefly explore the relationship of the Davidic cov-enant to the Abrahamic covenant to help establish the connection between David, Abraham and Melchizedek.

---

[20] Gentry and Wellum 2012: 399.
[21] The king's role as instructor of Torah also establishes his priestly function.
[22] Kaiser 1974: 314–315.
[23] Ibid. 315.
[24] Gentry and Wellum 2012: 400; emphasis original.

David and Abraham

In chapter 2, I highlighted some associations between Melchizedek, Abraham and David to begin building a biblical framework for understanding Psalm 110:4. Now we turn our attention to the Davidic covenant and its relationship to God's covenant with Abraham. There are at least three points of contact between the two covenants.

First, God's promise to David in 2 Samuel 7:9 – 'I will make for you a great name' (*wĕ'āśitî lĕkā šēm gādôl*) – alludes to Genesis 12:2, where God promised Abraham, 'I will make your name great' (*wa'ăgaddĕlâ šĕmekā*). Second, in 2 Samuel 7:10–11, God promises David that he will give the people of Israel a 'place' where they will experience rest from their enemies. Deuteronomy 11:24 defines Israel's 'place' in a way that recalls the geographical borders promised to Abraham in Genesis 15:18–21. In time, David's son Solomon governs these boundaries in his kingdom (1 Kgs 4:20–21). The point is that the Davidic covenant will bring the original land-promise to fruition.[25] Third, the Lord's promise to build David a house is the promise of an enduring dynastic lineage. In 2 Samuel 7:12, Yahweh tells David, 'I will raise up your offspring (*zera'*) after you who will come from your body.' The appearance of *zera'* in 2 Samuel 7:12 evokes God's covenant with Abraham, when he promised to multiply Abraham's seed (*zera'*) and to give his offspring the land of Canaan (Gen. 12:7; 13:15–16; 15:5, 18; 17:7–8; 22:17). Hamilton has noted that the phrase 'who will come from your body' evokes Genesis 15:4 where Yahweh tells Abraham that 'one who will come from your body, he will be your heir'.[26] The 'phrase used in both texts, "who will come from your body . . . ," appears nowhere else in the OT'.[27]

The parallels are not coincidental. Instead, Dumbrell rightly concludes that the writer of 2 Samuel clearly understood the Davidic covenant in the light of 'the underlying theology of the Abrahamic covenant'.[28] The Davidic covenant is 'presented as being within the process of the fulfillment of the Abrahamic covenant'.[29] But would David himself have recognized the Abrahamic overtones in the covenant described in

---

[25] Gentry argues along similar lines. See ibid. 423–424.
[26] Hamilton 2007: 268.
[27] Ibid.
[28] Dumbrell 2009: 149.
[29] Ibid. 127.

2 Samuel 7? The answer, again, is found in David's response to the covenant as 'a charter for all humankind' (2 Sam. 7:19).[30] Beecher explains the significance: 'There is no escaping the conclusion that the narrative represents that David recognized in the promise made to him a renewal of the promise made of old that all the nations should be blessed in Abraham and his seed.'[31] David and Abraham share a special connection in redemptive history.

If David perceived that God's promise to him carried forward the blessing of Abraham, then it should be no surprise that Melchizedek, the priest associated with the Abrahamic covenant, played a prominent role in David's eschatology. Just how Melchizedek rose to prominence in David's messianic theology remains to be explored. Nevertheless, the biblical-theological foundation for a Davidic and priestly messiah has been laid. Moving forward, the individual verses of Psalm 110 will provide the structure for the next chapter. I will consider relevant issues to the argument of this book as they arise from the text itself.

---

[30] Carl Armerding (2004: 41) notes the connection between the 'charter for humanity' and the Abrahamic covenant this way: '2 Samuel 7 becomes with the Abrahamic Covenant (Gen 12, 15, and 17), the universal "charter" by which Yahweh will confirm the universal promise of blessing ("to all nations") already articulated through Abraham.'

[31] Beecher 1905: 238.

5

Exegesis of Psalm 110

Psalm 110:1a

'A psalm of David'

The superscript attributes Psalm 110 to David. Though much modern scholarship denies Davidic authorship of this psalm, the New Testament authors attributed Psalm 110 to David.[1] Geoffrey Grogan says that the Davidic authorship of this psalm is 'basic and essential' to Jesus' argument in Mark 12:36–40.[2] To reject David as the author of Psalm 110 is to assume an interpretative perspective alien to Jesus and the apostles. The Africa Bible Commentary summarizes my own view:

> No other psalm in the entire Book of Psalms is as worthy of the heading *Of David. A Psalm*. And for no other psalm is the authorship quite so emphatically endorsed as here. To deny that David wrote this psalm is to be at war with the NT, which often attributed it to him.[3]

Pushing Psalm 110 into the post-exilic period or assigning it to someone other than David inevitably affects the psalm's interpretation and influences the kind of questions interpreters ask. But if we follow the canonical witness and affirm Davidic authorship, we are in a better position to ask the kinds of questions that can be answered by a biblical-theological investigation as opposed to a historically reconstructed one.

---

[1] See Matt. 22:43–45; Mark 12:36; Luke 20:42–43; Acts 2:34–35. For sources that hold to Davidic authorship of Ps. 110, see Paul 1987; Bateman 1992; Johnson 1992: 431; Davis 2000; Waltke 2008: 67–68; Hamilton 2021: 292. See also Grogan's (2008: 34–40) discussion.

[2] Grogan 2008: 35.

[3] Adeyemo 2010: 1595.

Jesus said that David spoke the words of Psalm 110:1 'in the Holy Spirit' (Mark 12:36).[4] The burden of this book has been to demonstrate how David, under divine inspiration, interpreted Genesis 14, the patterns of his own life and the Davidic covenant to conclude that the Messiah would be a priest-king like Melchizedek.

'The LORD said to my Lord'

The opening line of verse 1 introduces Yahweh as the speaker: 'The declaration (*nĕ'um*) of Yahweh to my Lord' (v. 1a). The most obvious question arising from verse 1 is: who is David's Lord?[5] Scholars have put forth many theories regarding the identity of David's Lord ('*ădōnî*).[6] Much of the debate focuses on whether Psalm 110 should be read as a messianic psalm. Critical scholarship generally rejects a messianic understanding of Psalm 110. However, recent articles by Bateman,[7] Davis[8] and Aloisi[9] have defended a messianic interpretation.[10] Aloisi comments on the major hurdle in securing a messianic reading of Psalm 110:

> One of the few difficulties with this view is the fact that it requires David to have a fuller understanding of the Messiah than is often thought possible at his point in history. No OT passage written prior to David indicated that the Messiah would sit at Yahweh's right hand, rule from Jerusalem, and be a priest after the order of Melchizedek. So how did David know about these messianic truths? . . . As the king of Israel and a writer of Scripture, David may have known more about the Messiah than was recorded in Scripture or revealed to Israelites in general at that time. Furthermore, if verses one and

---

[4] Hamilton 2021: 292.

[5] Graham Cole (2013: 75–95) discusses whether we should read Ps. 110:1 (and other OT messianic texts) as referring to a divine messiah. His conclusion seems right that Ps. 110:1 is consistent with the NT teaching of the deity of Christ but does not demand it in its own historical context. Clearly, the NT teaches that the one who fulfils Ps. 110 is the God-man, the Lord Jesus Christ.

[6] Obviously, these theories will vary depending on the position one takes regarding issues of historical setting, date of composition, and authorship. Herbert Bateman (2004: 645) identifies five possible options for the recipient of Ps. 110 contingent upon the acceptance of Davidic authorship of the psalm: (1) Saul, (2) Achish, (3) David, (4) Solomon, (5) heavenly King (Messiah).

[7] Bateman 1992.

[8] Davis 2000.

[9] Aloisi 2005.

[10] This is not to say that each of these articles takes the same approach regarding how one arrives at a messianic interpretation of Ps. 110.

four of Psalm 110 introduce prophetic oracles from Yahweh, David may have received new revelation about the Messiah in connection with the composition of this psalm.[11]

Neither of Aloisi's answers to the proposed difficulty of a messianic interpretation is ultimately satisfying. In his view, we must either assume that Scripture does not inform the logic undergirding David's messianic presentation, or default to the position that Psalm 110 was merely the result of 'new revelation'. While the use of *nĕ'um* in verse 1 suggests that David wrote Psalm 110 as a prophet pointing us towards an eschatological event, we need not conclude that David penned this psalm as a result of some visionary glance into the future.[12] If what I have argued thus far is correct, the messianic hope of Psalm 110 is deeply rooted in both the metanarrative and covenantal framework of Scripture.

When set against the backdrop of the Davidic covenant, the identity of David's *'ădōnî* begins to surface. In 2 Samuel 7:12–13, God promised David that one of David's offspring would reign from David's throne for ever. The *'ădōnî* of Psalm 110 is David's way of describing God's covenantal promise. David's heir will surpass the greatness of his father, establishing himself as David's 'Lord'. He will sit at Yahweh's right hand, mediating God's rule over the world in a kingdom that will never fail.

Moreover, Psalm 110 is not the first place in the Psalter where we discover a Davidic priest-king installed in the presence of God to rule the nations. Psalms 1 – 2 present us with a similar messianic expectation. Perhaps underdeveloped and underappreciated is the importance of Psalms 1 – 2 for understanding the identity of the Messiah in Psalm 110.[13]

Psalms 1 – 2:
the Psalter's interpretative lens

What do Psalms 1 – 2 have to do with Psalm 110? The answer to this question hinges on one's interpretative assumptions regarding the shape of the

---

[11] Aloisi 2005: 119–120.

[12] Waltke (2008: 68) notes that *nĕ'um* is used 375 times in the OT and always refers to divine speech. Jesus identified David as speaking 'in the Spirit' when he penned Ps. 110 (Matt. 22:43).

[13] I am not suggesting that David had access to Pss 1 – 2. I am now turning to a discussion of how Pss 1 – 2 inform a correct interpretation of the Psalter and, therefore, influence how we ought to understand Ps. 110.

Psalter. A form-critical approach to the Psalter finds little or no association between Psalms 1 – 2 and Psalm 110 because it assumes the psalms are tied together only by literary genre. Robert Cole has documented the pervasive influence of form criticism on modern scholarship's interpretation of Psalms 1 – 2.[14] He suggests that Hermann Gunkel's form-critical method had far-reaching effects: any type of progress towards a canonical reading of the Psalms was brought to a virtual halt for nearly a hundred years.[15]

Happily, form criticism's hundred-year regime has succumbed to the scholarly pursuit of canonical exegesis. A canonical approach to the Psalter assumes intentionality behind its arrangement and expects to find a metanarrative overlaying its individual parts.[16] Jamie Grant and Cole have argued at length that Psalms 1 – 2 are one literary unit that function as the interpretative lens through which the rest of the Psalter is to be read.[17] As such, Psalms 1 – 2 should be allowed to have an interpretative impact on other psalms, especially messianic and Davidic psalms. Psalm 110 in particular shares numerous linguistic and thematic parallels with Psalm 2.

Psalm 1: a royal psalm?

The focus of Psalm 1:1–3 is on 'the man' (hā'îš). The description of the 'îš as 'blessed' ('ašrê) indicates the psalm's intention to describe life experienced under God's divine favour. The blessed ('ašrê) man flourishes because he lives according to God's will as expressed in God's law (tôrâ). He 'meditates' on Torah continuously. The blessed man delights in Yahweh's Torah, internalizes Torah, dwells on Torah and allows Torah to consume him. Psalm 1:2 echoes Moses' instructions on kingship in Deuteronomy 17:18–20:

> And when he sits on the throne of his kingdom, he shall write for himself in a book a copy of this law, approved by the Levitical priests. And it shall be with him, and he shall read in it all the days of his life, that he may learn to fear the LORD his God by keeping all

---

[14] R. L. Cole 2013: 7–45.

[15] Ibid. 7.

[16] For studies on a canonical reading of the Psalms, see Whybray 1996; DeClaissé-Walford 1997; Mitchell 1997; Barber 2001.

[17] Grant 2004; R. L. Cole 2013.

the words of this law and these statutes, and doing them, that his heart may not be lifted up above his brothers, and that he may not turn aside from the commandment, either to the right hand or to the left, so that he may continue long in his kingdom, he and his children, in Israel.

(ESV)

As noted earlier, Israel's king was to embody the Torah. His life, kingdom and progeny would prosper if he ordered his life around God's covenantal instruction. The 'blessed man' in Psalm 1:1–3 exemplifies Deuteronomy's ideal of Israelite kingship.[18] His devotion to Torah sets the stage for his enthronement in Zion (Ps. 2:6).

In addition to Deuteronomy 17, Psalm 1:1–3 strongly alludes to Joshua 1:8 (see Table 5.1).[19] The Joshua allusion at the beginning of Psalm 1 hints that the blessed man will, like Joshua, enact a holy war (cf. Ps. 2:8–9) on the very ones he resists: the wicked, sinners and scoffers. The Messiah's conquest, described in Psalm 2, over the nations to the ends of the earth

Table 5.1 Linguistic parallels between Joshua 1:8 and Psalm 1:1–3

Joshua 1:8	Psalm 1:1–3
This book of the law (*tôrâ*) shall not depart from your mouth, but you shall meditate on it day and night (*wĕhāgîtā bô yômām wālaylâ*) . . . For then you will cause your way to prosper (*taṣlîaḥ 'et-dĕrākekā*) and you will understand.	Blessed is the man who walks not in the counsel of the wicked, nor stands in the way (*ûbĕderek*) of sinners, nor sits in the seat of scoffers; but in the law of the Lord is his delight, and on his law he meditates day and night (*ûbĕtôrātô yehgeh yômām wālāylâ*). He will be like a tree planted upon streams of water which gives its fruit in its season and its leaves will not wither and in all that he does, he will prosper (*yaṣlîaḥ*).

---

18 Grant (2004) has argued at length for the influence of Deuteronomy's kingship law (Deut. 17:14–20) on Pss 1 – 2 and the shaping of the Psalter in general.
19 For a brief discussion on the connection between Ps. 1 and Josh. 1:8, see Grant 2004: 46–48.

is, therefore, the logical outflow of Psalm 1's description of the Joshua-like king who prospers by meditating on *tôrâ*.[20]

The sequence in Psalms 1 – 2 of Torah meditation preceding kingly conquest follows the pattern of Joshua's own ministry. Before Joshua began his conquest, Yahweh commanded him to keep the law in terms similar to the kingship text of Deuteronomy 17:19–20. In Joshua 1:7, Yahweh commanded Joshua: 'do according to all the law that Moses my servant commanded you. Do not turn from it to the right hand or the left in order that you might prosper wherever you go' (see Table 5.2).

Table 5.2 Linguistic parallels between Deuteronomy 17:19–20 and Joshua 1:7

Deuteronomy 17:19b–20	*Joshua 1:7*
. . . that he may learn to fear the LORD his God by keeping (*lišmōr*) all the words of this law (*tôrâ*) and these statutes to do them (*la'ăśōtām*), that his heart might not be lifted up above his brothers, and that he may not turn from the commandment to the right hand or the left (*ûlĕbiltî sûr min-hammiṣwâ yāmîn ûśĕmō'wl*) in order that he might lengthen the days of his kingdom, he and his children in Israel.	Only be strong and exceedingly courageous to do according to all the law (*lišmōr la'ăśôt kĕkol-hattôrâ*) that Moses my servant commanded you. Do not turn from it to the right hand or the left (*'al-tāsûr mimmennû yāmîn ûśĕmō'wl*) in order that you might prosper wherever you go.

The purpose of the allusion is to depict Joshua as a kingly leader. Later biblical authors support the evidence for seeing Joshua as a royal figure in that they describe kings such as Solomon and Josiah after the mould of Joshua (2 Kgs 22:2; 1 Chr. 22:11–16; 28:3–20; 2 Chr. 7:11).[21] Putting the pieces together, it is clear that a substantial connection exists between kingship (Deut. 17), Joshua (conquest) and the 'blessed man' of Psalm 1. The parallels between Psalm 1, Deuteronomy 17 and Joshua 1 create a

---

[20] Like Adam in the garden, the kingly figure of Ps. 1 must learn the instruction of Yahweh before taking dominion over the earth.

[21] On the relationship between Joshua and Israel's monarchs, see Williamson 1976; Nelson 1981; Porter 2000; contra Goswell 2013: 42: 'None of the key features of Joshua 1 . . . are essentially royal in nature.'

kaleidoscopic picture of the blessed man as a Joshua-like king who prospers by meditating on Torah.

The Edenic priest of Psalm 1?

Not only does Psalm 1 portray the blessed man as Israel's king; it might also hint that he is a priestly figure. Psalm 1:3 depicts the *'îš* as a flourishing tree (*'ēṣ*) planted by streams of water (*palgê māyim*). The imagery of a tree bearing fruit (*pĕrî*) next to a flowing stream is reminiscent of Eden and parallels Ezekiel's description of the eschatological temple (Ezek. 47:12; cf. Gen. 2:9–14; see Table 5.3).[22]

Table 5.3 Linguistic parallels between Psalm 1:3 and Ezekiel 47:12

Psalm 1:3	Ezekiel 47:12
And he will be like a tree (*'ēṣ*) planted by streams of water (*palgê māyim*) that gives its fruit (*piryô*) in its season and its leaf does not wither (*wĕ'ālēhû lō'-yibbôl*), but in all that he does he prospers.	And on the banks will grow up . . . each type of tree (*'ēṣ*) for food. Its leaves will not wither (*lō'-yibbôl 'ālêhû*) and its fruit will not fail . . . because its water flows from the sanctuary. And its fruit will be for food and its leaves for healing.

In chapter 2, I highlighted the numerous parallels between the description of the eschatological temple in Ezekiel 47 and the garden of Eden. Ezekiel's temple is an eschatological restoration of the primeval garden-sanctuary. Perhaps the parallels between the garden of Eden, Ezekiel 47 and Psalm 1 indicate that the setting of Psalm 1 is an arboreal temple. Robert Cole is confident that this is the case:

> Parallel language between Ezekiel 47 and Psalm 1 and their similar use of Genesis 1–2 indicates a common eschatological thrust. The

---

[22] Terms found in both Ps. 1 and Gen. 1 – 2 include 'tree' (*'ēṣ*) and 'fruit' (*pĕrî*) (Gen. 1:11–12, 29; 2:9–14, 16). While the term for 'streams' (*peleg*) in Ps. 1 is different from the term for 'river' (*nāhār*) found in Gen. 2:10, the imagery is the same. R. L. Cole (2013: 82–85) argues that Edenic imagery is prevalent at major junctures of the Psalter. The opening of Ps. 1, the major juncture of Ps. 72 just before Book III towards the conclusion of the Psalter in Ps. 148 are all punctuated with Edenic imagery.

pious and perfect man at the head of the Psalter will ultimately be
established . . . in the eschatological sanctuary garden.[23]

If Cole is correct, the blessed man flourishes as one who lives and worships
in God's sanctuary. Is this man a priest who meditates on *tôrâ* in God's
garden-temple? In the light of Scripture's metanarrative, an affirmative
answer is attractive but a bit tenuous. More definitive is the blessed man's
kingship as defined by Deuteronomy 17. Nevertheless, the cumulative case
for seeing a royal *priestly* messiah in the opening of the Psalter becomes
stronger as we turn to Psalm 2.

Psalm 2: royal-priestly Son of God

The implicit regal identity of the messianic figure in Psalm 1 is made
explicit in Psalm 2. Yahweh's response to the raging nations and rebellious
kings of the earth is described in Psalm 2:6:

> Psalm 2:6:   Now as for me, I have installed my king
>   on Zion, my holy mountain.

God's solution to the rebellious nations is to instal his 'anointed
one' (*māšîaḥ*) as king in Zion (Ps. 2:2, 6). This messianic king will inherit
the nations and the ends of the earth as his possession (Ps. 2:7). The
picture is consistent with what we have seen throughout the metanarrative
of Scripture. God is going to establish his kingdom through a royal
human viceroy who will conquer the nations to the ends of the earth
(Ps. 2:8).[24]

Psalm 2:6 also points to the priestly role of this messiah. Yahweh will
establish his king in Zion, the 'holy mountain' (*har-qodšî*) of Yahweh
himself. The imagery is similar to Exodus 15:17, which describes redeemed
Israel dwelling on a mountain-sanctuary under the rule of Yahweh. The
messianic king of Psalm 2 now embodies what was to be true of Israel. In
Psalm 2:6 'my holy mountain' is appositional to 'Zion' – a term pregnant
with meaning. Zion often refers to Jerusalem, the city of David and site

---

[23] R. L. Cole (2013: 66–67) also observes parallels between Ps. 1:3 and Pss 46, 52 and 92 to
confirm the sanctuary setting of Ps. 1.

[24] Ps. 2:8 might also hint at the priestly role of the Messiah because he is one who intercedes
for the nations by 'asking' Yahweh for them. Dave Schrock pointed me to this observation in
a personal conversation.

of the temple. However, Zion can also refer to the heavenly city of God, the dwelling place of Yahweh himself (Pss 48:2–3; 110:1–2). If Zion in Psalm 2 is the heavenly Jerusalem, then the installation of the Messiah on this holy hill is the exact same picture presented in Psalm 110:1–3 where David's Lord (*'ădōnî*) sits at the right hand of Yahweh to rule the nations from Zion. Perhaps what is explicit in Psalm 110 is implicit in Psalm 2: Yahweh will mediate his rule through a priest-king who will exercise worldwide dominion from God's right hand.[25]

Psalm 2 uncovers one more fundamental component of the Messiah's identity: he is the son of God. Psalm 2:7b describes this filial relationship between the messianic priest-king and Yahweh:

Psalm 2:7b: He said to me, 'You are my son,
today I have begotten you.'

Not only is the Messiah enthroned as king, but he will also exist in a father–son relationship with Yahweh himself. Their filial relationship has the Davidic covenant in the background (2 Sam. 7:14). Furthermore, the familial bond between the king and Yahweh implies that the Messiah *images* God in the world. He will be Yahweh's viceroy who will receive the nations as his inheritance and the ends of the earth as his heritage. His eschatological reign will bring others into the state of his own blessedness (*'ašrê* [Ps. 2:12]).[26]

The Psalter, thus, begins by drawing the reader into a story that has been developing since the opening pages of the Bible. God will accomplish his creation project by establishing his kingdom through a royal son who has access to God's presence. Robert Cole's conclusion about the function of Psalms 1 – 2 is right: 'Indeed they belong together, not at all as a hypothesized coronation liturgy, but rather to open the entire Psalter with an integrated portrayal of the victorious eschatological priest-king.'[27]

---

[25] Whether Zion refers to the earthly temple mount or the heavenly Jerusalem in Ps. 2 does not change the fact that Zion, in heaven or on earth, is the special dwelling place of God.

[26] The use of *'ašrê* forms an inclusio around the beginning of Ps. 1 and the end of Ps. 2, further substantiating their literary unity and dependence.

[27] R. L. Cole 2013: 63 n. 75.

Parallels between Psalms 1 – 2
and Psalm 110

The analysis of Psalms 1 – 2 above may not be enough to convince everyone that Psalm 110 is to be read in the light of Psalms 1 – 2.[28] But an examination of the specific lexical and thematic parallels between the two passages should substantiate their interpretative interdependence.[29] The associations between these texts demonstrate that the Messiah in Psalms 1 – 2 is one and the same as the priest-king of Psalm 110. For the sake of space, these parallels are summarized in Table 5.4 opposite.

The numerous correspondences between Psalms 1 – 2 and Psalm 110 diminish any notions that the messianic theology of Psalm 110 is an anomaly. The apparent novelties of Psalm 110 – heavenly session and priestly identity of the Messiah – are accounted for in the opening pages of the Psalter.[30]

Summary

Contained in Psalms 1 – 2 is a snapshot of the biblical storyline. God's plan to secure his kingdom through a royal son sets the trajectory for the entire Psalter. In Psalm 1, the blessed man dwells in what appears to be a restored Eden. He is a royal figure whose existence echoes primal humanity in the garden of God. As Israel's ideal king, he is a student of Torah, meditating on God's instruction in God's garden-like sanctuary (cf. Deut. 17:14–20). Psalm 2 develops the identity and mission of this righteous king by describing him as a Joshua-like conqueror over the nations. He will reign over all the kingdoms of the earth from the heavenly location of God's sacred mountain. He will live in a covenant relationship with Yahweh as Yahweh's own son.

The royal son appears to embody the role set out for Adam and Israel. Adam bore the image of God in the garden-sanctuary, where he was to learn God's law before fulfilling the creation mandate. Like Adam (and Israel), the Messiah must meditate on Torah before mediating God's rule

---

[28] It is also important to note that the author of Hebrews juxtaposed Ps. 2:7 and Ps. 110:4 while arguing for Christ's high-priestly role. Clearly, the author of Hebrews believed that Ps. 2 and Ps. 110 were meant to be read in the light of each other.

[29] Feldmeier and Spieckermann (2021: 106–112) also observe the parallels between Ps. 2 and Ps. 110.

[30] Granted Pss 1 – 2 do not say anything specifically about a *Melchizedekian* priesthood.

Table 5.4 Parallels between Psalms 1 – 2 and Psalm 110

Psalms 1 – 2	Psalm 110
The wicked will not stand in the 'judgment' (Ps. 1:5)	He will execute 'judgment' on the nations (Ps. 110:6)
The *'ădōnî* 'sits in the heavens' (Ps. 2:4)	The *'ădōnî* sits at the right hand of Yahweh (Ps. 110:1)
Yahweh instals his king in 'Zion' (Ps. 2:6)	Yahweh sends forth from 'Zion' the king's sceptre (Ps. 110:2)
Reference to the 'decree' (*ḥōq*) of Yahweh (Ps. 2:7)	Reference to the oath (*šābaʿ*) of Yahweh (Ps. 110:4)
The Messiah will break the nations with a 'rod of iron' (Ps. 2:9)	The Messiah rules with a 'mighty sceptre' (Ps. 110:2)
The Messiah will 'break' and 'shatter' the nations (Ps. 2:9)	The Messiah will 'shatter' kings and chiefs (Ps. 110:5–6)
The Messiah will execute 'his wrath' (*'appô*), but 'his wrath' is easily kindled (Ps. 2:5, 12)	The *'ădōnî* will shatter kings on the day of 'his wrath' (*'appô*) (Ps. 110:5)
Judgment on 'kings' (Ps. 2:2–5, 10–12)	Judgment on 'kings' (Ps. 110:5)
Judgment on 'nations' (Ps. 2:8–9)	Judgment on 'nations' (Ps. 110:6)
The Messiah will rule the entire earth (Ps. 2:8)	The Messiah will rule the entire earth (Ps. 110:6)

to the rest of the world. As the covenantal son of God, he is God's image planted on God's mountain to usher in God's rule by bringing God's reign from heaven to earth. All those who take refuge in the royal son will have the privilege of entering into the state of blessedness (*'ašrê* [Ps. 2:12]). Such human flourishing is only possible as people live in a right relationship with God.

Psalms 1 – 2 look backwards and forwards. They powerfully draw the reader into the storyline that has been developing since Genesis 1, while simultaneously projecting the messianic shape of the remaining psalms. When Psalms 1 – 2 are allowed to fulfil their canonical purpose, we discover that the apparent novelties of Psalm 110 are already evident in the opening of the Psalter. The royal Melchizedekian priest of Psalm 110 is the blessed man and Davidic Messiah of Psalms 1 – 2.

Psalm 110:1b

'Sit at my right hand'

The session of David's Lord at the right hand of Yahweh puts him on the highest throne in the universe. God's 'right hand' metaphorically refers to power and authority.[31] The Messiah will not rule by his own authorization but 'as a vicegerent and representative, deriving authority from his divine counterpart'.[32]

The language of 'right hand' does more than metaphorically communicate authority, power and kingship; it also highlights the Messiah's privileged position of access to Yahweh. David's Lord will reign from the very heavenly throne room of God.[33] The spatial connotations of 'right hand' find support in the reference to 'Zion' in Psalm 110:2. Because the Messiah is at Yahweh's right hand, Yahweh will 'send forth' (yišlaḥ) the Messiah's 'staff of power' (maṭṭê-'uzzĕkā) from this heavenly locale (cf. Ps. 2:6).[34] Before the explicit statement concerning his priesthood in Ps. 110:4, verses 1–2 describe a kind of priestly access given to David's Lord. Much like the messianic picture in Psalm 2, Psalm 110 depicts the enthronement of the Davidic Messiah as a priest-king in Zion.[35]

The author of Hebrews may have picked up the priestly implications of Psalm 110:1. He viewed Jesus' entrance into the true Mount Zion – the

---

[31] Allen 2002: 115.
[32] Ibid.
[33] Waltke (2008: 69) suggests that the 'right hand', in its historical context, refers to the king's throne hall or Hall of Judgment located to the right of the place where the ark of the covenant (God's earthly throne) would have been situated in the temple. It seems to me that the eschatological thrust of the psalm suggests that there is more than the earthly spatial connotations of 'right hand'. David Mitchell (1997: 158–160) suggests that a case can be made for seeing the spatial referent of 'right hand' to be the heavenly realm.
[34] The heavenly connotations of 'right hand' are supported by the NT's use of Ps. 110:1 in Heb. 1:13 and Acts 2:33–35.
[35] Rooke (1998: 193) suggests that a 'key characteristic of sacral kingship is the understanding of the monarch as in some way either the embodiment of the god or as having been brought into a particularly close relationship with the deity by being chosen or imbued with divine power'. She goes on to argue that this 'particularly close relationship' is one of adopted sonship, and as such 'it was only natural that he [the king] should be answerable to Yahweh for the nation and should fulfil the function of national mediator between people and deity'.

heavenly Jerusalem and greater tabernacle (Heb. 9:11; 12:25) – as a fulfilment of Psalm 110:1. Furthermore, he connected Psalm 110:1 to Jesus' priestly ministry. Hebrews 1:3b says, 'After making purification of sins, he sat down at the right hand of the majesty on high.' According to the author of Hebrews, Christ's exalted position of authority, mediation and access to God's heavenly abode is the product of his priestly work of purification. Jesus takes his rightful seat at God's right hand in fulfilment of Psalm 110:1 because he is the successful high priest.

'Until I make your enemies a footstool for your feet'

The description of the Messiah's enemies as a footstool under his feet evokes similar scenes from Psalm 8 and Joshua's conquest described in Joshua 10. Psalm 8, a Davidic psalm, describes humankind's position of authority over creation. The language of Psalm 8:6 parallels David's description of the Messiah's rule in Psalm 110:1 (see Table 5.5).

Table 5.5 Linguistic parallels between Psalm 8:6 and Psalm 110:1

Psalm 8:6	Psalm 110:1
You have given him dominion over the works of your hands; you have put all things under his feet (*kōl šattāh taḥat-raglāyw*).	The LORD said to my Lord, 'Sit at my right hand until I make your enemies a footstool for your feet (*'ad-'āšît 'ōyĕbêkā hădōm lĕraglêkā*).'

As discussed in chapter 2, Psalm 8 functions as a commentary on Genesis 1:26–28. David reflects on humankind's regal authority over the created realm. God has placed (*šît*) all of creation under the feet (*regel*) of humankind (Ps. 8:6). In other words, God created humanity to rule the created realm. In Psalm 110, David applies the same language to the Messiah's authority over his enemies. After sin entered the world, the concept of dominion included the need to exercise rule over the human forces of evil.[36] David's Lord will be the one to fulfil this world-wide dominion, accomplishing what Adam failed to do in a pre-fallen world.

---

36 Beale 2004: 113.

Yahweh's injunction to the Messiah to 'rule' (*rādâ*) in Psalm 110:2 is the same command originally given to Adam (cf. Gen. 1:26, 28).[37] What God intended to do through the prototypical priest-king Adam, he will now do, in a heightened sense, through David's Lord. Creation *and its corruption* will be subjected to the rule of a righteous king.[38]

The conquest narrative of Joshua provides a second significant canonical insight into Psalm 110:1.[39] The imagery of the Messiah's enemies lying as a collective footstool under his feet echoes a dramatic scene from Joshua 10:24:

> And when they brought these kings to Joshua, Joshua called to every man of Israel and he said to the chiefs of the men of war who had gone with him, 'Come near. Put your feet on the necks of these kings.' So they drew near and put their feet on their necks.

Joshua's actions are a graphic picture of what it means for the people of Israel to subdue and rule their enemies. Joshua 10:24 is probably the Bible's most literal example of God's enemies being made footstools for the feet of God's people. The description of neck-stomping appears twice in Joshua 10:24, highlighting the event's prominence in the narrative.

Joshua 10:24 evokes the promise of Genesis 3:15 that a seed of the woman would crush the head of the seed of the serpent. Joshua 10:25 records Joshua's promise that subjugation is what the Lord will do to all the enemies of Israel. The neck-stomping event, coupled with Joshua's promise, drives the promise of Genesis 3:15 forward. The act of

---

[37] Dempster (2003: 60) suggests that the imperative 'powerfully echoes' the creation mandate.

[38] The NT clearly connects Ps. 8 and Ps. 110 in 1 Cor. 15:25–27, Eph. 1:19–23 and Heb. 1:13 – 2:9. Commenting on the relations between Ps. 8 and Ps. 110 in 1 Cor. 15:25–27, Keener (2013: 157) writes, 'In brief, when one reads Psalm 8, Psalm 110, and 1 Cor 15:20–28 in tandem, one begins to see the tension between king David, king Adam, and king YHWH resolved in the single person of Jesus the Messiah . . . these texts working together push the reader towards an encounter with the divine reality revealed in the person of Jesus.'

[39] It is plausible that the conquest narrative of Joshua helped shape David's understanding of the Messiah's identity. I argued earlier that the Davidic covenant informs Ps. 110. In 2 Sam. 7:10–11 God promises David that he will plant his people Israel in the land. No longer shall 'sons of injustice' afflict the people 'as they did in the former times' when the judges ruled over the people of Israel. There is a loud echo to the conquest in these verses. Joshua brought the people into the land, but the people did not finish the job of clearing out the pagan peoples. The book of Judges highlights this fact. God promises David in 2 Sam. 7:11 that he (God) will give David 'rest from all [his] enemies'. As noted earlier, the theme of rest is a strong allusion to the book of Joshua (Josh. 21:44; 22:3; 23:1; cf. 2 Sam. 7:1, 11).

head-crushing initially promised to the seed of the woman and picked up in Israel's conquest eventually became the symbol of victory for the Messiah (Ps. 110:1). He will make his enemies a footstool for his feet and, as Psalm 110:6 announces, he will shatter the 'head' (*rōʾš*) over the wide earth (cf. Gen. 3:15). Some might argue that the connection between Joshua 10:24 and Psalm 110:1 is a bit tenuous. However, the literary parallels between Joshua 10 and the Melchizedek narrative in Genesis 14 support my contention that Joshua's conquest is meant to inform our understanding of Psalm 110. There are at least six points of contact between Joshua 10 and Genesis 14. First, the mention of 'Adoni-zedek, king of Jerusalem' (*ʾădōnî-ṣedeq melek yĕrûšālaim*) in Joshua 10:1 recalls the figure 'Melchizedek, king of Salem' (*malkî-ṣedeq melek šālēm* [Gen. 14:18]). Second, both narratives describe a war with kings. In Joshua 10, five kings of the Amorites make war with Gibeon. Similarly, Genesis 14 describes a battle involving five kings against four kings, and the country of the Amorites is mentioned in Genesis 14:7. Third, in Joshua 10, Joshua and his army go to war to save Gibeon; in Genesis 14, Abraham goes to war to save his kinsman Lot. Fourth, in both narratives, God is the one who gives victory in battle. Fifth, Melchizedek's blessing upon Abraham in 14:20 is similar to Yahweh's statements to Joshua in 10:8a:

Genesis 14:20a: And blessed be God Most High who delivered
(*māgan*) your enemies into your hand (*bĕyādekā*)

Joshua 10:8a: The LORD said to Joshua, 'Do not fear them,
for I have given (*nātan*) them into your hand
(*bĕyādekā*).'[40]

Finally, both narratives include a commission to forsake any long-term fear after experiencing victory in battle. In Genesis 15:1, God tells Abram not to fear (*ʾal-tîrā*), for Yahweh will be his shield and give him a great reward. In Joshua 10:25, Joshua tells the people not to fear (*ʾal-tîrʾû*), for Yahweh will give them victory over all their enemies.

What is the significance of the parallels between Joshua 10 and Genesis 14 – 15? Why would the author of Joshua evoke the episode between

---

40 Joshua's statement in 10:19b is also similar: 'for the LORD your God has given them (*nĕtānam*) into your hand (*bĕyedkem*).'

Melchizedek and Abraham when describing Joshua's defeat of these pagan kings? I suggest that the link is meant to tie Joshua's holy war to the covenantal blessing of Abraham – a blessing that will have implications for the nations. Joshua's conquest was the means to bring the land promise to fruition. Through Joshua's leadership, Abraham's seed (the people of Israel) will possess the gate of their enemies (Gen. 22:17) in order to acquire the Promised Land (Gen. 12:1; 15:18). Just as Melchizedek pronounced God's blessing of deliverance on Abraham, so too God will bless the people of Israel with deliverance from their enemies in Canaan (Josh. 10:8, 9; cf. Gen. 14:20). Like Genesis 14, Joshua 10 highlights God's plan to bless the nations through Abraham and his offspring (cf. Gen. 22:17–18). Abraham delivered Lot (Gen. 14:1–16), and Gibeon was spared from warring kings by being in covenant with the Israelites (Abraham's offspring).

At the very least, the above analysis of Psalm 8, Joshua 10 and Psalm 110 shows the interconnectedness between God's original design for humanity, Melchizedek, Joshua and David's Lord. Resembling Adam, David's Lord advances God's creation project in a fallen world by subduing and ruling the enemies of Yahweh (Ps. 110:1, 6). Resembling Joshua, he fills the nations with corpses (Ps. 110:6), just as Joshua devoted everything with breath in the pagan nation to destruction (Josh. 10:40).[41] Resembling Melchizedek, his eschatological victory is set in the context of the Abrahamic covenant. The 'wide earth' (Ps. 110:6; cf. Rom. 4:13) has become this Melchizedek's promised land.

---

[41] The connection between Ps. 110 and Joshua may have informed the logic of the author of Hebrews in Heb. 4:8–14. In Heb. 3 – 4, the author exposits Ps. 95 (a psalm attributed to David in Heb. 4:7) to encourage his audience to enter the eschatological rest that awaits the people of God. He draws a typological connection between the ministry of Joshua and the ministry of Jesus. Heb. 4:8–10 describes the failure of Joshua (Ἰησοῦς) to give the people of God rest in the Promised Land and holds out the promise for a future sabbath rest. The author interjects a word of exhortation in 4:11–13 before returning to his argument in 4:14. The inferential conjunction *oun* in 4:14 links Jesus' high-priestly ministry to the mention of Joshua in vv. 8–10. The author establishes the typological connection between Joshua and Jesus by identifying the great high priest in 4:14 as 'Jesus' (*Iēsoun*). The association between Joshua and Jesus is strong in the Greek because they share the same name: 'For if *Iēsous* [Joshua] had rested them, he would not have spoken about another day after this . . . Therefore, having a great high priest who has passed through the heavens, namely *Iēsoun* [Jesus], the Son of God, let us hold fast our confession' (Heb. 4:8, 14). What does any of this have to do with Ps. 110? The significance of the typological association is that Jesus' Joshua-like work is a function of his priesthood. In Hebrews, Jesus' high priesthood is grounded in Ps. 110:4: 'You are a priest for ever after the order of Melchizedek.' What biblical basis did the author of Hebrews have for associating the conquest work of Joshua with the priestly work of Jesus? If what I have argued is correct, then it would appear that Ps. 110 is the answer. The royal-priestly Messiah carries out a Joshua-like conquest over the entire earth and lays claim to the heavenly Zion.

Psalm 110:2

'The LORD sends the staff of your power from Zion'

The 'staff of your power' (*maṭṭê-ʿuzzĕkā*) represents the regal authority of the Messiah. In verse 1, the *ʾădōnî* is simply a passive agent sitting at Yahweh's right hand while Yahweh brings his enemies into subjection. Here in verse 2, the construct phrase *maṭṭê-ʿuzzĕkā* is placed at the beginning of the clause to emphasize the Messiah's kingly rule.[42] Nevertheless, even the Messiah's power flows from Yahweh, for it is Yahweh who 'sends forth' (*yišlaḥ*) the king's staff from Zion. The composite picture is that of a king exercising his rule from the privileged position of priest-like access to the throne room of God.

'Rule in the midst of your enemies'

David's Lord does not begin his reign only after his enemies become footstools under his feet. His rule from Zion is active 'in the midst' (*bĕqereb*) of his enemies (Ps. 110:2). He sits on the highest throne in the universe while his enemies continue to resist his kingship. The imperative 'rule' (*rĕdēh*), as noted above, loudly echoes the creation mandate (cf. Gen. 1:28). Like Adam, David's Lord exercises a kind of priestly rule, mediating Yahweh's justice from the sanctuary of God. He will bring the heavenly realm of Zion to bear on a world that is hostile to God. When the enemies of this priest-king are finally made a footstool for his feet, the will of Yahweh will be done on earth as it is in heaven (Zion).

Psalm 110:3

Psalm 110:3 is a notoriously complex verse to translate and interpret.[43] Numerous studies exist on the text-critical and translational issues

---

42 See also Davis 2000: 164.

43 Referencing R. Tournay, Allen (2002: 110) comments that Ps. 110:3 'has been called the most obscure verse in the whole Psalter'. Brown (1998: 93) notes the difficulties concerning Ps. 110 as a whole and 110:3 in particular. He writes, 'Psalm 110 is one of the most difficult of the psalms to interpret. Despite its many textual conundrums, the psalm is widely recognized as a royal liturgy of some sort ... Although some level of agreement regarding the psalm's liturgical nature has been reached, no unanimity has emerged regarding the translation and meaning of 3ay–b, particularly the last five words of the verse.' David Hay (1973: 21) regards 110:3 in the Hebrew as 'virtually unintelligible'.

involved.[44] It is not my intention to rehearse all of the textual problems or get bogged down in matters not immediately relevant to this study. My comments will be based on the text of the MT. However, at critical points I will point out possible emendations to the vowel-pointing of the MT. From the outset, it will be helpful to juxtapose a literal rendering of the MT and the LXX since most of the translational variations are apparent in the differences between these two versions (see Table 5.6).[45] Virtually all of the differences between the MT and LXX concern matters of vowel-pointing, not variants in the consonantal text.

Table 5.6 Translations of Psalm 110:3

MT	LXX (109:3)
Your people will offer themselves freely on the day of your power. In holy garments, from the womb of the dawn, to you belongs the dew of your youth.	Authority is with you in the day of your power, with the brightness of the holy ones. I have begotten you from the womb before the dawn.

'Your people will offer themselves freely on the day of your power'

The LXX translator interpreted 'ammĕkā as the preposition 'with' ('im) with a second-person masculine singular pronominal suffix (meta sou, 'with you'), and probably read nĕdābōt as the noun nĕdîbâ meaning 'nobility of rank'. The LXX thus supplies hē archē ('authority') for the Hebrew nĕdābōt. The rendering of the LXX is attractive in that it keeps the focus on the Messiah. However, Allen believes the MT 'has the merit of continuing the military vein of v. 2'.[46] If we adopt the MT, then what are we to make of this clause? The scene shifts from the military prowess of the Messiah to the Messiah's mighty army. Led by the king, these warriors will lead a holy war to conquer the nations. The language parallels Judges 5:2

---

[44] For various translations, see Brown 1998; Rendsberg 1999; Allen 2002: 110–111; Barthélemy 2005: 736–748; Grohmann 2010.

[45] Interestingly enough, Barthélemy argues for a reading that more closely follows the LXX. He proposes four corrections to the MT: 'Si l'on accepte les quatre corrections que nous proposons pour ce verset, on pourra traduire: "Avec toi est le principat au jour où [se déploie] ta valeur sur les saintes montagnes, du sein de l'aurore sors comme la rosée: je t'ai engendré!"' (Barthélemy 2005: 748).

[46] Allen 2002: 110.

where the people of Israel are said to have 'voluntarily' (*nādab*) joined their leaders to battle their enemies. A similar scene appears in Psalm 110:3. The Messiah's army needs no coercing to engage in war. His troops fight with loyalty and allegiance. They are a faithful, obedient and willing group of volunteers ready to do the king's bidding.[47]

'In holy garments, from the womb of the dawn'

Scholars dispute the vocalization of every word in the remainder of 110:3. It is entirely possible that the MT's *běhadrê* (in garments) should be rendered *běharărê* (on mountains).[48] The latter appears in Symmachus, Jerome and many medieval manuscripts. The rendering is attractive because Psalm 110 has numerous parallels with Psalm 2. The phrase *běharărê-qōdeš* (mountains of holiness) recalls Psalm 2:6 where the king reigns from the Lord's holy mountain (*har-qodšî*). In this sense, we might understand the Messiah's army as a band of holy warriors proceeding from Yahweh's sanctuary. While the reading is attractive, most of the manuscript evidence supports the consonantal text of the MT.

Perhaps the *běhadrê-qōdeš* (holy garments) of the royal army are meant to recall Aaron's priestly attire (*bigdê-qōdeš* [Exod. 28:2]).[49] In 2 Chronicles 20:21, the phrase *lěhadrat-qōdeš* (in holy attire) describes the garb of the Levitical priests who march before Israel's army. Keil and Delitzsch conclude that the Messiah's army in Psalm 110 is 'a priestly people which leads forth to holy battle, just as in Apoc. xix. 14 heavenly armies follow the Logos of God upon white horses'.[50] The priestly connotations of 'holy garments' might also find support in Psalm 96:5–9. Here

---

[47] Ibid.
[48] Allen (ibid.) argues for this rendering. He comments, 'MT בהדרי־קדש could mean "in holy vestments" (cf. NIV, REB), which would fit better after v 4 than before it. The pl. of הדר is not found elsewhere . . . An alternative MS reading . . . is בהררי־קדש "on the holy mountains," with which one may compare קדשי הר "my holy mountain," in Ps 2:6 and the very phrase in a Zion psalm, 87:11. Barthélemy et al. (*Preliminary and Interim Report*, 3:394) prefer this reading and so does NRSV. The following reference to טל "dew," suits it (cf. Ps 133:3). It is possible that even more ancient support for this reading is forthcoming from Joel 2:2, set in a passage redolent with echoes of other biblical material, including Ps 97. There the juxtaposition of שהר, "dawn," הרים, "mountains," and עם, "people," in connection with the day of Yahweh (cf. Ps 110:5) may be intended as a prophetic reversal of Ps 110:3, in the light of the reversal of Isa 2:4 in Joel 4(3):10, with the message that the victorious army backed by Yahweh is not Israel but a force directed against Israel.'
[49] Davis 2000: 165.
[50] Keil and Delitzsch 1996: 696.

the families of the earth are summoned to worship Yahweh in his cosmic temple. Specifically, they are to worship Yahweh in 'holy attire' (*bĕhadrat-qōdeš* [Ps. 96:9]).[51]

The imagery may also remind the people of Israel of their corporate royal priesthood as described in Exodus 19:6. In addition, the noun *hādār* could serve as a subtle allusion to Psalm 8:5, where humankind (*'ādām*) receives regal glory and 'honour' (*hādār*) from God at creation (cf. Gen. 1:26–28). The Messiah's army would, therefore, embody the priestly authority inherent in humanity's original design and later given to Israel (Exod. 19:6). The evidence may suggest that the 'holy attire' of these messianic warriors hints that they share, to some extent, in the priestly identity of their royal leader (Ps. 110:4).[52]

The next phrase *mērehem mišhār* – vocalized in the MT as 'from the womb of the dawn' – poses, yet again, many textual difficulties.[53] Thankfully, the debates about this phrase have little impact on its overall meaning.[54] The metaphor depicts the army as eager to engage in the Messiah's holy war. These fighters are not latecomers to the battle, but rather they arrive at dawn, 'implying their immediate readiness'.[55]

---

[51] Commenting on the cosmic symbolism of temples in the ANE, Beale (2004: 43 n. 31) writes, 'The word "beauty" is also contextually associated with astronomical phenomena in Is. 62:1, 3 . . . and Ps. 110:3 ("Thy people will volunteer . . . in the *beauty* of holiness, from the womb of the dawn"). Ps. 96:5–9 strikingly combines elements of the heavens, beauty, the temple, and priestly attire: directly following mention of the created "heavens", it says, "splendor and majesty are before Him, strength and *beauty* are in His *sanctuary*", followed by a command to "bring an offering into His courts" and to "worship the LORD in the splendor of holiness" (NASB renders "holy array")'; emphasis original.

[52] Allen (2002: 110) argues against the 'holy attire' reading in 110:3, suggesting that it would make better sense after 110:4. However, if what I have argued is correct, then the Messiah's priestly identity is already apparent in 110:1.

[53] See Allen (ibid. n. 3e) for a brief summary of the numerous debates concerning *mērehem mišhār*.

[54] The differences centre mainly on whether to translate the phrase with directional movement 'out of the womb, towards the dawn' or simply 'from the womb of the dawn' or 'from the rain of the dawn'. In all of these instances, the inherent imagery is retained.

[55] Rendsberg 1999: 550. According to Mitchell (1997: 261–262), *mērehem mišhār* evokes multiple associations. He writes, 'What can be most simply maintained is that it denotes the army's place of origin, a place both splendid and supernatural. It may be the place of the dawn. It may also suggest the dawning of a new age, described elsewhere in sunrise imagery (cf. Isa. 60.1; Mal. 3.20 [4.2]). It might even contain a reference to the resurrection of the dead. For there is a striking parallel with the language of Isa. 26.18–19, probably the earliest unmistakable reference to resurrection in Hebrew literature, in the imagery of birth, dew and dawn: *For dew . . . of the dawn . . . is your dew; the earth to the dead . . . will give birth.* The idea that the faithful dead will rise at Messiah's appearing is, of course, well-attested in later Hebrew literature.'

'To you belongs the dew of your youth'

The most significant translational issue centres on the final word of verse 3: *yalduteka*. Pointed as such, this word is from the feminine noun *yaldût* in construct with a second-person masculine singular suffix. Thus the translation 'your youth' is appropriate. What is meant by 'your youth' is more difficult to determine. A common proposal is that 'youth' connotes prime strength and vitality for either the Messiah himself or his army.[56]

A slight repointing of the vowels, however, reveals an intriguing and viable interpretation for the thesis of this project. It is quite possible that *yalduteka* should be taken as a qal perfect first-person common singular verb with a second-person masculine singular suffix: *yĕlidtîkā*. In this case, the meaning of *yĕlidtîkā* would be 'I have begotten you' from the root *yālad* meaning 'to beget'.[57] The only other occurrences of *yaldût* in the Old Testament appear in Ecclesiastes 11:9 and 11:10. In Ecclesiastes 11:9, *yaldût* also ends with a second-person masculine singular suffix (*bĕyaldûtêkā*). The inseparable preposition *bet* identifies the form as a noun. In both 11:9 and 11:10 the context indicates that a young man is being addressed. Thus, in the only other uses of *yaldût* in the Old Testament, the context and syntax clearly identify them as nouns. Psalm 110:3 lacks both syntactical and contextual indicators that *yalduteka* must be from the noun *yaldût*. Also of significance is the fact that the LXX, Origen and the Syriac Peshitta rendered *yalduteka* as the verbal form. The LXX supplies the verb *exegennēsa*, meaning 'I have begotten'. It is noteworthy that Barthélemy argued for *yĕlidtîkā* as the original reading: 'je t'ai engendré!'[58]

I have already pointed out the numerous parallels between Psalm 110 and Psalm 2. Interestingly enough, the verb *yĕlidtîkā* appears in Psalm 2:7: 'today I have begotten you.' The appearance of the verbal form of *yalduteka* in Psalm 2 might suggest that the LXX translator's use of *exegennēsa* in

---

[56] Allen (2002: 116) argues that the 'dew' represents an army of divine origin that is given to the Messiah at just the right time. Thus the 'dew of your youth' is a metaphorical description of the Messiah's army, which will fight for the Messiah during the prime of his strength. Waltke (2008: 72–73) takes 'youth' as a reference to the Messiah's army. He writes, '"Youth" connotes freshness, prime strength, prowess, promise and endurance (cf. Lam 4:7). Holy war is a time when God and humans in their true strength join forces against impious and immoral despots.'

[57] Brown (1998: 95) argues for the verbal reading. See also Kraus 1986: 114.

[58] Barthélemy (2005: 748). Feldmeier and Spieckermann (2021: 108) also adopt the LXX translation.

Psalm 110:3 was an attempt at harmonization. However, harmonization may not be the best explanation because the verbal forms of *gennaō* differ between the two psalms. Psalm 2:7 employs the perfect *gegennēka* while Psalm 110:3 uses the aorist compound form *exegennēsa* from *ekgennaō*. The different tenses and numerous parallels between Psalm 2 and Psalm 110 may actually strengthen the notion that *yaldutekā* should be rendered as the verbal form ('I have begotten you') in Psalm 110:3.

If *yĕlidtîkā* is the verbal form from the root *yālad*, then the question remains as to how the syntax of this final clause fits together. In other words, how does *ṭal* (dew) and *lĕkā* fit syntactically with the verb *yĕlidtîkā*? I suggest that *ṭal* could be read as an adverbial modifier of *yĕlidtîkā*: 'I have begotten you *as the dew.*' If this reading is correct, then what becomes of *lĕkā*? *lĕkā* does not fit as a prepositional phrase (i.e. 'to you') with the proposed reading. However, if the vowels are repointed from *lĕkā* to *lēk*, then we end up with the imperative form of *hālak* meaning 'Go!' The imperative at the beginning of the clause would parallel the imperative form of *rādâ* at the beginning of the final clause of verse 2. Thus, the final clause of verse 3 would read, 'Go forth! I have begotten you as the dew.' However, if we read *lēk* as an imperative, then it is possible that *ṭal* adverbially modifies *lēk*, which would render the phrase, 'Go forth as the dew.' Either possibility makes little difference for the general meaning of the passage.

Though hard to prove beyond all reasonable doubt, rendering *yĕlidtîkā* as 'I have begotten you' is an attractive proposal in the light of the development of the Bible's storyline thus far. How so? I have already demonstrated the interconnectedness between the office of royal priesthood and the concepts of covenant, image of God and sonship. Furthermore, the language of 'begotten' in 110:3 would further link the messianic theology of Psalm 110 with Psalm 2. Cole argues that 'begetting', in Psalm 2, refers 'to the official act of installation or enthronement'.[59] With respect to Psalm 110, he concludes, 'Certainly Ps. 110.2–3 with its similar vocabulary (בהדרי ... ביום ... מציון ... ילדתיך ... קדש – Zion, a special day, holy place, birth) likewise portrays the same coronation and establishment of this king.'[60]

[59] R. L. Cole 2013: 115.
[60] Ibid. Cole also observes an interesting connection between dew and the oil used for anointing the priest Aaron in Ps. 133:2–3. He writes (ibid. n. 133), 'The enigmatic "dew" of 110

It is also interesting to note that the author of Hebrews juxtaposes Psalm 2:7 and Psalm 110:4 in Hebrews 5:5–6. Both verses are used by the author of Hebrews as support for the priesthood of Jesus Christ. Psalm 2:7 says nothing about priesthood; it only mentions the sonship of the Messiah. Furthermore, Psalm 110:4 appears to have nothing in common with Psalm 2:7; it mentions nothing of sonship. However, if we allow the contexts of each passage to inform the logic of the author of Hebrews, we discover that Psalm 2:6 describes the priestly access and installation of the Messiah in the holy dwelling place of Yahweh before describing the Messiah's sonship (Ps. 2:7). Similarly, Psalm 110:3 describes the Messiah's sonship ('begotten') before moving into a statement concerning his priesthood. Obviously, this line of reasoning assumes that the author of Hebrews read *yĕlidtîkā* in Psalm 110:3 as 'begotten'. But this is exactly what we would expect since the author of Hebrews relies heavily on the LXX, and the LXX supplies *exegennēsa* for *yĕlidtîkā* in Psalm 110:3.

When David's Lord is installed (begotten) at the right hand of Yahweh, he is anointed (Messiah) as king and exists in a father–son relationship with Yahweh. These are the characteristics of the true image of God in humankind and reflect the promises of the Davidic covenant (2 Sam. 7:12–16).

Psalm 110:4

Psalm 110:4 presents its own unique interpretative challenges. Even a cursory glance at 110:4 raises immediate questions about the oath, eternal priesthood and the order of Melchizedek. It will be necessary to linger over verse 4 to present a compelling case for how David arrived at his messianic Melchizedekian theology. In what follows, my objective is to answer more specifically the question of why David applied the Melchizedekian priesthood to the Messiah. I will analyse Yahweh's oath and the narratives of 1–2 Samuel to argue that David saw in his own life a reflection of the redemptive-historical roles of Abraham and Melchizedek. To prove this case, it will be necessary to demonstrate the

---

(טל ילדתיך) would appear to be metaphorical for oil as in Ps 133.2–3 . . . Consequently, there would appear to be a connection between נסכתי of 2.6, in the sense of anointing, and the begetting (ילדתיך) of 2.7.' Perhaps, then, the 'dew' (anointing) of Ps. 110:3 describes the installation (begetting) of the king in terms of a father–son relationship.

typological correspondences between David and Melchizedek, and David and Abraham.[61]

'The Lord has sworn and will not change his mind'

The priesthood of the Messiah is grounded in a divine oath: 'The Lord has sworn'. When did Yahweh swear an oath to David? More specifically, how did David arrive at the conclusion that the Messiah's priesthood would be a function of this unchangeable oath? The answer is probably bound up in the nature of the Davidic covenant. While no mention is made of an oath in 2 Samuel 7:1–16, Psalms 89 and 132 reflect on God's covenant with David in terms of oath-taking. Following Hahn's lead here, I will briefly discuss each of these psalms to get at the meaning of Yahweh's oath in Psalm 110:4.[62]

Psalm 89

Psalm 89:3 references the Davidic covenant in terms of an oath: 'I have made a covenant with my chosen; I have sworn (*nišba'tî*) to David my servant.' Nowhere does this psalm state that the Lord's oath conferred upon David the status of a Melchizedekian priest. Nevertheless, in Psalm 89:20, Yahweh anoints David with 'holy oil' (*běšemen qodšî*). The Torah reserved holy anointing oil for the priests alone (Exod. 30:32). Aaron and his sons were anointed with 'holy anointing oil' (*šemen mišhat-qōdeš* [Exod. 30:25]). Numbers 35:25 also mentions the 'holy oil' (*běšemen haqqōdeš*) in reference to the high priest's anointing. The close relationship between holy oil and the priestly anointing may imply that David's anointing in Psalm 89:20 has priestly connotations.[63]

Psalm 89 also establishes David as the firstborn, servant and highest of the kings of the earth (Ps. 89:27). Yahweh – David's Father by covenant (Ps. 89:26) – will grant worldwide dominion to his firstborn son (Ps. 89:23,

---

[61] In his book on typology, Hamilton (2022: 163–169) argues for typological correspondences between the events described in Gen. 14, Judg. 6 – 8 and 1 Sam. 30. Hamilton similarly argues that David would have understood the events of his own life (1 Sam. 30) in the light of Gen. 14 and Judg. 6 – 8 to conclude that he himself typified a future messianic king from his line (Ps. 110).

[62] Hahn 2009: 184–194.

[63] It must be noted that the language of 'anointing' or 'anointed one' (Messiah) can also refer to kingship in the Bible. 1 Sam. 2:10 ends with the statement, 'He [Yahweh] will give strength to his king and he will exalt the horn of his anointed.' See Alexander 2003: 69.

24, 27). A Davidic king will subdue the sea and the rivers with his own hands (Ps. 89:25). Psalm 89's description of David's regal authority echoes Adam's original royal commission as the divine image-bearer. Just as Adam was to exercise dominion over the earth as Yahweh's firstborn son, servant and viceroy, David now inherits this creational commission.[64] At the very least, Psalm 89 weaves together the concepts of a divine oath (covenant) and kingship. The priestly anointing may also belong to David in this particular psalm. We can conclude, then, that Yahweh's oath to David establishes David and his offspring as the inheritors of the Adamic role.

Psalm 132

Hahn points out that scholars commonly read Psalm 132 'against the backdrop of God's covenant with David, along with the procession of the ark of the covenant into Jerusalem that David led in 2 Samuel 6'.[65] Seow has shown that Psalm 132 possesses a bipartite structure that reflects the narrative progression of 2 Samuel 6 – 7.[66] The psalm divides into two halves of ten lines each. The first half (132:1–10) pertains to David's oath to Yahweh, while the second half (132:11–18) pertains to Yahweh's oath to David.[67] David swore (šābaʿ) to build a 'dwelling place' (miškān) for Yahweh (Ps. 132:2–5). In response, Yahweh swore (šābaʿ) to build David a dynasty in Zion (132:11–18). The first half of Psalm 132 points to the procession of the ark into Jerusalem described in 2 Samuel 6, and David's desire to make Jerusalem the place where Yahweh's temple would reside (2 Sam. 7:1–3). The second half points to Yahweh's response to the events of 2 Samuel 6:1 – 7:4, namely his covenantal promises of 2 Samuel 7:4–16:

> Psalm 132 reveals that God refused David's request in order to grant him something far greater: an everlasting dynasty established by a divine covenant oath with one of his sons, who was destined to

---

[64] Hamilton (2007: 270) observes a possible allusion to Gen. 3:15 in Ps. 89:10. The phrase 'You crushed Rahab like one who is slain' evokes the head-crushing ministry of the seed of the woman. Granted, in Ps. 89:10, the head-crushing is an act of Yahweh, not the Davidic king. Nevertheless, the allusion serves as another link between Ps. 89 and the early chapters of Genesis.

[65] Hahn 2009: 187. See also Routledge 2009: 15. My discussion of Ps. 132 is largely dependent on Hahn's analysis of this psalm in Hahn 2009: 187–189.

[66] Seow 1989: 148.

[67] Ibid.

build the 'Temple-house' of Yahweh. According to Psalm 132, all of this was in response to David faithfully executing his oath to bring the ark into Jerusalem.[68]

Thus Psalm 132 establishes an important connection between the divine oath, Zion and the narrative events of 2 Samuel 6 – 7 – events that, I will later argue, reveal David's own priestly behaviour.

To sum up, Psalms 89 and 132 associate the Davidic covenant with a divine oath. In Psalm 89, the oath establishes a Davidide as the royal (priestly?) Messiah and inheritor of the Adamic role. In Psalm 132, the Davidic heir will rule from Jerusalem. When read against the backdrop of 2 Samuel 6 – 7, Psalm 132 reveals that the divine oath established Zion as the throne-city of the Davidic kingdom in response to David's own priestly behaviour. The composite picture is that of a royal-priestly figure who will build God's temple and reign from Jerusalem to the ends of the earth. By virtue of an oath, a royal priest of Jerusalem (a new Melchizedek?) will fulfil God's creation project (cf. Gen. 14:18). By connecting the divine oath to royal priesthood and Zion (Jerusalem), Psalms 89 and 132 further inform the biblical logic undergirding Psalm 110:4. Yet the question remains: is there evidence in the biblical narratives that reveals how David himself would have made the connections between Jerusalem, priesthood and Melchizedek?

'"You are a priest for ever after the order of Melchizedek"'

The narratives of 1–2 Samuel point to two instances where David acted as a priest. The first is found in 2 Samuel 24, and the Chronicler's description of the same event in 1 Chronicles 21. The narrative describes David's sinful census of Israel and the consequences of that sin. After the census, the Lord comes to David through the prophet Gad and offers David a choice between one of three punishments. David, knowing that Yahweh is merciful, abounding in steadfast love and forgiveness (Exod. 34:6–7), chooses to fall into the hands of Yahweh, 'for his mercy is great' (2 Sam. 24:14). David's choice brings three days of pestilence upon the people, and 70,000 men die (2 Sam. 24:15). When the angel of the Lord stretches out

---

[68] Hahn 2009: 189.

his hand towards Jerusalem, Yahweh intervenes and prevents any further destruction (2 Sam. 24:16). The Lord's mercy appears to be the result of David's desperate plea: 'Please let your hand be against me and the house of my father' (2 Sam. 24:17). David had previously faced the giant Goliath on behalf of his people, and now he is ready and willing to face Yahweh's wrath in their stead. Yahweh exercises mercy when David builds an altar and offers sacrifices to Yahweh at the threshing floor of Araunah the Jebusite (2 Sam. 24:18–25). The Chronicler documents David's response to Yahweh's mercy: 'This here shall be the house of the LORD God and here the altar of burnt offering for Israel' (1 Chr. 22:1).

The events of 2 Samuel 24 recall Abraham's faithful obedience in offering up Isaac at Mount Moriah (cf. Gen. 22). Numerous parallels exist between these two episodes. In both episodes the events unfold at Mount Moriah, the future site of the Jerusalem temple. In 2 Chronicles 3:1 the threshing floor of 'Ornan' ('Araunah' in 2 Sam. 24) the Jebusite is identified as a location on Mount Moriah. In both narratives, the chosen seed is under the threat of extinction. In Genesis 22, Isaac, the heir of the promises of God, is threatened with death. In 2 Samuel 24, David himself is ready to endure extinction to save the people of Jerusalem. In both passages, God intervened to thwart disaster at the last minute. God spared Isaac after Abraham stretched out his hand to take hold of the knife (Gen. 22:10–11), while in 2 Samuel 24, God prevented the angel of the Lord from destroying Jerusalem after the angel had stretched out his hand to destroy the city (2 Sam. 24:16). In both texts, the 'angel of the Lord' is a prominent character in the story. Furthermore, several intertextual connections exist between Genesis 22 and the narratives of 2 Samuel 24 and 1 Chronicles 21 (see Table 5.7 on page 116).

What is the point of the parallels between David's actions and Genesis 22? First, David's sacrifice at Araunah is the only place in the Old Testament – other than 2 Samuel 6 – that depicts David performing priest-like actions in connection with the future site of the temple. If Hahn is right, 'this incident represents both the cause for and the occasion of David coming to know that God had chosen Jerusalem'.[69] Second, the typological association between David and Abraham reveals that the promises made to Abraham will come to pass through David. Just as God spared the seed of promise in Genesis 22, he also spares the holy city of

---

69 Ibid. 192.

Table 5.7 Linguistic parallels between Genesis 22 and 2 Samuel 24 (1 Chr. 21)

Genesis 22	2 Samuel 24 and 1 Chronicles 21
Abraham 'stretched forth his hand' (*yišlaḥ . . . 'et-yādô*) and took the knife 'to slaughter' (*lišḥōṭ*) his son (Gen. 22:10)	The angel 'stretched forth his hand' (*wayyišlaḥ yādô*) towards Jerusalem 'to destroy' (*lĕšaḥătāh*) it (2 Sam. 24:16)
Yahweh will provide (*yahweh yērā'eh*) (Gen. 22:14)	Yahweh saw (*rā'āh yahweh*) (1 Chr. 21:15)
Abraham 'lifted up his eyes and saw' (*wayyiśśā' 'abrāhām 'et-'ênāyw wayyar'*) (Gen. 22:13)	David 'lifted up his eyes and saw' (*wayyiśśā' dāwîd 'et-'ênāyw wayyar'*) (1 Chr. 21:16)

Jerusalem and the chosen line of David from death. God has not forgotten his promise, or shall we say his oath, to Abraham (cf. Gen. 22:16). Third, if the David–Abraham typology identifies David as a *new* Abraham, then we gain more insight into David's understanding of a Melchizedekian messiah. Just as Abraham submitted to the priest-king Melchizedek by paying him tithes and receiving Melchizedek's blessing, so too will David submit to his greater 'Lord', the priest-king after the Melchizedekian order (Ps. 110:1, 4). Finally, David's own participation in offering sacrifices (2 Sam. 24:18–25; cf. 2 Sam. 6:13, 17) might suggest that David would have regarded the offering of sacrifices as an integral part of the Melchizedekian priest's ministry. Psalm 110 does not ascribe sacrificial offerings to the Melchizedekian priest, but sacrifice was probably a necessary element of David's perception of the office of the priesthood.[70] With these connections in mind, we turn now to 2 Samuel 6, the final and possibly most significant narrative informing Psalm 110:4.

David as a new Melchizedek (2 Sam. 6)

In 2 Samuel 6, we are given a description of the events involving the return of the ark to Jerusalem. The author of 2 Samuel explains the ark with this

---

[70] The author of Hebrews develops Christ's self-sacrifice as an integral part of his Melchizedekian priesthood (Heb. 8:3; 9:11–28; 10:1–14).

important editorial comment: '[the ark] which is called by the name of Yahweh who sits above the cherubim' (2 Sam. 6:2). Bearing God's name, the ark symbolized the presence of God and his lordship – he sat enthroned over the cherubim. The ark also housed the Decalogue. God's Word regulated Israel's identity. Dumbrell explains:

> Where God's word was, there was the divine presence, and as we well know in other connections, the Old Testament gave great prominence to the power of God expressed through his word as well as to his presence mediated by the word. Thus a close association between the ark and sanctuary (i.e., the demands which kingship made, and the symbol of divine rule itself) was always maintained.[71]

The appearance of the ark at the beginning of 2 Samuel 6 sets the stage for the actions of a royal priest (David) who maintains the close association between the divine rule and the sanctuary (2 Sam. 7:1–2).

The episode in 2 Samuel 6 contains the greatest amount of evidence pointing to priestly behaviour in David. At least four observations bear this out. First, David sacrificed several oxen and fattened animals to the Lord (2 Sam. 6:13). Second, David wore the 'linen ephod' (2 Sam. 6:14), which was among the priestly garments assigned to Aaron in the book of Exodus (Exod. 28:4; 29:5). The author of 1 Samuel also mentions the ephod in several passages about priests (1 Sam. 2:18, 28; 14:3; 22:18). By choosing to mention David's ephod in 2 Samuel 6:14, the author of 2 Samuel links David to these priestly counterparts. Third, David offered 'burnt offerings' and 'peace offerings' before Yahweh (2 Sam. 6:17; cf. Lev. 6:5). Finally, David pronounces a priestly blessing (*bārak*) on the people 'in the name of the LORD of armies' (*běšēm yahweh ṣěbā'ôt*) and distributes to them a gift of bread, meat and raisins (2 Sam. 6:18–19). David's blessing evokes Yahweh's instructions to the Levitical priests to 'bless in the name of the LORD' (*ûlěbārēk běšēm yahweh* [Deut. 21:5; cf. Deut. 10:8]).[72] David's blessing accompanied by the distribution of gifts also mirrors Melchizedek's

---

[71] Dumbrell 2009: 143.

[72] In Deut. 10:8, mention is made of the Levites' role of carrying the ark and blessing in the name of Yahweh. The care of the ark and the duty to bless appear together as marks of the priestly office. Routledge (2009: 15) argues that the relationship between David and Melchizedek centres on 'blessing'. To be a priest after the order of Melchizedek is, according to Routledge, to be a channel of divine blessing. In Ps. 110, 'the emphasis is on the Davidic king as a channel of divine blessing to the descendants of Abraham' (ibid.).

encounter with Abraham. The ancient priest-king gave the battle-tested Abraham gifts of bread and wine and pronounced a blessing on him (Gen. 14:18–19).

David's priest-like behaviour in 2 Samuel 6 is the clue that opens the door to David's interpretation of the ark's procession into Jerusalem. David understood himself to be a priestly ruler who would mediate God's reign from Jerusalem, the place chosen by Yahweh for a dwelling place (cf. Ps. 132:13). David's actions were, in Merrill's words, '[t]he strongest suggestion of a Davidic royal priesthood'.[73]

The evidence indicates that David viewed himself as a royal priest similar to the ancient priest-king Melchizedek. Melchizedek was the priest-king of (Jeru)salem (Gen. 14:18; cf. Ps. 76:2). Melchizedek's place in redemptive history tied him directly to Abraham and the Abrahamic covenant. More specifically, a Melchizedekian priesthood would mediate the blessings of the Abrahamic covenant.[74] Similarly, David acted as a priest-king of Jerusalem who, like Melchizedek, blessed the people of Israel (Abraham's seed). The composite picture we get of David is that of a priest-king like Melchizedek delivering God's blessing to the children of Abraham.[75]

Up to this point, my focus in analysing key narratives in 2 Samuel has been, admittedly, to arrive at a 'behind-the-text' conclusion. I have attempted to argue, in part, for David's historical self-awareness of a messianic Melchizedekian typology that lies behind the narratives. Such a behind-the-text approach is necessary and appropriate assuming David was the author of Psalm 110. Nevertheless, a canonical study must ask the

---

[73] Merrill 1993: 60.

[74] See my discussion of this point in chapter 2.

[75] If this is true, then how do we make sense of the point made in Heb. 7:13–14 that no-one from the tribe of Judah 'has ever served at the altar'? The point I am arguing is not that David was appointed a priest under the Mosaic covenant. David was not appointed to the office of priesthood, for that would have required a change in the law (cf. Heb. 7:12). As the author of Hebrews makes clear, the law could not be put aside without a sufficient sacrifice (Heb. 9:16 – 10:14). The point is that David was a model and type of the Melchizedekian priest that would fulfil Ps. 110. David's priest-like behaviour does not mean he served at the altar under the same terms and conditions as the Levites. His priestly behaviour does show, however, that he may have viewed himself as a type of the Melchizedekian priest that would fulfil Ps. 110. Indeed, David himself appears to have recognized the insufficiency of Israel's cultic system in Ps. 40:6–8: 'In sacrifice and offering you have not delighted, but you have given me an open ear. Burnt offering and sin offering you have not required. Then I said, "Behold, I have come; in the scroll of the book it is written of me: I delight to do your will, O my God; your law is within my heart"' (esv). David of course recognized that he was not the promised priest of Ps. 110.

question: did the author of 1–2 Samuel intend to depict David as a royal priest of the Melchizedekian order?

The priest-king of 1–2 Samuel

In his article 'Priest and King or Priest-King in 1 Samuel 2:35', Karl Deenick argues that the narratives of 1–2 Samuel unfold the promise of 1 Samuel 2:35 to present David as a model of 'what the ultimate priest-king would be'.[76] Deenick's argument begins with an analysis of 1 Samuel 2:35. He emends the MT of 1 Samuel 2:35 from *wĕhithallēk lipnê-mĕšîḥî* to *wĕhithallēk lipānai-mĕšîḥî* so that *mĕšîḥî* becomes the subject of the verb. Deenick's translation of 1 Samuel 2:35 in its entirety is thus:

And I will raise up for myself a faithful priest, he will do just as in my heart and my soul. And I will build for him a sure house and *my anointed one will walk before me all the days.*[77]

Unlike the standard interpretation of 1 Samuel 2:35, Deenick's translation identifies the faithful priest and the anointed one as the same person. Admittedly, the major weakness of Deenick's proposed emendation is that it lacks textual support. His broader argument, however, does not hinge on this emendation. It is quite possible that even if the promise of 1 Samuel 2:35 differentiates the priest and the Messiah, the author of 1–2 Samuel could have crafted his narrative to hint that the priest and Messiah would be one and the same person.[78]

The remainder of Deenick's article demonstrates how the narrative of 1–2 Samuel unpacks the promise of 1 Samuel 2:35. He concludes that the author of 1–2 Samuel presents David as a model of the 'kind of priest-king

---

[76] Deenick 2011: 338.

[77] Ibid. 325; emphasis mine.

[78] Deenick's proposal is not the only way to justify a reading that brings together the Messiah and the priest in 1 Sam. 2:35. Mary D'Angelo (1979: 84–85) analysed the same passage (1 Sam. 2:35) in her discussion of Heb. 3:1–6. She argues that 1 Sam. 2:35 could be translated: 'I will build him a sure house and *it* shall go in and out before my anointed always' (emphasis original). In this case, the house is the priestly line that serves in the sanctuary before the Lord and the messianic priest. D'Angelo's reading is not unreasonable because, as she notes, in the immediate context the 'house' of 1 Sam. 2:30 is the priestly line that goes in and out before Yahweh for ever. See my discussion of Heb. 3:1–6 in chapter 8 where I quote D'Angelo at length (in n. 37) to show how her reading of 1 Sam. 2:35 fits well with the logic of Heb. 3:1–6.

about which 1 Samuel 2:35 was prophesying'.[79] At least three observations from Deenick's essay deserve mention here.

First, Deenick rightly argues that in 1 Samuel 2:27–35 the demise of the Aaronic priesthood begins. The promise of a new 'faithful priest' in 1 Samuel 2:35 is Yahweh's response to the disobedience of Eli and his sons. Since Eli and his sons were of the lineage of Aaron, their disobedience 'has consequences not only for Eli's house, but for the whole house of Aaron'.[80] The faithful priest of 1 Samuel 2:35 will, therefore, come from neither Eli's house nor Aaron's house.[81] It is commonly suggested that the transfer of priestly authority from Eli and his house to the Zadokites fulfils the prophecy concerning Eli's demise. But Zadok's reception of the priesthood is only a partial fulfilment of God's word to Eli.[82] Zadok cannot ultimately be the 'faithful priest' since he is of the house of Aaron. Who, then, is the recipient of the promise in 1 Samuel 2:35? Or in Deenick's words:

> Given the disinterest throughout the books of Samuel in connecting the promise of a faithful priest with either Samuel or Zadok, are these early chapters and the promise of 1 Sam 2:35 to be taken as a kind of useless appendage, a kind of banal distraction before the real meat of the kingship issue arises?[83]

His point is well taken. The reality is that 1 Samuel 2:35 is not a 'banal distraction'. Instead, as we shall see, it finds partial fulfilment in David and ultimate fulfilment in David's greater Lord.

---

[79] Deenick 2011: 338.

[80] Ibid. 329.

[81] Ibid.

[82] Why is Zadok's reception of the priesthood only a partial fulfilment of the word of the Lord in 1 Sam. 2? 1 Kgs 2:27 indicates that Solomon's removal of Abiathar (Eli's descendant) from the high priesthood fulfilled the word that the Lord had spoken concerning the house of Eli in Shiloh. But this does not necessarily mean that Zadok is the fulfilment of the promised priest of 1 Sam. 2:35. Nor should 1 Kgs 2:27 be taken to mean that all of the events depicted in 1 Sam. 2:27–36 are fulfilled once Abiathar is rejected. In 1 Sam. 2:31, the Lord promises to cut down the strength of Eli and the strength of his father's house. Eli's 'father' in this context is Aaron, who was chosen to wear the ephod after Israel's exodus from Egypt (1 Sam. 2:27–28; cf. Exod. 28:1–4). The promise of 1 Sam. 2:35 is, therefore, not a promise to raise up a new Aaronic priest – i.e. Zadok – but a priest of a different order entirely, for it is the house of Eli *and the house of Aaron* that is rejected. Thus, 1 Kgs 2:27 cannot mean that 1 Sam. 2:35 is fulfilled in Zadok because Zadok is of the lineage of Aaron. Instead, 1 Kgs 2:27 indicates that the Lord's rejection of Eli's lineage (house) has now been fulfilled once Abiathar is rejected, yet the dismantling of the Aaronic priesthood – the house of Eli's father – will have to wait for a future fulfilment. See Deenick 2011: 328–330.

[83] Deenick 2011: 331.

Second, Deenick develops his argument by demonstrating how 1 Samuel 2:35 shares 'strong connections' with David and the Davidic covenant. In brief, the parallels include (1) the language of 'walking before';[84] (2) the theme of establishing a 'house';[85] (3) David's faithfulness as the one who does 'according to what is in my heart and mind';[86] and (4) David's priestly activity in 2 Samuel 6. Deenick concludes, 'When all the evidence is pulled together it certainly suggests that the writer is trying to make a strong link between David and the promised priest of 1 Sam 2:35.'[87]

Finally, Deenick observes that while everything up until 2 Samuel 6 points to David as the promised priest, the Davidic covenant and the remainder of 2 Samuel indicates that David falls short of fulfilling the prophecy. David will not live for ever (2 Sam. 7:12) even though his throne will be eternal. Furthermore, David falls into sin, proving himself not to be the 'faithful' promised priest of 1 Samuel 2:35. Why, then, the connections between the promise of 1 Samuel 2:35 and David? Deenick answers that while David is not the promised priest, the connections between 1 Samuel 2:35 and the Davidic covenant demonstrate that 'God intends to fulfill the promise of 1 Sam 2:35 through David and his line'.[88] David, despite his flaws, 'is held up as a model, as a picture, albeit still a shadowy one, of what the ultimate priest-king would be.'[89]

If Deenick is right, the books of Samuel become pivotal for understanding the development of royal priesthood in both historical and canonical contexts. It is worth quoting Deenick at length:

---

[84] Deenick (ibid.) writes, 'The language of "walking before" Yahweh is used often in connection with the Davidic covenant (2 Kgs 2:4; 8:23, 25; 9:4; 2 Chr 6:14, 16; 7:17).' Deenick admits that this language does not appear in Samuel in connection to the Davidic covenant.

[85] The promise of Yahweh to establish David's 'house' appears twice in 2 Sam. 7 (2 Sam. 7:16, 27). Deenick (2011: 331–332) observes, 'Both are clear reflections on the same idea in 1 Sam 2:35 where Yahweh will "build him a sure house."' Interestingly enough, Deenick says, 'the promise of a "sure house" is never again mentioned in connection with a priest'.

[86] Deenick (ibid.) observes a parallel between the description of the faithful priest in 1 Sam. 2:35 as the one who does 'according to what is in my heart and in my mind' and the description given of David in 1 Sam. 13:14 as a man 'after his [Yahweh's] own heart'. He also notes how the theme of David's faithfulness is developed in 1 Sam. 16:7; 25:28, and even outside Samuel in 1 Kgs 11:38. Deenick therefore concludes that 'the books of Samuel, and the Bible more broadly, portray David as the one who does, at least for the most part, all that is in Yahweh's heart and mind'.

[87] Ibid. 334.

[88] Ibid. 335.

[89] Ibid. 338.

Part of the purpose of the books of Samuel, then, appears to be identifying what kind of priest will fulfill the promise of 1 Sam 2:35. Perhaps most surprising to the careful reader is that it is a king who is intended to function as a priest not after the mold of Aaron, but, as Ps 110 and the writer of Hebrews make clear (Heb 7), after the mold of a superior priesthood (Heb 5:1–7:28), after the mold of Melchizedek. Melchizedek, the writer of Hebrews tells us, means 'king of righteousness.' In fact, the writer of Hebrews points out, 'the law appoints men in their weakness as high priests, but the word of the oath [i.e. Ps. 110:4], which came later than the law, appoints a Son who has been made perfect forever' (Heb 7:28). In Heb 5:1–2 the 'weakness' of the earthly high priests is identified as their sinfulness. In contrast, the oath of Ps 110:4 appointed Jesus as a priest who is without such weakness. This is the central thought of the Melchizedekian priesthood. So, although the books of Samuel show that the fulfillment of the promise of 1 Sam 2:35 was to be found in the house of David, they also show that the ultimate fulfillment of the 'anointed priest' lay not in David, but in Jesus Christ.[90]

David's statement in Psalm 110:4 – 'The LORD has sworn and will not change his mind, "You are a priest for ever after the order of Melchizedek"'[91] – is in perfect harmony with the Davidic covenant, the evidence

---

[90] Ibid. 337. Deenick (ibid. 338) also helpfully comments, 'At another level, it makes perfect sense that if the kind of priest being promised in 1 Sam 2:35 is not a Levitical priest, then neither David nor any of his descendants could be appointed without some major adjustments to the law. They are from the tribe of Judah and "in connection with that tribe Moses said nothing about priests" (Heb 7:14). In fact, no one from that tribe has ever served at the altar (Heb 7:13–14). If there is to be a change of priesthood, then there must be a change of the law, since the law required that only Levites could be priests, and more specifically only sons of Aaron (Heb 7:12; cf. Num 16–18). The only way someone from the tribe of Judah could be appointed is if the law covenant could be put aside. It is that very idea that the writer of Hebrews goes on to discuss after having mentioned the high priesthood of Jesus; he discusses the putting aside of the Mosaic covenant and the establishment of the new covenant. Thus, neither David nor any of his descendants could function as another kind of priest until something was done about the Mosaic covenant, and it could not be put aside without death (Heb 9:16–17).'

[91] Exactly what is meant by the phrase 'after the order of' ('al-dibrātî)? M. J. Paul (1987: 209) persuasively argues from Heb. 7:3 that the phrase 'after the order of' in Ps. 110:4 refers to the fact that the divine oath serves as the basis for the Melchizedekian priesthood. He writes, 'The meaning is: You are a priest not by descent but by oath, as was the case with Melchizedek.' However, I don't think that the phrase 'after the order of' should be limited to the concept of the oath. As the author of Hebrews argues, fundamental to Melchizedek's priesthood was its enduring nature (Heb. 7:3, 15–17).

of David's understanding of his own priestly identity, the David–Abraham typology (2 Sam. 24) and 1–2 Samuel's narrative development of a Davidic priest-king. There is no need to reduce Psalm 110:4 to political propaganda. Instead, biblical and theological convictions gave rise to the expectation of a coming priest-king after the order of Melchizedek.

Psalm 110:5

'The Lord is at your right hand'

After the explicit statement concerning the priesthood in verse 4, David returns to the theme of conquest and the imagery of the 'right hand' of Yahweh. Debate exists as to whether the *'ǎdōnî* of verse 5 is Yahweh or the Messiah. It seems appropriate to see the Messiah as the subject of the sentence: 'The Lord (Messiah) is at your right hand.' The parallels between verse 5 and verse 1 are strong enough to identify the *'ǎdōnî* of both verses as the messianic priest-king, even if they are pointed differently. Both verses refer to the *'ǎdōnî* as occupying the position of authority at Yahweh's right hand. We would expect the subject in verse 5 to be *yahweh* if a clear distinction was intended. Also, the third-person singular subject of the verbs in verse 7 clearly refers to the Messiah. If the subject of the verbs in verse 7 is the Messiah, then we must conclude that the subject of the third-person singular verbs in 110:5b–7 is also the Messiah. In this case, it would be a virtually unintelligible use of language to suggest that the second-person singular pronoun 'your' of *yěmînkā* (your right hand) also refers to the Messiah.[92] The resulting translation would be, 'The Lord (Yahweh) is at your (Messiah's) right hand. He (Messiah) will shatter kings on the day of his wrath.' Such a construction strains the normal use of language.[93] Furthermore, the 'day of' language in verse 5 parallels the 'day of' language in verse 3, which, in the latter, is a reference to a messianic eschatological day.

Commentators are quick to suggest that verse 5 is a transition away from priesthood and a resumption of the Messiah's ministry as king. For example, Allen writes:

---

92 See Anderson 2001: 59.
93 Perhaps the ambiguity is intentional. Mitchell (1997: 263) proposes, 'There seems to be a conflation of Yhwh and the king, in a way not dissimilar to what was noted in Zech 12.8, 10 and Ps 45.7 [6]. This is presumably to stress their oneness of will and purpose.'

Comparatively little use seems to have been made of the honor of v 4 in a cultic capacity, and it may be for this reason that the poet does not proceed to give a direct exposition of this oracle. It reminds him rather of the capture of Jerusalem that made historically possible the endowment of Jebusite kingship.[94]

David, however, does not divide the Messiah's activity into royal duties and priestly duties. Everything the Messiah accomplishes, he accomplishes as priest-king. Schrock is right to conclude: 'it seems better to understand verses 5–7 not as a royal explanation hermetically sealed off from the Messiah's priestly duties, but as a royal victory accomplished by the holy warfare of a Melchizedekian priest-king (cf. Rev 19:11–16).'[95]

'He will shatter kings on the day of his anger'

Verse 5 parallels verse 3 in that both refer to an eschatological 'day'. In verse 5, the 'day of anger' is the day the priest-king will 'shatter' (*māḥaṣ*) kings of the earth.[96] Davis notes that the 'day of' phrases on either side of 110:4 'highlight the fact that a Melchizedekian priest is more than one who performs worshipful ritual. He is, in fact, one who does powerful and successful battle for the glory of Yahweh.'[97]

The imagery here echoes Genesis 14 and the battle of kings, and Psalm 2 where the Messiah conquers the kings (*malkê*) who take counsel against him (Ps. 2:2). Like Abraham who defeated kings to rescue Lot, the Messiah's warfare is against hostile kings (Gen. 14:17). I argued earlier that the Messiah of Psalms 1 – 2 was a Joshua-like figure embarking on the ministry of universal conquest. Since the royal priest of Psalm 110 shares the same identity with the Messiah of Psalms 1 – 2, it is no surprise that Psalm 110 also ascribes to the Messiah a Joshua-like conquest. The book of Joshua repeatedly describes Joshua's conquest as warfare against 'kings'. The word *melek* appears 109 times in Joshua with virtually every occurrence serving as a reference to the recipients of Joshua's subjugation.[98] In canonical perspective, it would be difficult not to see a connection between the Melchizedekian priest's worldwide triumph over the kings

---

[94] Allen 2002: 117.
[95] Schrock 2013: 217.
[96] The perfect verb *māḥaṣ* should be understood as a proleptic perfect.
[97] Davis 2000: 166.
[98] Josh. 12:7–24 specifically catalogues thirty-one kings whom Joshua defeated.

of the nations and Joshua's conquest of the pagan kings occupying the Promised Land.

Psalm 110:6

'He will execute judgment among the nations, filling them with corpses'

David's Lord will have the right to 'judge' (*dîn*) among the nations. Such authority is an attribute regularly assigned to God in the Old Testament.[99] But in Psalm 110 it is the Messiah who executes judgment on the nations (110:5). From God's right hand he mediates God's wrath upon the world. Once again, the Messiah's ministry of judgment and conquest cannot be separated from his priestly position of access to God. All that he accomplishes in Psalm 110, he accomplishes as a priest-king.

The second half of verse 6 explains and clarifies what it means for the royal priest to execute judgment. His judgment will result in the death of his enemies. The imagery is graphic: he will fill the nations with 'corpses' (*gĕwiyyâ*). His holy war recalls the conquest of Joshua, who was to put to death everything that breathed in the land of Canaan (Josh. 10:40; 11:11; cf. Deut. 20:16, 17).

'He will shatter [the] head over the wide earth'

The verb *māḥaṣ* appears in verses 5 and 6. In verse 5, the Messiah shattered (*māḥaṣ*) kings, but now he shatters (*māḥaṣ*) the 'head' (*rō's*). Some English versions render *rō's* as 'chiefs' or 'the chief'. The translation 'chief' makes sense in the light of its parallelism with 'kings' in verse 5. However, the more literal rendering of 'head' is to be preferred. The 'head over the wide earth' is probably David's way of reflecting on Chedorlaomer in Genesis 14.[100] Chedorlaomer conquered a broad land and was a leader among the kings. David's description of the 'head over the wide earth' in Psalm 110:6 is his way of recasting Chedorlaomer as the eschatological enemy of the Messiah. The priest-king's ministry of conquest has now reached its

---

99 See e.g. Gen. 15:14; Deut. 32:6; Pss 50:4, 135:14; Isa. 3:13.
100 Peter Gentry informed me in a conversation that he thinks Ps. 110:4–6 is a sustained meditation on Gen. 14.

climax. He smote individual kings in verse 5 and entire nations in the first half of verse 6, but now he smites the supreme ruler – 'the head' – of all evil forces.

The head-crushing victory of the priest-king also recalls the promise of Genesis 3:15. David's Lord will crush the *head* of the serpent and thereby accomplish what Adam failed to do. He will be a new and better Adam who fulfils his priestly mandate by wresting humanity's lost authority from the serpent's clutches. His victory will be universal, as the entire earth (*'eres*) will finally be subject to human rulership.

Psalm 110:7

'He will drink from the brook by the way'

The first line of verse 7 is relatively obscure. What does it mean? Allen identifies a common interpretation among commentators: 'Reference is frequently seen to a rite of drinking from a Gihon spring as part of the enthronement ceremony (cf. 1 Kgs 1:38).'[101] Davis finds the notion of 'refreshment' in the imagery. He writes, 'Here in verse 7 . . . the refreshment comes after the battle when, victorious and "tired" from the battle, Messiah stoops to drink water from a flowing stream.'[102] Anderson proposes that the imagery of verse 7 captures the dual nature of the coming Messiah as both human and divine: 'Could not the drinking by the way be an expression of his humanity and humiliation, while the lifting of the head would symbolize his deity and exaltation.'[103] Indeed, none of these proposals is mutually exclusive and the imagery is difficult to discern.

Drinking by the brook after a victorious battle may allude to a scene from Judges 15:9–20.[104] In this passage, Samson (a messianic figure), empowered by the Spirit of Yahweh, defeats 1,000 Philistines with the jawbone of a donkey (Judg. 15:14–16). After his victorious battle, God

---

[101] Allen 2002: 118. See also Kraus 1978: 936.

[102] Davis 2000: 167.

[103] Anderson 2001: 61. A similar interpretation is found in Chrysostom's commentary (1998: 29): 'Here he shows the lowliness of his lifestyle, the meanness of his existence, no swagger about him, no bodyguards in attendance, no visible display when he performs this; instead, his way of life was simple to the extent of his drinking from a torrent . . . These words refer not to divinity, however, but to humanity – drinking from a torrent, being raised up.'

[104] Peter Gentry pointed me to the parallel between Ps. 110:7 and Judg. 15.

provides Samson with water and Samson drinks (*šātâ*) so that his soul is revived (Judg. 15:19).

Another possible interpretation is that the imagery of verse 7 may serve as a subtle echo of Psalms 1 – 2. The 'brook' (*naḥal*) by the 'way' (*derek*) recalls the 'streams' (*peleg*) of water in Psalm 1. The noun *derek* appears four times in Psalms 1 – 2. I argued earlier that the imagery in Psalm 1 of the flourishing fruit-bearing tree by a flowing stream situated the Messiah in an Edenic sanctuary. Perhaps the imagery of Psalm 110:7 is similar.[105] If this is the case, then the royal priest finds refreshment in the brook flowing out of the eschatological sanctuary (Ezek. 47). His source of strength comes from being in the presence of the source of life himself. It might be that David's Lord, like Samson, drinks from a water supply that only God can provide. If Psalm 110 is a sustained meditation on Genesis 14, then 'the way' may recall Salem, the future site of the temple, where Abraham received refreshment from the priest-king Melchizedek.

'Therefore he will lift [up his] head'

The contrast between the 'head' of verse 6 and the 'head' of verse 7 is explicit. The Messiah crushes the head of his arch-enemy in verse 6 and, as a result, he now has his own head exalted in triumph. He is the final and victorious priest-king who will turn God's enemies into a footstool and crush the head of Satan himself. The *lifting of his head* signals 'that he has distinguished himself, is worthy of honor and dominion (cf. Gen 40:13; Judg 8:28; 1 Sam 2:10; Ps 3:3 [MT 3:4]; 27:6), and is full of joy (Ps 27:4, 9)'.[106] The emphasis on the Messiah's victory in verse 7 is a fitting conclusion to the psalm and probably forms an inclusio with verse 1. In verse 1, Yahweh promised David's Lord victory through the metaphor of turning enemies into a footstool for his feet. In verse 7, his victory is finished as he lifts his head in triumph.

Conclusion

Chapters 4–5 have argued for an interpretation of Psalm 110 that situates David's messianic priest-king in the unfolding storyline of Scripture.

---

[105] Mitchell (1997: 263) concurs: 'Some mythological river may be indicated, possibly the eschatological stream that the prophets envisage flowing from the latter-day house of Yhwh (Ezek. 47; Joel 4 [3] . . . ; Zech. 14.8).'

[106] Waltke 2008: 79.

These chapters demonstrated that the theology of the Torah, the Davidic and Abrahamic covenants and the patterns of David's own life all undergird the logic of Psalm 110. Chapter 5 highlighted the parallels between Psalms 1 – 2 and Psalm 110 in order to dig deeper into the Psalter's messianic understanding. Furthermore, the narratives of 1 – 2 Samuel solidified the typological connections between David and Abraham, and David and Melchizedek.

Psalm 110 is a theological masterpiece. How unfortunate in the modern period that such a beautiful symphony of biblical theology has been reduced to a solo of one politically motivated performer! Psalm 110 is much more than political propaganda for the Israelite monarchy. It is the sound of several major biblical-theological themes coming together in perfect harmony. Kingship, priesthood, covenant and sonship all find their part in the textual orchestra bringing scriptural unity to David's messianic prophecy.

6

Royal-priestly messianism: Psalm 110 in the intertestamental literature

This chapter will explore the influence of Psalm 110 on the Jewish intertestamental literature. The goal here is to discover how the authors of the intertestamental literature interpreted and applied David's conception of a royal-priestly Messiah to their own messianic expectations. But why devote an entire chapter to extra-canonical literature in a project of biblical theology? First, the intertestamental literature reveals the Jewish interpretative perspective of the Old Testament leading up to the arrival of Jesus Christ. By examining these Jewish writings, we gain greater insight into how ancient writers understood Psalm 110 in the light of the entire Old Testament. Does their reading of Psalm 110 support the argument of this book? Second, the intertestamental literature reveals the theological convictions and world view of the historical culture from which the New Testament was birthed. Thus, an examination of these writings should shed more light on the interpretative perspective and historical background of the New Testament texts.

Surprisingly, explicit use of Psalm 110 is almost non-existent in the intertestamental Jewish documents. Lange and Weigold do not list a single reference to Psalm 110 in their book *Biblical Quotations and Allusions in Second Temple Jewish Literature*.[1] David Hay's study of Psalm 110 led him to conclude, 'Evidence for pre-Christian interpretations of Ps 110 is ambiguous.'[2] Yet Hay and others have identified several portions of

---

[1] Lange and Weigold 2011: 175. Bauckham (1999: 62) also concludes, 'There is no convincing case of allusion to Psalm 110:1 (or to any other part of the psalm) in Second Temple Jewish literature, apart from Testament Job 33:3, where it used quite differently.'

[2] Hay 1973: 23.

intertestamental literature where Psalm 110 appears to have had a significant influence on the theology and world view of the ancient authors.[3]

Messianic portraits in the Second Temple period: priest, king and priest, or priest-king?

Fletcher-Louis has helpfully summarized Jewish messianic expectations
during the Second Temple period. He has observed three possible forms
of messianic identity and national rule in the Second Temple literature.
The nation of Israel would be ruled by: (1) a high priest alone, (2) an
anointed priest-king, or (3) an anointed priest and an anointed king.[4]
Evidence for each of these messianic expectations exists in the Jewish
literature, although the union of priesthood and kingship in a single figure
is the least attested.[5] The second option in Fletcher-Louis's taxonomy is
most relevant to this project. Did Psalm 110 influence those documents
that anticipated the Messiah to be both priest and king over the people
of God?

It is beyond the scope of this chapter to examine every possible allusion
to Psalm 110 in the intertestamental sources or to offer a detailed exegesis
of every Jewish text that unifies priesthood and kingship in a single figure.
Instead, this chapter will focus more narrowly on those passages that were
probably influenced by Psalm 110's expectation of a messianic priest-king.
The following sources deserve attention: the *Testament of Reuben*, the
Testament of Levi, *1 Enoch*, *2 Enoch* and *11QMelchizedek*. The lengthiest
treatment will be given to *11QMelchizedek*. Before diving into these texts,
a word needs to be said on the relationship of Psalm 110 to the Hasmonean
dynasty.

---

[3] Ibid. 19–33.

[4] Fletcher-Louis 2006: 164–167.

[5] Some of the sources listed by Fletcher-Louis to support each form of government include:
(1) high priest alone: Ben Sira, Judith, the Animal Apocalypse, the *Epistle of Aristeas*, the
Testament of Moses and Samaritan sources; (2) priest-king: the Aramaic Levi Document, some
material in the *Testament of the Twelve Patriarchs*, the Hasmoneans, Josephus's preferred state,
the Similitudes of Enoch and *2 Enoch*; (3) priest and king: *Jub.* 31:11–20, Qumran-Essenism,
some material in the *Testament of the Twelve Patriarchs*, Pseudo-Philo's *Biblical Antiquities*
and possibly Sirach (ibid. 164–166).

Hasmonean rule

The Hasmoneans were high priests in Jerusalem from roughly 152 to 37 BC.[6] They ruled Jerusalem not merely as priests but also as royal monarchs.[7] According to Rooke, the Hasmoneans 'epitomized the combination of kingship and priesthood'.[8] Their claim to both the priesthood and kingship has led many scholars to believe that Psalm 110 was used to support their rise to power. Again Rooke writes, 'Their acceptance of the high priesthood followed their rise to prominence, and can perhaps be compared with the way in which the king of Psalm 110 is also granted priesthood as a function of kingship.'[9] For this reason, among others, some critical scholarship argues that Psalm 110 was actually written during the Hasmonean era.[10] Hay is on firmer ground to suggest that the Hasmoneans probably used Psalm 110 'to defend their claims to priestly and royal prerogatives'.[11]

The Hasmoneans chose for themselves the title 'priests of the Most High God'.[12] Commenting on this title, Hay writes, 'If the Hasmoneans deliberately selected a title recalling the precedent of Melchizedek, they probably also appropriated the one scriptural passage besides Gen 14 which mentions him – Ps 110.'[13] An allusion to Psalm 110:4 is found in 1 Maccabees 14:41. In this passage, Simon is appointed *archierea eis ton aiōna* (cf. Ps. 110:4). The application of Psalm 110 to the Hasmonean dynasty does not necessarily add any biblical-theological insight to the interpretation of Psalm 110. It does, however, provide one example of how Psalm 110 was applied to a historical dynasty before the coming of Jesus.

Testament of Reuben

The *Testament of Reuben* describes Levi as an anointed priest and king:

---

6 Babota 2014: 1.
7 Nickelsburg (1981: 92) describes the Hasmonean rise to power as an occupation of both the priesthood and the 'princely' authority.
8 Rooke 1998: 206.
9 Ibid. 207.
10 See e.g. Davidson 1900.
11 Hay 1973: 24.
12 Hay (ibid.) suggests that the language of 'priest of the Most High God' in *As. Mos.* 6:1 and *Jub.* 32:1 is an allusion to the Hasmonean rulers.
13 Ibid. 25.

It is for this reason that I command you to give heed to Levi, because he will know the law of God and will give instructions concerning justice and concerning sacrifice for Israel until the consummation of times; he is the anointed priest of whom the Lord spoke . . . For he will bless Israel and Judah, since it is through him that the Lord has chosen to reign in the presence of all the people. Prostrate yourselves before his posterity, because (his offspring) will die in your behalf in wars visible and invisible. And he shall be among you as an eternal king.[14]

(*T. Reub.* 6:8, 11–12)

Beale identifies this passage as one of the Jewish texts that merge the offices of priesthood and kingship into one figure 'on the basis of Psalm 110'.[15] The mere fact that kingship and priesthood both find expression in the person of Levi might be enough to assign dependence on Psalm 110 since no other biblical text so clearly unites these two roles in a single figure. Furthermore, the eternality (*aiōn*) of Levi's kingship may have been influenced by Psalm 110:4 and Melchizedek's eternal (*aiōn*) status as priest-king (*T. Reub.* 6:12). Beale may be correct to assert that Psalm 110 is the biblical basis that gave rise to the union of priesthood and kingship in *Testament of Reuben* 6:8–12, but without any direct citations, linguistic parallels or more robust thematic parallels, any attempt to connect the two must be considered tenuous.

Testament of Levi

Psalm 110 may have played a significant influence on the messianism of the *Testament of Levi*. When Levi is clothed in priestly garments, he and his progeny are promised an eternal priesthood:

And they severally carried (these things) and put (them) on me, and said unto me: From henceforth become a priest of the Lord, thou and thy seed for ever. And the first anointed me with holy oil, and gave to me the staff of judgment. The second washed me with

---

[14] This translation is adapted from Kee 1983: 784–785.
[15] Beale 2011: 319 n. 4.

pure water, and fed me with bread and wine (even) the most holy things, and clad me with a holy and glorious robe.[16]
(*T. Levi* 8:3–5)

Several parallels exist between this verse and Psalm 110. First, Levi and his progeny receive the priesthood 'for ever' (*aiōn*), just as the Melchizedekian Messiah of Psalm 110 receives the priesthood 'for ever' (*aiōn*). Second, like David's Lord, Levi wields a 'staff' (*rhabdos*) representing his authority to judge (cf. Ps. 110:2, 6). Furthermore, Levi is fed with bread and wine, the same elements Melchizedek offered to Abraham in Genesis 14:18 (cf. Ps. 110:4).

Later, in chapter 8 of the *Testament of Levi*, reference is made to a king from Judah who will establish a new priesthood according to the pattern of the Gentiles (*T. Levi* 8:14). Here, the roles of kingship and priesthood are unified in the same individual. Judah's priest-king is also identified as a beloved 'prophet of the Most High' and seed of Abraham (*T. Levi* 8:15). Kee asserts that this 'new role . . . may allude to the Maccabean priest-kings, with their increasingly secular discharge of the dual role'.[17] But perhaps this royal figure who receives a new priesthood 'after the pattern of the Gentiles' (*kata ton typon tōn ethnōn*) is meant to recall the Davidic king who receives a priesthood 'after the order of' (*kata tēn taxin*) the Gentile priest-king Melchizedek. The fact that *Testament of Levi* 8:14–15 describes this figure as a prophet in the service of the 'Most High' in conjunction with his familial tie to Abraham only strengthens the likelihood that the Melchizedek narrative of Genesis 14:18–24 (and by extension Ps. 110:4) had an influence on the author's messianic expectation.

Chapter 18 of the *Testament of Levi* also speaks of a coming priest who embodies the role of king. The two roles come together in 18:2–3:

Then shall the Lord raise up a new priest. And to him all the words of the Lord shall be revealed; And he shall execute a righteous judgment upon the earth for a multitude of days. And his star shall arise in heaven as of a king. Lighting up the light of knowledge as the sun the day.[18]

---

16 Adapted from Charles 1913: 308–309.
17 Kee 1983: 791 (d).
18 Charles 1913: 314.

With a subtle echo of 1 Samuel 2:35, the *Testament of Levi* anticipates the day when the Lord will raise up a new priest.[19] This new priest will never have a successor, for he will remain a priest 'for ever' (*aiōn* [*T. Levi* 18:8]). He will exercise universal authority by executing judgment over the entire earth (*T. Levi* 18:2).

An allusion to Numbers 24:17 in *Testament of Levi* 18:3 establishes the future kingship of the priest. The priest's 'star' shall ascend in heaven like that of a king to emanate the light of knowledge over the earth. The allusion evokes the broader context of Numbers 24:17, where the 'sceptre of Judah' crushes the head of Moab, thus fulfilling the promise of Genesis 3:15 that a seed of the woman would crush the head of the serpent. In a similar manner, the priest-king of *Testament of Levi* 18 will be the one to conquer the demonic Beliar (*T. Levi* 18:12) and will enable his children 'to tread' (*tou patein*) upon evil spirits (*T. Levi* 18:12; cf. Ps. 110:6). His eschatological success will reopen the gates of the garden-paradise. The flaming sword that kept Adam out of the garden will vanish, and the saints will be free to eat from the tree of life once more (*T. Levi* 18:10–11). Finally, the ministry of the priest-king is directly connected to the heavenly temple, for it is from the 'temple of glory' in the heavens that the priest-king is made holy (*T. Levi* 18:6).

Though direct verbal correspondences are lacking, several thematic parallels exist between Psalm 110 and chapter 18 of the *Testament of Levi*. First, both texts expect the eschatological Messiah to be both priest and king (*T. Levi* 18:2–3; Ps. 110:1, 4). Second, both texts speak of the eternal priesthood of the Messiah (*T. Levi* 18:8; Ps. 110:4). Third, both passages assign the rule of judgment to the priest-king (*T. Levi* 18:2; Ps. 110:6). Fourth, the respective priest-kings are victorious over the demonic world (*T. Levi* 18:12; Ps. 110:6). Fifth, both figures are connected to the heavenly realm (*T. Levi* 18:6; Ps. 110:1).

Enochic literature

1 Enoch

Scholars such as Hay, Martin Hengel and Fletcher-Louis believe that Psalm 110 influenced the Enochic literature.[20] According to Hay, '[t]here

---

[19] The verbiage in 1 Sam. 2:35 and *T. Levi* 18:2 is different, but the Lord, in both texts, will 'raise up' a priest.

[20] Hay 1973: 26; Hengel 1995: 185–186; Fletcher-Louis 2006: 164–166.

is no strong verbal parallelism, but the possibility of allusion is undeniable'.[21] Hengel argues that *1 Enoch* combines the imagery of Daniel 7 and Psalm 110 to describe the heavenly enthronement of the Messiah over the nations.[22] Several verses in *1 Enoch* describe the eschatological reign of the Messiah in terms of his being seated on God's throne and executing judgment over the earth:[23]

On that day Mine Elect One shall sit on the throne of glory
And shall try their works,
And their places of rest shall be innumerable.
(45:3)

And the Elect One shall in those days sit on My throne,
And his mouth shall pour forth all the secrets of wisdom and
    counsel:
For the Lord of Spirits hath given (them) to him and hath glorified
    him.
(51:3)

Ye mighty kings who dwell on the earth, ye shall have to behold
Mine Elect One, how he sits on the throne of glory and judges Azazel,
and all his associates, and all his hosts in the name of the Lord of
Spirits.
(55:4)

And the Lord of Spirits placed the Elect One on the throne of glory.
And he shall judge all the works of the holy above in the heaven,
And in the balance shall their deeds be weighed.
(61:8)

And the Lord of Spirits seated him on the throne of His glory,
And the spirit of righteousness was poured out upon him,
And the word of his mouth slays all the sinners,
And all the unrighteous are destroyed from before his face.
(62:2)

---

[21] Hay 1973: 26.
[22] Hengel 1995: 185–186.
[23] The following quotations are taken from Charles 1913: 214–235.

And he sat on the throne of his glory,
And the sum of judgment was given unto the Son of Man,
And he caused the sinners to pass away and be destroyed from
    off the face of the earth,
And those who have led the world astray.
(69:27)

In these verses, the Son of Man is a king reigning from the throne of God at the end of time. The picture of this heavenly king is very similar to the royal ideology of Psalm 110, where the Messiah sits at God's right hand to execute his righteous judgment over the nations. Though verbal connections to Psalm 110 are lacking in these verses, it is quite likely that the author combined the imagery of Daniel 7 and Psalm 110 to describe the Messiah's end-time reign.[24] Such a combined reading of Psalm 110 and Daniel 7 is not without parallel. For example, in Mark 14:62, Jesus responds to the high priest's question concerning his messiahship by applying Psalm 110:1 and Daniel 7:13 to his own ministry.

2 Enoch

In *2 Enoch* 68 – 72, the author describes the establishment of the priesthood after Enoch's departure.[25] Enoch's ascent to heaven leaves his family without a priest. Methusalam, Enoch's son, asks the Lord to raise up a priest in Enoch's absence, implying that Enoch himself held the priestly office during his earthly existence (*2 En.* 69:4). The priesthood is transferred to Methusalam (*2 En.* 69:15) and eventually transferred to a child named Melchizedek (*2 En.* 71:21). Melchizedek will be preserved from the great flood that is coming to the earth. He will be placed in the paradise of Eden, the centre of the earth, where Adam was created (*2 En.* 71:35; 72:1). Melchizedek will arise in the last generation as the final priest. He 'will be the head of all, a great archpriest, the Word and Power of God, who will perform miracles greater and more glorious than all the previous ones' (*2 En.* 71:34).[26]

---

[24] Commenting on *1 En.* 62:2, Hamilton (2014b: 174) writes, 'Here the Chosen One is enthroned with the Lord of Spirits, calling to mind Daniel 7 and Psalm 110.'

[25] All references to *2 Enoch* are taken from Charlesworth 2009.

[26] It seems that this eschatological Melchizedek is different from the priest-king of Salem we meet in Gen. 14. The Melchizedek who is preserved in the paradise of Eden is said to remain there for ever (*2 En.* 72:5). A 'righteous man' is born in the twelfth generation who will go to the mountain where stands the ark of Noah. This righteous man will meet 'another Melchizedek'. He will bring this Melchizedek out of hiding to be a priest and king in Salem in the style of the other Melchizedek, 'the originator of the priests' (*2 En.* 72:6).

Although, once again, direct verbal correspondences are lacking between the Enochic literature and Psalm 110, the imagery of an enthroned messiah in *1 Enoch* and the priestly Messiah of *2 Enoch* draws in both cases from the logic of Psalm 110. The fact that the eschatological figure is a priest-king named Melchizedek in *2 Enoch* only strengthens the likelihood that Psalm 110 shaped the messianic expectation of the author of *2 Enoch*. It is also interesting that Melchizedek's royal priesthood in *2 Enoch* appears to be an expression of Adam's prototypical reign as a priest-king in God's sanctuary (*2 En.* 71:35; 72:5).[27] Perhaps the author of *2 Enoch* understood Psalm 110 in the light of creation and Adam's role as God's vicegerent.

11QMelchizedek

A. S. van der Woude first published *11QMelchizedek* (11QMelch) in 1965.[28] Paul Kobelski dates 11QMelch approximately to 50 BC.[29] The text itself is a commentary on several different Old Testament texts. For this reason, 11QMelch is often labelled as a thematic *pesher* similar to other Qumran documents.[30] As the title suggests, the main character in this Qumran scroll is an eschatological figure bearing the name 'Melchizedek'.

Surprisingly, 11QMelch contains no single citation or clear allusion to Psalm 110. Yet the simple fact that the central figure in this document is a hero named *Melchizedek* is evidence enough that Melchizedek in 11QMelch was 'consciously modeled' after the biblical portraits of Melchizedek in Genesis 14:18–20 and Psalm 110.[31] According to Anders Aschim, '[t]hese scriptural texts are certainly a formative impulse behind the Melchizedek image of 11QMelch'.[32] Hay puts it this way:

[C]ould any Jew acquainted with those scriptural passages fail to think of them when mentioning Melchizedek? If the author of this Qumran writing did have the psalm in mind, he must have applied

---

[27] Fletcher-Louis (2006: 166 n. 45) has written that Enoch is in the seventh generation from Adam and, as such, he possesses Adam's divine kingship (*2 En.* 30:12).
[28] Van der Woude 1965.
[29] Kobelski 1981: 3.
[30] Ibid. *Pesharim* are interpretative commentaries on Scripture.
[31] Ibid. 54.
[32] Aschim 1999: 140.

at least its fourth verse to the heavenly Melchizedek; and he may have taken its first verse as a testimony to Melchizedek's celestial enthronement.[33]

Aschim's conclusion also seems right:

> While the state of preservation precludes certainty, there are nevertheless enough clues extant in 11QMelch to indicate probable dependence on Psalm 110. Like the 'you' of the Psalm, Melchizedek occupies a position close to God in heaven (Ps 110:1; 11QMelch II 9–14). He 'rules' from 'Zion' (Ps 110:2; 11QMelch II 23–25). He is involved in battle (Ps 110:1.3.5–6; 11QMelch II 13–14) and judgment (Ps 110:6; 11QMelch II 9–13.23).[34]

These parallels, and others, are enough to establish the influence of Psalm 110 on 11QMelch.[35]

Overview

The narrative of 11QMelch describes a messianic figure (Melchizedek) who liberates a people in captivity to Belial and his evil spirits. The captives are the prisoners described in Isaiah 61:1–3 as the 'broken-hearted' and those who 'mourn in Zion' (11QMelch 2:4). Melchizedek will proclaim liberty to these captives on the Day of Atonement at the end of the tenth jubilee (2:7). He will liberate them from Belial's power by freeing them from the debt of all their iniquities (2:6, 25). The Day of Atonement in 11QMelch is an eschatological event when Melchizedek will 'carry out the vengeance of God's judgments' on Belial and his evil spirits (2:13). Melchizedek's judgment will usher in the rule of God in accordance with Isaiah 52:7 – 'Your God reigns!' (2:16; cf. 2:23). The success of Melchizedek's

---

[33] Hay 1973: 27.

[34] Aschim 1999: 136.

[35] Kobelski (1981: 54–55) concludes the following: 'These similarities between Psalm 110 and 11QMelch are too numerous and too basic to the interpretation of each document to be coincidental, and the occurrence of the name Melchizedek in Ps 110:4 strongly suggests that the Melchizedek presented in 11QMelch was consciously modeled after the figure addressed in v 1 of Psalm 110 as *'dny*. The exaltation with Yahweh, the promise of victory to a king, the mention of Melchizedek, the eschatological setting represented by the "day of wrath," and the theme of judgment on the enemies are all elements that form the basis for the presentation of Melchizedek in 11QMelch.'

eschatological victory appears to be the fruit of his role as both king and priest. Each of these anointed offices deserves a closer look.

Kingship in *11QMelchizedek*

Various proposals have been put forth regarding the identity of Melchizedek in 11QMelch. The majority of scholars take the position that Melchizedek is an angelic being, possibly the archangel Michael.[36] Others, such as Jean Carmignac and Paul Rainbow, have argued that Melchizedek is a messianic human being.[37] In fact, Rainbow posits that the Melchizedek figure is a Davidic messiah. Franco Manzi argues that *mlk ṣdq* is not a personal name in 11QMelch but is a title for Yahweh himself: 'King of Justice'.[38] At the very least, these discrepancies reveal that the identity of Melchizedek in 11QMelch is not easily discerned.

Part of the difficulty is that Melchizedek appears to occupy a dual identity in 11QMelch. He is both identified with God and distinct from God at the same time. The author uses two biblical passages referring to God and applies them to Melchizedek. The words of Psalm 82:1–2 and Psalm 7:8–9 shape Melchizedek's identity in 11QMelch 2:9b–11:

> As is written about him in the songs of David, who said: Elohim will stand up in the assem[bly of God,] in the midst of the gods he judges. And about him he said: Above it return to the heights, God will judge the peoples. As for what he sa[id: How long will yo]u judge unjustly and show partiality to the wicked? Selah.[39]

The 'gods' and the 'wicked' in this passage are Belial and his evil spirits (2:12). The title 'Elohim', however, is applied to Melchizedek as the one who wields the authority to judge evil spirits. Another link between Melchizedek and God appears in 11QMelch 2:9. Here, the author substitutes Melchizedek's name for Yahweh's name in a line taken from Isaiah 61:2 (see Table 6.1 on page 140). The year of 'Yahweh's favour' becomes, in 11QMelch, the year of 'Melchizedek's favour'. For these reasons, scholars have identified Melchizedek as a heavenly being or Yahweh himself.

---

[36] De Jonge and van der Woude 1966; Hay 1973: 137 n. 37; Kobelski 1981: 1–74.

[37] Carmignac 1970: 365–369; Rainbow 1997.

[38] Manzi 1997. I am relying on Aschim's (1999: 134–135) essay for this observation on Manzi's interpretation.

[39] Martínez 1996: 140.

Table 6.1 Comparison of Isaiah 61:2 and 11QMelch 2:9

Isaiah 61:2	11QMelch 2:9
šnt-rṣwn lyhwh	lšnt hrṣwn lmlk ṣdq

Yet it is also clear that Melchizedek is distinct from God in his ministry as the eschatological judge. According to 11QMelch 2:13, Melchizedek mediates God's authority as the one who 'carries out the vengeance of God's judgments'. Here, Melchizedek executes the eschatological judgment, not as God but as one who is separate and distinguished from God. How can Melchizedek be both identified with God and distinct from God? The answer, I suggest, may be found in Melchizedek's role as king. The king in the ancient world represented God to the people and executed God's authority on earth. As the king, Melchizedek mediates the divine rule of God. His authority is closely associated with God's authority, but he remains distinct from God as God's viceroy, not God himself.[40]

Knohl has proposed that Melchizedek in 11QMelch is a human messianic king and that the identification of Melchizedek with God is based on Jeremiah 23:5–6: 'I shall raise unto David a righteous shoot and he shall reign as king and prosper, and execute judgment and justice in the land . . . and this is the name whereby he shall be called: "YHWH is our righteousness."'[41] Knohl's proposal has some merit. Jeremiah 23:5–6 directly compares the righteous king and messianic 'shoot of David' with God himself. To call the future king 'Yahweh is our righteousness' implies representational authority and, to some extent, shared identity. Furthermore, like Melchizedek, this messianic king administers a ministry of judgment by establishing justice and righteousness in the land (Jer. 23:5). However, the problem with Knohl's proposal is that nothing in the text of 11QMelch establishes a direct link to the Jeremiah passage. Jeremiah's influence on the identity of Melchizedek cannot move beyond the realm of speculation.

Alternatively, why not let one Melchizedek inform the identity of the other Melchizedek? In other words, the Melchizedek of Psalm 110 was

---

[40] Commenting on the relationship between God and Melchizedek, Mason writes, 'The point of the text seems to be that Melchizedek actually is the person carrying out – on God's behalf – those things ascribed to God in the passages of Scripture cited; if God indeed is acting directly, one would question the need for a pesher explanation of the obvious' (Mason 2008: 190).

[41] The citation of this verse is taken directly from Knohl's (2009: 261) essay.

probably the primary influence on the messianic portrait of Melchizedek in 11QMelch. After all, they share a name only twice mentioned in the entire Old Testament. Hamilton agrees. He points out that the author of 11QMelch chose Davidic passages to describe Melchizedek and his ministry (i.e. Isa. 52:7; 61; Dan. 9:25). He writes:

> These texts are heavily Davidic, with Isaiah 61 speaking of the Spirit-anointed Messiah and the anointed of Daniel 9:25 being spoken of in the same terms. This seems to indicate that the reference to 'Melchizedek' in this passage should be understood along the lines of the Davidic Psalm 110.[42]

As I argued in chapter 3, the priest-king of Psalm 110 is one who reigns from the heavenly Zion (Ps. 110:1–2; cf. Heb. 1:13). He mediates the rule of God from the location of God's right hand (Ps. 110:1, 5). In this sense, the author of 11QMelch may have viewed the priest-king of Psalm 110 as a heavenly figure or as one who shares in God's royal authority. Furthermore, Melchizedek in Psalm 110 wields the authority of heaven from heaven over both human and spiritual forces of evil. From the position of God's right hand, he 'executes judgment' on the eschatological day of his wrath (Ps. 110:5–6). The final object of the Messiah's judgment is the satanic 'head' (Ps. 110:6; cf. Gen. 3:15). This arch-enemy (Belial in 11QMelch?) of God is the last casualty of the Messiah's eschatological conquest.[43] Thus, both Psalm 110 and 11QMelch depict a Melchizedekian figure who shares in the divine rule of God and judges the spiritual forces of evil.

As the eschatological king and judge, 11QMelch implies that Melchizedek will be the one to usher in the kingdom of God. The author mentions the final 'day' ('this day' [hzw't hw'h ywm]) of judgment in reference to Isaiah 52:7: 'How beautiful upon the mountains are the feet of the messenger who announces peace, of the mess[enger of good who announces salvation,] saying to Zion: "your God [reigns"]' (2:15–16).[44] The messenger

---

[42] Hamilton 2014b: 162.
[43] Hamilton (ibid. 163) sees a connection between Belial and the seed of the serpent in 11QMelch. He writes, 'The liberation of the sons of light comes through the defeat of "Belial and the spirits of his lot" who show partiality to the wicked (Col II, 11–12; Ps 82:2), and the mention of Belial calls to mind the way that the wicked are sometimes referred to as "sons of Belial", that is, seed of the serpent, in the Old Testament (e.g. Deut 13:13 [MT 13:14]; Judg 19:22; 1 Sam 2:12; 1 Kgs 21:10; 2 Chr 13:17).'
[44] Martínez 1996: 140.

is the Spirit-anointed messenger of Isaiah 61:1–3 (2:19). The righteous king Melchizedek proclaims liberty to the captives in the power of the Spirit by announcing that the reign of God has finally arrived (2:16–20). He will destroy Belial and thereby usher in an era of peace under the rule of God's glorious kingdom.

Priesthood in *11QMelchizedek*

Melchizedek is never specifically identified as a priest in 11QMelch. Without explicit mention of a priestly office, should we conclude that Melchizedek in 11QMelch lacks the priesthood held by his namesake in the biblical text? Some scholars think so.[45] I contend, however, that the priesthood is fundamental to Melchizedek's programme of eschatological salvation.

Melchizedek's ministry is to free the community from the rule of Belial. Significantly, Melchizedek accomplishes this redemption on the Day of Atonement (2:7). Who is more central in the ritual of the Day of Atonement than the high priest of Israel? Describing what was to take place on the Day of Atonement, Leviticus 16 focuses almost entirely on God's instructions to Moses about the high priest's (Aaron's) role in making atonement for the sins of the people. Like Israel's high priest under Mosaic law, Melchizedek will liberate the members of his community by freeing them 'from [the debt of] all their iniquities' (2:6). Concerning the Day of Atonement in 11QMelch, Aschim writes:

> In the context of 11QMelch, this is much more than a date notice. It is a matter of great importance that the eschatological liberation takes place on this very day. Probably, Melchizedek is the subject of the verb 'to atone' (כפר) in the following sentence (II 7–8). If so, he enacts the role of the high priest in the Day of Atonement ritual according to Leviticus 16: 'And the 'D[ay of Aton]ement' i[s] the e[nd] of the tenth [ju]bilee, to atone that (day) for all the sons [of light and] men of the lot of Mel[chi]zedek.'[46]

Melchizedek's eschatological liberation is a function of his priesthood. As a priest, he nullifies Belial's power by providing atonement for the sins of

---

[45] Hay 1973: 27; Laub 1980: 39. Laub's work is cited in this regard by Aschim (1999: 139).
[46] Aschim 1999: 132.

142

the community. Melchizedek's priestly service 'at least partly explains the author's choice of the name "Melchizedek" to designate him in this work (cf. Ps. 110:4)'.[47] 11QMelch also alludes to Leviticus 16 by mentioning two lots: the 'lot of Melchizedek' (2:8) and 'Belial and the spirits of his lot' (2:12). On the Day of Atonement, the high priest was to cast lots over the two goats, 'one lot for Yahweh and the other lot for Azazel' (Lev. 16:8). Knohl suggests that the lots that were given to Yahweh and Azazel in Leviticus 16 are reassigned to Melchizedek and Belial in 11QMelch.[48] This reassignment sets the stage for the high priest Melchizedek to atone for the sins of the people and destroy Belial and his lot for ever. In Aschim's words:

Appearing in the final phase of history as a heavenly warrior, judge, and high priest, he is expected to complete a series of actions on God's behalf. He will conquer evil powers, liberate the human 'sons of light' from the dominion of evil, act as a high priest on their behalf in the Yom Kippur ritual, and pronounce judgment on their enemies, 'Belial and his lot.'[49]

Kobelski offered one of the most extensive and persuasive arguments for the priesthood of Melchizedek in 11QMelch. He observed several similarities between 11QMelch and the 'new priest' in *Testament of Levi* 18:2–14. Melchizedek in 11QMelch and the 'new priest' of *Testament of Levi* 18 are eschatological judges who defeat Belial, usher in the new age and dispel the darkness by illuminating the world with 'light'. Kobelski concluded that it was impossible to separate the royal Melchizedek from his office of priesthood:

He reigns as king and his dominion is characterized as a time of peace and joy (11QMelch 2:9–16). With the destruction of Belial's power the period of sin and evil, which had affected even the righteous, is at an end; and the sons of light are restored to their position among the sons of heaven. Although the priesthood of Melchizedek is not explicitly referred to in 11QMelch, the identification of him as

---

47 Rainbow 1997: 192.
48 Knohl 2009: 261–262.
49 Aschim 1999: 133.

a priest of El Elyon in Genesis 14, the mention of the everlasting priesthood of Melchizedek in Psalm 110, and the use of Genesis 14:18b–19 in 1QapGen 22:15, make it impossible to separate the mention of him from the thought of his priesthood.[50]

Summary

Though specific references to Psalm 110 are lacking in 11QMelch, the connection between the two texts cannot be missed. Knohl concurs:

> We have seen that Melchizedek of Psalm 110 is a priestly King, who rules over his people and judges the nations. The same combination is developed in *11QMelchizedek*. The hero of this *pesher* is a messianic king who rules over his community, judges the evil spirits and atones for his people on the eschatological Day of Atonement.[51]

While some intertestamental literature anticipated a messianic diarchic rule, where an anointed priest and an anointed king would establish God's kingdom, 11QMelch is one text that clearly brought kingship and priesthood together in a central figure. Knohl again comments:

> *11QMelchizedek*, however, rejects the separation of kingship and priesthood. The savior and redeemer of the eschatological Day of Atonement combines kingship and priesthood within a single personality. Thus, it is no wonder that he is described as heir to the biblical figure Melchizedek.[52]

Conclusion

This chapter singled out a small body of intertestamental literature influenced by Psalm 110 and its conception of a messianic priest-king. The evidence from the *Testament of Levi*, *1 Enoch*, *2 Enoch* and *11QMelchizedek* indicates that their authors interpreted Psalm 110 as an eschatological text describing God's anointed priest-king and his role in establishing God's kingdom. The author of *2 Enoch* appeared to attach the messianic

---

[50] Kobelski 1981: 68.
[51] Knohl 2009: 263.
[52] Ibid.

Melchizedek's eschatological ministry to Adam's prototypical priestly rule in God's garden-paradise, thus hinting at a reading of Psalm 110 similar to the argument being advanced here. 11QMelch most fully developed Psalm 110 by unfolding Melchizedek's end-time conquest in royal and priestly categories connected to major biblical themes: eschatological judgment, atonement, the establishment of God's kingdom and triumph over the spiritual forces of evil. At the very least, we may conclude that these intertestamental works understood the royal-priestly messianism of Psalm 110 as part of the larger biblical narrative, even if just at the thematic level. For these authors, Psalm 110 was certainly not a novel prophecy devoid of any biblical-theological connections or merely a political charter isolated to a single event in Israel's history, namely David's rule in Jerusalem.

7

Jesus, Psalm 110
and the Gospel of Mark

The purpose of chapters 7 and 8 is to explore the New Testament's presentation of Jesus as the royal priest of Psalm 110. The New Testament authors cite Psalm 110 more than any other Old Testament passage. A whole series of books could be written on the New Testament's use of Psalm 110. Such comprehensive analysis is not necessary for this book. Instead, these chapters will focus on the New Testament's development of both priesthood and kingship in the life and ministry of Jesus on the basis of Psalm 110. Chapters 7 and 8 do not constitute a systematic theology of the offices of Christ's priesthood and kingship that neatly divides the offices and evaluates them from an atemporal perspective. Instead, I am aiming at a biblical-theological and redemptive-historical development of royal priesthood and Psalm 110. Chapter 7 will give attention to the Gospel of Mark, while chapter 8 will examine the epistle to the Hebrews.

Gospel of Mark

The New Testament continues to unfold the Old Testament's story of the kingdom of God. Jesus' life and ministry is the beginning of the final chapter in the story of God's reign over the world – a reign that began with creation in the life of Adam and was later passed on to the people of Israel. The belief that an individual priest-king (Adam) or corporate priest-king (Israel) would bring about the fulfilment of God's kingdom is fundamental to the Old Testament's storyline and intricately bound up with the covenantal framework of Scripture. We would expect, then, that Jesus would hold the offices of both kingship and priesthood in the pages of the Gospels. But is this the case?

While the kingship of Jesus pervades the pages of the New Testament, it appears, at least on the surface, that only the epistle to the Hebrews offers any developed treatment of the priesthood of Christ, and that on the basis of Psalm 110. Eugene Merrill represents the majority of scholars by saying that the Gospels are 'virtually silent' on the topic of Jesus as priest.[1] But not everyone is so convinced. Scholars such as Broadhead,[2] Fletcher-Louis[3] and Perrin[4] remain persuaded that the Gospels depict the person and work of Christ from the perspective of his priesthood.[5]

The Gospel of Mark references Psalm 110 twice during Jesus' last days in Jerusalem. In Mark 12:36, Jesus, in the temple, quotes Psalm 110:1 in reference to the Messiah as the Davidic son. In Mark 14:62, Jesus responds to the questioning of the high priest by conflating the imagery of Daniel 7:13 and Psalm 110:1 to reveal his own messianic identity. Psalm 110:4, 'You are a priest for ever after the order of Melchizedek,' never appears in Mark's Gospel. Nevertheless, Mark's use of Psalm 110 in settings associated with the temple and the Jerusalem high priesthood naturally evokes the broader context of the psalm. Is the reader in these moments meant to understand Jesus as David's Lord who will sit at God's right hand, but to refrain from applying the remainder of the psalm (Melchizedekian priesthood) to Jesus' identity? An affirmative answer creates an awkward tension, to say the least.

But is there more evidence for a priestly Jesus in the Gospel of Mark? Does Jesus' self-referential use of Psalm 110 in the closing act of the narrative come as a surprise or has Mark prepared his readers for these stunning affirmations ahead of time? Admittedly, the answers to these questions are difficult and rely heavily on narrative subtexts and textual implications. Where one lands on the issue of Jesus' priestly identity in the Gospels may never escape accusations of eisegesis from one scholarly camp or hermeneutical shallowness from the other.

At the very least, the evidence deserves a fresh hearing. This chapter will argue that Mark intended his readers to identify Jesus as the priest-king of Psalm 110 even though he is not officially installed in the Melchizedekian office until his resurrection and ascension, as Hebrews

---

[1] Merrill 1993: 51.
[2] Broadhead 1992.
[3] Fletcher-Louis 2000; 2006.
[4] Perrin 2013.
[5] See also Schrock 2013: 258–297.

will make clear. The Gospels depict Jesus as the Messiah; he is David's Lord (Ps. 110:1). Hebrews unpacks the *timing* of his installation in the messianic office of priest-king. It makes sense, then, that the Gospel-writers do not explicitly identify Jesus as a priest during his earthly life. He is the Messiah of Psalm 110, but he is not of the tribe of Levi. Only after he fulfils the old-covenant types and shadows, through his sacrificial death and resurrection, does he enter into his office of priest-king.

Mark's use of Psalm 110 in the closing narrative is the culmination of the development of Jesus' priestly identity already begun in 'act one' of Mark's Gospel (Mark 1:1 – 8:26).[6] Defending this argument will depend on building a cumulative case by presenting multiple lines of evidence. No single strand of evidence in Mark 1:1 – 8:26 proves that Mark intended to portray Jesus' ministry as a priestly ministry. Nevertheless, the cumulative effect of pulling the individual strands of evidence together should present a compelling case that Jesus' earthly ministry is a priestly ministry.

The kingdom of God is near

Jesus arrives on the scene in Mark's Gospel proclaiming the gospel of God and the nearness of God's kingdom (Mark 1:14–15). No explanation of the meaning of the kingdom of God is given and none is needed.[7] The opening words of Mark's Gospel connect the 'beginning' (*archē*) of Jesus' arrival in human history to the story that has been unfolding since the 'beginning' (*archē*) of the world (cf. Gen. 1:1). The creation of the world described in Genesis 1 – 2 and the initial establishment of God's kingdom through Adam, God's covenantal son, informs the mission of Jesus Christ, the 'Son of God' (*huiou theou*).[8] Without denying the fact that the title 'Son of God' carries ontological connotations – Jesus is the Son of God from eternity – its functional purpose is to fasten Jesus' sonship to typological figures in the Old Testament.[9] As Son of God, Jesus is not only the new Adam; he is also the new Israel, and the Davidic son-king (Exod. 4:22–23; 2 Sam. 7:12–16). His life and ministry will bring to pass God's

---

6 Broadhead 1992: 23 n. 5.
7 Goldsworthy 2002: 73.
8 According to Treat (2014: 89), 'Mark's first word (ἀρχή) is not simply telling the reader where to begin, but is rather a reference to Gen 1:1 (ἐν ἀρχῇ LXX), which places Mark's story about Jesus within the story of the world from creation (Gen 1–2) to new creation (Isa 65:17–25), and more specifically (as is clear in the next verse) within the story of Israel'.
9 See Wellum's (2016: 158–163) discussion of the title 'Son of God'.

promises to Israel concerning redemption and the establishment of God's worldwide reign.

In the opening chapter, Mark conflates two important Old Testament passages anticipating the coming reign of God from heaven to earth. First, Malachi 3:1 predicted a forerunner who would prepare the way for the coming of the Lord. The Lord's coming in Malachi 3:1–4 is his coming to the temple to exercise judgment. The Lord will occupy sacred space to refine his people from the epicentre of his presence on earth. The second Old Testament citation comes from Isaiah 40:3. The reference to Isaiah evokes the broader context of Isaiah 40 – 55 and the themes of new exodus, new creation and the establishment of the kingdom of God.[10] Treat rightly observes that 'the influence of Isaiah 40–55 on Mark includes not only the Isaianic new exodus, which culminates in God's enthronement in Jerusalem (Isa 52:7), but also its agent and means – the servant and his atoning death (Isa 52:13 – 53:12)'.[11] The kingdom-through-cross framework casts its shadow over Mark's entire narrative.[12] Jesus has arrived in human history to usher in the reign of God by leading a new exodus through his death on the cross, which, in the theology of the narrative, is a covenant sacrifice making atonement for sins (Mark 14:12–25).[13] In other words, the kingdom will come through covenant sacrifice.

If kingdom and cross (covenant sacrifice) are so intricately linked in Mark's Gospel, then perhaps we should also expect the offices of king (kingdom) and priest (covenant sacrifice/r) to inform Jesus' mission and identity. The broader narrative of the Old Testament – Psalm 110 in particular – attached the arrival of God's kingdom to a figure who was both a king and a priest. Jesus appealed to Psalm 110 twice in Mark's temple narrative implying that the Melchizedekian priest-king had arrived in his own person. But how does the explicit application of Psalm 110 to Jesus in the final section of Mark's narrative fit with all that has come before?

There is little doubt that Jesus is the royal Son of God in Mark's Gospel.[14] The opening verse establishes him as the 'Christ' (*christos*) and

---

[10] For a full development of the influence of the Isaianic new exodus in Mark's narrative, see Watts 2000.

[11] Treat 2014: 89.

[12] Ibid. 91.

[13] Mark 14:12–25 identifies the Passover meal with Jesus' own sacrifice as the 'blood of the covenant'. In Matthew's account of the Lord's Supper, Jesus' blood is specifically identified as the means to effect the forgiveness of sins (Matt. 26:28).

[14] On the development of royal Christology in the Gospel of Mark, see Donahue 1979: 72–79; Rowe 2002; Vickers 2004: 21–23.

'Son of God' (Mark 1:1). Both titles are pregnant with royalty. Psalm 2 describes the *christos* (anointed) as God's chosen king ruling the nations to the ends of the earth. Psalm 18:51 (LXX 17:51) identifies the *christos* as the Davidic king and object of God's steadfast love.

God's promise to David was that the Messiah-king would exist in a father–son relationship with Yahweh (2 Sam. 7:12–16). Upon ascending from the waters of baptism, the voice from heaven revealed Jesus' messianic identity, echoing the words of Psalm 2:7: 'You are my beloved Son; with you I am well pleased' (Mark 1:11 ESV). On the outskirts of Jericho, blind Bartimaeus accurately assessed Jesus' identity as the 'Son of David' (Mark 10:47–48). Similarly, the crowds hailed him as the one who would bring the coming kingdom of David (Mark 11:10).

More difficult to discern than his royalty is the priestly identity of Jesus in Mark's Gospel. Mark never explicitly identifies Jesus as a priest, but this is no surprise because Jesus was not of the lineage of Levi. To call Jesus a priest would have made Jesus not a fulfiller of the law but a changer of the law (cf. Heb. 7:12). The lack of explicit reference to Jesus as priest does not negate the fact that the Gospel narratives portray Jesus as a priest of a different order. To suggest that the office of priesthood, which was such a major part of Old Testament theology, messianic expectation and Israel's political existence, had no bearing on the Christologies of the Gospel-writers seems dubious. Broadhead is more certain: 'This priestly image, though briefly-developed, has been woven into the larger tapestry of the Gospel of Mark and contributes to its wider Christological portrait.'[15] Act one of Mark's Gospel (1:1 – 8:26) develops the arrival and outworking of the kingdom of God in Jesus' ministry not just in regard to his kingship but also as a component of his priestly authority.

Jesus the priest

Mark 1:21–28 and 5:1–20

Mark 1:21–28 describes Jesus' first exorcism. Jesus is in the synagogue on the sabbath and a man possessed by an unclean spirit confronts him. The fact that Mark describes this evil spirit as 'unclean' (*akathartos*) is

---

15 Broadhead 1992: 22.

significant (Mark 1:23, 26). The concept of clean and unclean evokes the holiness code of Leviticus:

> You are to distinguish between the holy and the common, and between the unclean and the clean, and you are to teach the people of Israel all the statutes that the LORD has spoken to them by Moses. (Lev. 10:10–11 ESV)

> And the priest shall examine [any person with a skin disease] again on the seventh day, and if the diseased area has faded and the disease has not spread in the skin, then the priest shall pronounce him clean; it is only an eruption. And he shall wash his clothes and be clean. (Lev. 13:6 ESV)

The priests were responsible for regulating Israel's worship by separating the clean from the unclean.[16]

In its narrative context, Jesus' encounter with the unclean spirit in Mark 1:21–28 is meant to address the issue of Jesus' identity. As the narrative begins, Jesus' authoritative teaching is set in contrast with the teaching of the scribes (Mark 1:22). He is in a different class altogether from the religious authorities of Israel. When the unclean spirit appears on the stage, it immediately makes a statement concerning Jesus' identity: 'the Holy One of God' (*ho hagios tou theou* [Mark 1:24]). *Ho hagios* is a title repeatedly used of God in the Old Testament, especially in the book of Isaiah (Ps. 70:22; Isa. 12:6; 30:12, 15; 40:25; 41:20; 43:3, 14, 15; 45:11; 48:17; 49:7; Hab. 1:12; 3:3).[17] However, the title 'the Holy One *of God*' on the lips of an *unclean* spirit suggests another possible Old Testament backdrop, namely the priesthood.

Moses gave instructions concerning the priesthood in Leviticus 21:6–8, grounding the priests' responsibilities for maintaining cleanness in the holiness of their office:

> They shall be holy to their God (LXX *hagioi esontai tō theō autōn*) and not profane the name of their God. For they offer the LORD's

---

[16] As I argued in the previous chapter, Jewish texts such as the *Testament of Levi*, *1 Enoch*, *2 Enoch* and *11QMelchizedek* demonstrate that many in Jesus' day were expecting a royal-priestly messiah to destroy the spiritual forces of evil.

[17] Most of the uses of *ho hagios* refer to 'the Holy One of Israel'.

food offerings, the bread of their God; therefore they shall be holy. They shall not marry a prostitute or a woman who has been defiled, neither shall they marry a woman divorced from her husband, for the priest is holy to his God (LXX *hagios estin tō kyriō theō autou*). You shall sanctify him, for he offers the bread of your God. He shall be holy to you, for I, the LORD, who sanctify you, am holy. (Lev. 21:6–8 ESV)

The priests were to be 'holy to their God' as they followed the ordinances for maintaining cleanness. Even the garb of the high priest reflected the standard of holiness attached to the office. Fastened to his turban was a plate of pure gold with the engraving 'Holy to the LORD' (*hagiasma kyriou* [Exod. 28:36]). Furthermore, Aaron is twice identified as 'the holy one' in the Old Testament (Num. 16:7; Ps. 106:16).[18] In Psalm 106:16 (LXX Ps. 105:16), he is 'the holy one *of the Lord*' (*ton hagion kyriou*). Holiness, in the Old Testament, was a fundamental component of priestly identity.

Perhaps it is a mistake to limit the background of the phrase *ho hagios tou theou* either to God's holiness or to the priest's holy character as though the two are mutually exclusive. God is holy and his priests, as his representatives, were called to be holy. The reference to Jesus as *ho hagios*, in Mark, associates Jesus with the holy God of Israel, but the qualifier *tou theou* makes him distinct from God, acting as God's representative. The unclean spirit knows Jesus' true identity. Jesus is God's representative, a holy one (priest) with authority over all things unclean, even unclean spirits.

A similar scene appears in Mark 5:1–20. A man with an 'unclean spirit' confronts Jesus (Mark 5:2, 8, 13). Again, the confrontation reveals something about Jesus' identity. The unclean spirit identifies Jesus as 'Son of the Most High God' (*huie tou theou tou hypsistou* [Mark 5:7]). There are only seven places in the LXX where the adjective *hypsistos* modifies the noun *theos*. Three of them occur in the Psalms (LXX Pss 56:3; 77:35, 56); the other four appear in the Melchizedek episode in Genesis 14:17–24. Four times in the span of five verses, God is identified as 'God Most High' in Genesis 14:

---

[18] Fletcher-Louis (2007: 63) observes, 'The only precedent for a singular "*the* Holy One of God" is Aaron (Ps. 106.16; Numb. 16.7 "the holy one (of the LORD)")'; emphasis original. See also Marcus 2000: 188.

Genesis 14:18:	*ēn de hiereus **tou theou tou hypsistou***
Genesis 14:19:	*eulogēmenos abram **tō theō tō hypsistō***
Genesis 14:20:	*kai eulogētos **ho theos ho hypsistos***
Genesis 14:22:	*ektenō tēn cheira mou pros **ton theon ton hypsiston***

The phrase *huie tou theou tou hypsistou* in Mark 5:7 is nearly identical to the description of Melchizedek's priesthood in Genesis 14:18:

Genesis 14:18:	*hiereus tou theou tou hypsistou*
Mark 5:7:	*huie tou theou tou hypsistou*

Ironically, the unclean spirits rightly recognize Jesus' true identity while others do not (cf. Mark 1:27). He is the Son of the Most High God. His authority over the demonic world is a function of his sonship. Throughout the Old Testament, divine sonship entailed representation (imaging) and the authority to rule on behalf of God. God's son mediated God's reign on earth. In other words, he was a priest and a king. The same understanding of Jesus' sonship here in Mark's narrative is probable, especially in the light of the allusion to the Melchizedek episode in Genesis 14. A new priest-king, not of the tribe of Levi, overpowers an 'unclean' spirit (Ps. 110; cf. 11QMelch). Before Jesus identifies himself as the messianic priest-king of Psalm 110 in the temple narrative (Mark 11:35–37; 14:62), he has already begun ridding the land of spiritual uncleanness.[19]

Mark 1:40–45 and 5:21–43

Jesus' interaction with the leper at the end of Mark 1 continues the development of Jesus' priestly identity in the context of ceremonial uncleanness. The leper begs Jesus to make him 'clean' (Mark 1:40). As noted from Leviticus, it was the priests who were responsible for pronouncing someone or something as clean or unclean (Lev. 13:6). Jesus, however, is a greater priest than those of the Levitical order. Jesus not only pronounces clean; he actually makes clean. He responds to the leper's request by touching (*haptō*) him and making him clean (Mark 1:41). Anyone who came into

---

[19] Perrin (2010: 168) argues that Jesus' exorcisms substantiate his role as the eschatological Melchizedek.

contact with a leper, including priests, would have become unclean. Yet Jesus is able to touch the leper and not only remain clean himself but also make that which was unclean clean.

Similarly, in Mark 5:21–43, Jesus comes into contact with two people who should have rendered him ceremonially unclean: the woman with the issue of blood and Jairus's dead daughter (cf. Lev. 15:27; Num. 19). In narrative context, these events follow right after Jesus' healing of the man with the unclean spirit (Mark 5:1–20). Having been identified as the 'Son of the Most High God' (keeping in mind the likelihood that this title echoes the Melchizedek narrative [Gen. 14:17–24]) Jesus proceeds to heal, by touch, two ceremonially unclean women (Mark 5:21–43).

Jairus appears on the scene first. He is one of the 'rulers of the synagogue' (Mark 5:22). Mark refers to Jairus three more times in this narrative, each time using the description 'ruler' or 'ruler of the synagogue' instead of his name (Mark 5:35, 36, 38). His position is obviously an important part of the narrative, but why? Maybe Mark wants his readers to see that this ruler of the synagogue came to Jesus to find something that the law was unable to provide.[20] The daughter (*thygatrion*) of the ruler of the synagogue is ill and on the verge of death (Mark 5:23). He has found no solution for her condition in the law, so he falls at Jesus' feet imploring him to put his hand on her so that she might 'be made well and live' (*sōthē kai zēsē* [Mark 5:23 ESV]).

Jesus agrees to go with Jairus, but his journey is interrupted. Jairus's daughter is under the shadow of death, but so are the daughters (*thygatēr*) of Israel (cf. Mark 5:34). A desperate woman has been suffering from a discharge of blood for twelve years. The law renders her ceremonially unclean, but it has no power to remedy her situation either. Even the physicians (*iatros*) of the land have offered no solution (Mark 5:26). Perhaps the physical condition of these two *daughters* and the failure of the physicians evokes Jeremiah 8:22 to show that these physical ailments are symptoms of a much bigger problem in Israel. Israel's idolatry provoked Jeremiah's questions:

Is there no balm in Gilead?
Is there no physician (*iatros*) there?

---

[20] David Schrock pointed out this observation and the following reference to both women as 'daughters' in a personal conversation.

Why then has the health of the daughter (*thygatros*) of my people
 not been restored?
(Jer. 8:22 ESV)

Jeremiah lamented the spiritual epidemic in the land. Everyone from
'prophet to priest' was corrupt and there was no righteous king in Zion
(Jer. 8:10, 19). Fast-forward several hundred years to the setting in
Mark 5 and the situation is similar. Israel is spiritually ill and nobody –
not the rulers of the synagogues, not the physicians, not the priests, not
the law – has the remedy. There is no balm in Gilead and no physician who
can heal.

Happily, for the two daughters in Mark 5, there is a priest-king roaming
Israel who can heal. In the case of the woman with the issue of blood,
Mark emphasizes the fact that she was healed simply by touching Jesus'
'garment' (*himation*), a detail reaffirmed three times in the narrative
(cf. Mark 5:27–28, 30). Contact with an unclean woman and a corpse did
not render Jesus unclean, but instead, power went forth from Jesus
through his garments to bring healing.[21]

In this respect, scholars are right to refer to Jesus' healing power as his
contagious holiness. There is no Old Testament precedent for a priest (or
anyone for that matter) ever making an unclean person clean – although,
as Fletcher-Louis has observed, Ezekiel 44:19 indicates that the priestly
vestments could communicate holiness to the people:[22]

And when they go out into the outer court to the people, they shall
put off the garments in which they have been ministering and lay
them in the holy chambers. And they shall put on other garments,
lest they transmit holiness to the people with their garments.
(Ezek. 44:19 ESV)

A similar concept appears in the law of the sin offering in Leviticus 6:27:
'Whatever touches its flesh shall be holy, and when any of its blood
is splashed on a garment, you shall wash that on which it was splashed
in a holy place' (ESV). Assuming the garment (*himation* [LXX 6:20]) in

---

[21] Mark 5:30 (ESV) says that Jesus perceived that 'power had gone out from him' when the
woman touched his garment.

[22] Fletcher-Louis 2007: 64–70.

Leviticus 6:27 is or at least includes the priest's clothing, it is apparent that the garment itself became holy by coming into contact with the blood or flesh of the sacrifice. Though not the priest himself, the garments worn by the priest (Ezek. 44:19) and the sacrifice made by the priest (Lev. 6:27) were able to render other objects and people holy. Similarly, by touching unclean objects (e.g. the corpse of Jairus's daughter [Mark 5:41]) with his flesh, or by bringing unclean people (e.g. the woman with the issue of blood) into contact with his garment, Jesus transmits holy healing power. Surely, Jesus' garment did not contain any special power in and of itself. Its ability to heal was a function of the person wearing it, much like the fact that the garment of the priest communicated holiness because it was the *priest's* garment and because it had come into contact with the holy sacrificial offering. Jesus' flesh and the garments on his flesh could heal unclean people because, in part, he was a superior kind of priest, and, perhaps, because his flesh would become this priest's superior sacrifice.[23]

Mark 2:1–12

Mark 2:1–12 describes a confrontation between Jesus and the scribes. The issue of Jesus' identity is at the heart of the controversy because Jesus claims authority as 'the Son of Man' to forgive sins (Mark 2:10). The religious elites question Jesus' ability to forgive sins by asking in their hearts, 'Who can forgive sins but God alone?' (Mark 2:7 ESV). Their question is appropriate, and it is what drives the interpretation of Jesus' healing miracle. By healing the paralytic and thereby proving that he has the authority to forgive sins, Jesus reveals that he shares in God's divine authority over fallen humankind.

But in the light of Jesus' self-referential use of the title 'Son of Man', we should not limit the meaning of this pericope to a revelation of Jesus' divine nature. Though the subject of much debate, the meaning of 'Son of Man' in Mark's Gospel has Daniel 7 as its primary referent (Mark 8:38; 13:26; 14:62).[24] In Daniel 7, one like a son of man is a 'human figure described in divine language' who appears before the Ancient of Days to receive dominion, glory and a kingdom (Dan. 7:14).[25] Daniel 7 is not the

---

23 Broadhead (1992: 25) argues that the phrase *martyrion autois* in Mark 1:44 should be translated 'as a testimony against them'. The leper is, therefore, to present himself to the priests as a testimony that their ministry is insufficient.
24 Treat 2014: 96.
25 Ibid.

first place in the biblical narrative where we discover a human king reigning over the nations from the throne room of God (cf. Ps. 110). Psalm 110 and Daniel 7:13–14 both picture a human king in the presence of God ruling over the earth. As we will see below, Jesus combines the imagery of Daniel 7:13 and Psalm 110:1 to describe the nature of his messiahship to the high priest. For now, the point is that Daniel's son of man is a picture of the ideal human king. That the Son of Man has authority on earth to forgive sins may imply that a human king is restoring human dominion over a sin-cursed earth and a sin-cursed people.

Kings, however, did not forgive sins in the Old Testament. Instead, a human priest had the authority to mediate God's forgiveness to the people. The priest's role on the Day of Atonement bears this out (cf. Lev. 16:32–34). Through the atonement ritual, Israel's priest was able to offer the forgiveness of sins on behalf of God. Broadhead's conclusion on this passage seems accurate: 'Jesus does in Mark 2:1–13 what only a priest of God can do – offer God's forgiveness for sin.'[26] Joel Marcus similarly writes, 'Part of Jesus' offense, then, may be his usurpation of priestly prerogatives, and this makes particularly good sense if scribes were priests.'[27] In addition, Jesus' use of the title 'Son of Man' may also pick up on the high-priestly character of the one like a son of man in Daniel 7 (see my discussion below).

But forgiveness happened at the temple, and here Jesus offers forgiveness apart from the temple and its priesthood.[28] What are we to make of this? Beale answers this question by noting the importance of the title 'Son of Man':

> The temple was the divinely instituted place where sacrifices were offered for the forgiveness of sins, but now Jesus has become the divinely instituted location where forgiveness is to be found, since he himself is also the sin offering. Matthew 9:2–6 (=Mark 2:1; Luke 5:18–26) says that 'the Son of Man has authority on earth to forgive sins', which may suggest that this pardoning of sins, formerly obtained at the temple, is part of his work as the priestly last Adam. Hence, again, we have the close association of temple function

---

[26] Ibid. Perrin (2013: 171) similarly concludes, 'The pronouncement of forgiveness was an activity that had traditionally been reserved for the priesthood.'

[27] Marcus 2000: 216.

[28] On the relationship between the temple and forgiveness, see Wright 1997: 406–412.

(albeit echoed) with the Adamic commission to have authority over the earth.[29]

If we allow the plotline of Scripture to inform Jesus' use of the title 'Son of Man' and his claim to authority, then surely this scene is more than a revelation of Jesus' divine character. It is a revelation of Jesus' full humanity manifesting itself in his kingly and priestly work as the final Adam.

Mark 2:23 – 3:6

Mark 2:23 – 3:6 describes two confrontations between Jesus and the religious authorities over the issue of the sabbath. In Mark 2:23–28, the Pharisees accuse Jesus and his disciples of breaking the law by plucking heads of grain on the sabbath. Jesus responds by appealing to David's actions during the time of Abiathar, the high priest.[30] David entered the house of God and ate the bread of the Presence, which was reserved by law for the 'priests' alone (Mark 2:26). So, were Jesus and his disciples exceptions to the rule like David and his men? Or were they, like David and his men, partaking in a priestly prerogative?[31] The latter better accounts for the cultic dimensions of 1 Samuel 21:1–9 and Mark 2:23–28, and the shared priest-king typology between David and Jesus. Just as David's priestly typology had its roots in covenants prior to the Mosaic covenant and its Levitical priesthood – namely the Melchizedekian priesthood and the Abrahamic and creation covenants – so too did Jesus' royal priesthood transcend Mosaic law.[32] For Jesus did not appeal to sabbath

---

[29] Beale 2004: 177–178. Beale (ibid. 176–177) points to the Great Commission in Matt. 28 as another example of the association between the temple and Adamic authority.

[30] It is not necessary to address the Abiathar problem here. For an excellent treatment of the Abiathar problem in Mark 2:23–28, see Perrin 2013.

[31] Perrin (2013: 174–175) poses a similar question: 'This raises the question as to whether Mark's Jesus intends to say that David's men (and by extension his own disciples) were exceptions to the for-priestly-consumption-only rule or were, in fact, confirmation of it.' My questions above are dependent on his reasoning.

[32] I developed the arguments for seeing David as a kind of Melchizedekian royal priest in chapter 4. Commenting on the relationship between David and his warriors and Jesus and his disciples, Perrin (2013: 175) writes, 'Reading the pericope of the disciples' plucking grain in anticipation of the subsequent narrative, it becomes clear that Jesus permits the disciples to "desecrate the Sabbath" precisely because, like David's men, they had priestly prerogatives as part of a new temple regime. If as a rule the temple showbread was reserved for the priests, then David's men and the disciples were both exceptions that proved the rule. The scene contained in 2:23–28, then, is not to be understood as Jesus' attempt to engage in casuistic discussion over the scope of the Law (as it is so often taken) but rather an eschatological announcement that YHWH is about to transfer the priestly mantle from the official cult leadership, who in their resistance to the true Son of David were liable to judgment.'

regulations instituted at Sinai to justify his priestly prerogative. He reminded his audience that the sabbath was a creation ordinance: 'the Sabbath was made for man, not man for the Sabbath' (Mark 2:27 ESV). The sabbath rest lost through Adam's failure is now being restored in a priest-king better than Adam himself. For the 'Son of Man [Adam] is lord even of the Sabbath' (Mark 2:28 ESV).[33]

Once again, Jesus' priestly behaviour occurs outside temple confines. In 1 Samuel 21, David acted as a royal priest at the 'house of God', a setting proper for priestly activity. Jesus and his disciples, however, are in a grainfield, a setting not proper for priestly activity and out of sync with the precedent set by David in 1 Samuel 21. What should we make of this? Fletcher-Louis speculates:

> If Jesus is the true eschatological high priest, then it stands to reason that wherever he may be there rests the sacred space of the true temple. And if David's men can eat the bread of the presence at a sanctuary in Nob (1 Sam. 21.1), why cannot Jesus set up a new sanctuary for his disciples in the Galilean countryside?[34]

In Mark 3:1–6, Jesus, as Lord of the sabbath, does on the sabbath what would be expected from the eschatological priest-king: he overcomes the effects of the curse by healing a man with a withered hand, thereby restoring him to the creational harmony reflected in the original Edenic state of sabbath rest (Mark 3:1–6; cf. Gen. 2:1–3). As in the previous confrontation, Jesus heals the man with the withered hand in the context of opposition. Broadhead draws out the irony in these confrontational encounters. He writes, 'Jesus does what any good priest should do – he ministers to the people on the Sabbath. In contrast, the priests of Israel use the Sabbath to plot Jesus' death (3.6).'[35]

Mark 7:14–23

One final narrative worth noting is Mark 7:14–23. Here Jesus teaches on food laws as they relate to personal holiness. The old-covenant law demarcated clean and unclean foods (cf. Lev. 11), but Jesus took it upon

---

[33] Fletcher-Louis 2007: 75–77.
[34] Ibid. 76.
[35] Broadhead 1992: 28.

himself to redefine these dietary regulations. For Jesus, the difference between purity and defilement is not a matter of eating and drinking, but a matter of the heart. By redefining the nature of purity codes, Jesus embodies priestly authority: he declares all foods 'clean' (*katharizō*) (Mark 7:19). The implications of such a declaration are massive. If Jesus redefined ceremonial cleanness in relation to food laws, then he also de facto redefined the nature of temple worship. On this point, Perrin writes:

> When Mark later recounts Jesus declaring that 'nothing outside a man can make him unclean' (Mark 7:15), the Evangelist is not seeking, as so many interpreters want us to believe, to prioritize a warm, inner spirituality over cold, external rites. More to the point, Mark's intention is to recount a Jesus who, in revising the existent purity codes, is also redefining who may and who may not have legitimate access to the temple. Apparently possessing an authority that allows him to either circumvent or preempt standing temple regulations, Jesus is redefining temple membership along the lines of a new more radical ethic (Mark 7:18–23).[36]

The temple narrative

The use of Psalm 110 in the temple narrative must be understood in the light of Mark's development of Jesus' identity leading up to these events. Jesus enters the temple in Jerusalem with opposition from the religious authorities. The spiritual leaders repeatedly challenge Jesus until their opposition reaches its climactic confrontation in Mark 14:53–65. Here the high priest is Jesus' final adversary, and Jesus' self-referential application of Daniel 7 and Psalm 110 becomes the final statement of self-identification that leads to his crucifixion.

The hostility that characterizes Jesus' reception in Jerusalem comes as no surprise because Mark has already shown his readers that Jesus' ministry grew in the soils of escalating conflict (cf. 2:1 – 3:6). Joanna Dewey has demonstrated that the controversy stories of Mark 2:1 – 3:6 form a single literary unit with a chiastic structure.[37] Dewey asserts that 'Mark employed the conflict stories theologically to place Jesus' life in the context

---

[36] Perrin 2013: 171–172.
[37] Dewey 1973.

of his death, and he used them in his narrative construction to show how Jesus' death historically was to come about'.[38]

Jesus' early controversies with 'temple-based leadership' are therefore linked in the narrative to his run-ins with temple-based leadership at the Jerusalem temple.[39] In both cases, Jesus' identity is central to the conflict. In three of the controversy scenes, Jesus' priestly identity is set over and against the religious authorities (Mark 2:1–12, 23–28; 3:1–6). The superior priesthood of Jesus in contrast to the hostile religious establishment in Mark's early narrative prepares the reader for Jesus' more explicit self-referential use of Psalm 110 and for his controversial encounters in the temple, which lead to his death. Over and against the false priests of the temple, Jesus is the eschatological priest-king who will establish God's kingdom through his sacrificial death on the cross.

The timing of Jesus' use of Psalm 110:1 in Mark 12:35–37 is significant. Now that Jesus has entered the temple as the Davidic Messiah, he explicitly states what his actions have already demonstrated: he is the Davidic priest-king of Psalm 110.[40] Watts concurs:

> It is intriguing that although Jesus has been engaged throughout in the priestly activities of teaching (often on purity) and declaring individuals clean, it is only after his Davidic entry and his actions and masterfully confounding teaching in the temple precincts that he appeals to Psalm 110 – the one text that explicitly speaks of a Davidic priest-king.[41]

Jesus' use of Psalm 110 in this narrative is quite remarkable. In the city of David, in the temple, Jesus claims the highest authoritative offices the Old Testament had to offer: Davidic kingship and Melchizedekian priesthood. By virtue of his kingly authority and superior priesthood, he will

---

[38] Ibid. 400.

[39] Broadhead (1992: 29) has argued more extensively for the connection between the priestly portrait of Jesus and the religious controversy theme in Mark.

[40] Mark 12:36 employs the verb ὑποκάτω instead of ὑποπόδιον when citing Ps. 110:1 (LXX 109:1). It is possible that the use of ὑποκάτω is the result of a conflation of Ps. 110:1 and Ps. 8:6 (LXX 8:7) where ὑποκάτω appears. Ps. 8 is a commentary on Gen. 1:28 and the meaning of the image of God. At the very least, Mark 12:36 might reflect a tradition that held the royalty of the Davidic Messiah (Ps. 110) and the royalty of Adam (Ps. 8) in close connection. Moreover, Adam's royalty was attached to his priestly identity in the same way that the Davidic Messiah embodied a priestly royalty.

[41] Watts 2007: 319.

render the temple, its leadership and the entire Mosaic programme null and void.[42]

The timing of Jesus' appeal to Psalm 110:1 may also anticipate the judgment that is coming to those who stand against him (Mark 12:36).[43] Mark cites Psalm 110:1 on the heels of the temple-cleansing and several of Jesus' encounters with the hostile religious authorities (Mark 11:12 – 12:35). Jesus has silenced all of his opponents so that, even before his cross-work, he appears to be ruling in the midst of his enemies, and that from Zion no less (Mark 12:34; Ps. 110:2).

Upon silencing his enemies (Mark 12:34), Jesus issues a stunning revelation to all who oppose him: the Melchizedekian priest-king will subject his enemies to his authoritative rule (Mark 12:35–36). These enemies of Jesus are not just the religious authorities occupying the temple but also the satanic spirits behind them. Perrin says that 'wherever you find false leaders in Israel, an unclean spirit and ensnaring idols are not far below the surface'.[44] Here in Jerusalem, in the temple, the place of God's own sacred presence, the seed of the serpent has set up camp. Jesus won the skirmishes with the unclean spirits on his way to Jerusalem, but now the climactic battle will ensue. Jesus will cast the serpent out of the garden by bruising its head through his death on the cross (cf. Ps. 110:6).

The high priest on trial

Psalm 110 appears a second time in 'act three' of Mark's Gospel as part of the climactic confrontation concerning Jesus' identity. Jesus is brought before the council of temple-based leaders. Not surprisingly, the trial opens with statements concerning Jesus' relationship to the temple (Mark 14:58). Much of Jesus' earlier ministry stirred up controversy, in part, because he performed temple-based actions outside temple confines (Mark 2:1–12, 23–28; 3:1–6). Wright believes that in this final encounter

---

[42] Commenting on Mark 12:35–37, Benjamin Gladd (2021: 181) says, 'Jesus also fulfills the priestly aspect of Psalm 110:4. Mark has taken great pains to demonstrate how Jesus is a priest-king throughout the narrative. As such, he has just cursed the fig tree and judged Israel's temple, and now he ensures the inauguration of a new temple through his death and resurrection! Above all, Mark's readers must recognize that Jesus' identity as a preexistent priest-king is not a radically new doctrine but something that was enigmatically anticipated in the OT itself.'

[43] For an insightful discussion of the use of Ps. 110:1 in Mark 12:35–37 and its implications for Jesus' eschatological holy war, see Marcus 1992: 130–152.

[44] Perrin 2010: 163.

between Jesus and the council, the temple and Jesus' identity come to a head: 'Together they said that Jesus, not the Temple, was the clue to, and the location of, the presence of Israel's god with his people.'[45]

Wright is right, but I suggest that Jesus' *priesthood* – an office inseparable from the temple – is also an underlying concept in the narrative function of the trial scene. How so? The irony of this final confrontation between Jesus and the religious authorities is that the high priest of Israel is the primary prosecutor in the case. The high priest appears to wield authority over Jesus, yet it is Jesus who is the true messianic priest and king – a fact substantiated by Jesus' self-referential appeal to Psalm 110 and Daniel 7 in Mark 14:62. Hamilton agrees:

> Jesus declared to the wicked high priest of Israel that he was indeed the Christ, the Son of God, and at the same time Jesus asserted himself to be the Son of Man who would come on the clouds of heaven to receive everlasting dominion (Dan. 7:13) as the Melchizedekian high priest (Ps. 110:4). Naturally, the rebel holding the role would not appreciate Jesus declaring himself the true high priest-king of Israel.[46]

By conflating the imagery of Psalm 110:1 and Daniel 7:13 in response to the high priest's question concerning his identity, Jesus does not merely combine what appear to be two very different, yet prominent, Old Testament messianic texts. Instead, as Hamilton asserts, '[i]n his reply . . . Jesus made a profound biblical-theological connection'.[47] The profundity of Jesus' biblical-theological insight is amplified if the Son of Man in Daniel 7 is himself both king and *priest* like the Melchizedekian Messiah of Psalm 110. Indeed, this appears to be the case. Hamilton has argued that Psalm 110 is part of the biblical-theological logic informing Daniel's vision of the son of man in Daniel 7:9–14.[48] He asserts that:

---

45 Wright 1997: 644.
46 Hamilton 2014b: 190.
47 Ibid.
48 Hamilton (ibid. 148–149) highlights Daniel's use of plural 'thrones' in Dan. 7:9. This prompts him to ask, 'Why would "thrones" – more than one – be placed in the vision of Daniel 7:9–10? Assuming Daniel had access to the Davidic Psalm 110 . . . his perception and interpretation of what he saw in the vision could have been influenced by the statement in Psalm 110:1 . . . The fact that Jesus connected the Daniel 7:13 son of man with Psalm 110:1 strengthens this possibility . . . Rather than simply one throne for the Ancient of Days, Daniel saw "thrones", and in view of what takes place in the vision, where the one like a son of man receives the

Daniel understood his vision as an enactment of what David described in Psalm 110:1, connecting the Daniel 7 vision with the hope for a king from David's line and validating the way that Matthew [also Mark] presents Jesus interpreting these texts.[49]

If Hamilton is right that Daniel 7 is an enactment of Psalm 110:1, then I would add that David's Lord and Daniel's son of man share more than the office of Davidic kingship; they share a priestly office as well. Fletcher-Louis has offered the most extensive argumentation for the high-priestly character of Daniel's son of man.[50] The imagery of Daniel 7:13 evokes the Day of Atonement ritual when the high priest entered the Most Holy Place where the ark (God's throne on earth) was located and where the cloud of God's presence rested (Lev. 16:2). The scene is similar in Daniel 7:13. The son of man enters God's heavenly throne room (Most Holy Place), with the clouds of heaven, to be 'presented' (*qĕrēb*) before God:[51]

> The implicit liturgical scene fits the text's life setting: the day that the high priest fully comes to God is Yom Kippur and this is also the day that provides a cosmic purification of the world that has been defiled by pagan impurities.[52]

Daniel's son of man is ultimately given the global dominion that the priest-king Adam failed to achieve (Dan. 7:14), and he receives the eternal kingdom promised to David's greater son (2 Sam. 7:12–14). The son of man in Daniel 7 is a priest-king much like the Messiah of Psalm 110. Both exercise royal authority over all the nations; both enjoy priestly access to God's throne room; both are expressions of the Adamic prototype.

When the high priest, in Mark 14:61 (esv), asked Jesus, 'Are you the Christ, the Son of the Blessed ["son of God"; cf. Matt. 26:63]?' Jesus replied by pulling together two Old Testament passages that most clearly embodied God's eschatological programme begun from the creation of

---

kingdom (cf. Dan. 7:14), the natural conclusion is that there is a throne for the one like a son of man.' Hay (1973: 26) also believed that the use of 'thrones' in Dan. 7 was informed by Ps. 110:1.

[49] Hamilton 2014b: 149.

[50] Fletcher-Louis 1997; 2007: 58–60.

[51] As one who 'draws near' (*qĕrēb*), the son of man has priestly access to God. Notice the use of *qĕrēb* in texts related to the priest's privileged position of access to the tabernacle and temple. See e.g. Lev. 8:13, 24; Num. 3:6, 10, 38; Ezek. 40:46; 45:4.

[52] Fletcher-Louis 2007: 59.

the world: a son of God who is a royal priest with access to the presence of God will establish God's kingdom over the earth.[53]

Conclusion

If Mark wanted us to see a priestly Jesus in the early chapters of the narrative, it was because Jesus' rightful claim to be Israel's eschatological priest-king at the end of the narrative is what ultimately leads to his enthronement on the cross. Herein lies the irony that inundates Mark's Gospel. The priest-king conquers through his own sacrificial death. The cross is his kingly throne, and the blood shed there is his priestly sacrifice. The royal priest who cast out unclean spirits, made a leper clean, claimed authority over the sabbath, reconstituted sacred space (the temple) and redefined purity codes finally brings the kingdom through the supreme covenantal sacrifice of his own body (Mark 14:22–25).

Melchizedek's bread and wine, which blessed Abraham, have become a symbol for the body and blood of a new Melchizedek who has brought covenantal blessing to Abraham's descendants (Mark 14:22–25). The kingdom will finally come through a covenant mediator. A priest-king

---

[53] Hamilton (2014b: 189–190) also observes the massive biblical-theological import apparent in Jesus' response. He writes, 'The use of Daniel 7:13 in Matthew 26:64 and Mark 14:62 does not explore the chronological relationship between events of the end, but it does engage with the profound biblical-theological theme of the royal priest whose ultimate manifestation is Jesus. Adam in the garden was a royal figure with priestly overtones . . . Melchizedek was king and priest in Salem (Gen. 14:18). The priest-kings Adam and Melchizedek prepare the way for a nation of king-priests: God announced that the nation of Israel was his son (Exod. 4:22), and brought Israel out of Egypt to be a kingdom of priests (19:6). The anointing oil flowed over both kings and priests: though the only people Moses was instructed to anoint in the Torah were the priests (Exod. 28:41; 29:7; 30:30, etc.), God instructed Samuel to anoint David king over Israel, giving the anointed king a kind of priestly overtone. As king, David wore a linen ephod not unlike that of the priests (2 Sam. 6:14), and in Psalm 110 he spoke of his Lord being made a priest for ever, according to the order of Melchizedek . . . These themes are significant because Jesus, "the son of David, the son of Abraham" (Matt. 1:1), was hauled before the high priest of Israel, who asked if he was claiming to be king: "the high priest said to him, 'I adjure you by the living God, tell us if you are the Christ, the son of God'" (Matt. 26:63; cf. Mark 14:61). The "son of God" language here has passages like 2 Samuel 7:14 and Psalm 2:7 in the foreground, but in the near background is the reality that Adam (Luke 3:38) and Israel (Exod. 4:22) were also "son of God". The high priest asked Jesus if he claimed to be that long-awaited anointed king of Israel who descended from and fulfilled everything to which Adam and David pointed as the one who would relate to God the Father as the divine son. In his reply to this question, Jesus made a profound biblical-theological connection.' That profound biblical-theological connection is that Jesus unites Ps. 110 and Dan. 7 in reference to his own person as the Son of God who brings God's programme of the kingdom through a royal-priestly viceroy to its eschatological head.

will, at last, succeed when Jesus takes his throne on the cross to usher in God's kingdom through the covenant-sacrifice of his own blood. A royal priest after the order of Melchizedek has arrived.

8

Psalm 110 and the Christology of Hebrews

The Old Testament saturates every page of the epistle to the Hebrews, and Christ absorbs it all as the one who fulfils all previous revelation (Heb. 1:1–2). No Old Testament passage has a more significant influence on the theology of Hebrews than Psalm 110.[1] Royal and priestly Christology rooted in David's articulation of a royal Melchizedekian priest undergirds the argument of the entire epistle. It is probably safe to say that Hebrews is the interpretative trump card regarding the meaning of Psalm 110 in the context of Scripture.

The purpose of this chapter is to demonstrate how the author of Hebrews interpreted Psalm 110 as a part of the canonical story of the Bible. The question under investigation is: how did the author of Hebrews understand Psalm 110 within the biblical storyline and in reference to its culmination in Jesus Christ? Is there evidence that the author of Hebrews interpreted the priest-king theology of Psalm 110 as part of the covenantal metanarrative I have developed thus far? This chapter will walk through the major theological sections of Hebrews to demonstrate how Psalm 110 shapes the Christological and soteriological logic of the epistle at nearly every stage of the author's argument.

The following pages will develop six key ideas. First, the author of Hebrews understood Psalm 110 as part of the covenantal storyline of Scripture that began with Adam – the archetypal son, priest and king – and advanced in Israel, God's corporate firstborn son and kingdom of priests (cf. Exod. 19:6).[2] In the logic of Hebrews, Christ's universal reign

---

[1] The following sources develop the significance of Ps. 110 in the logic of Hebrews: Stanley 1994; Kurianal 2000; Wallace 2003; Kistemaker 2008; Jordaan and Nel 2010; Compton 2015. Buchanan (1972) described Hebrews as basically a midrash on Ps. 110.

[2] The concept of Christ as son, king and priest is what Hahn (2009: 278) calls 'royal priestly primogeniture'. He writes, 'For the author of Hebrews, Christ's threefold role as firstborn son,

from the heavenly tabernacle as the king and priest of Psalm 110 is the fulfilment of God's original design for humanity (Adam) to rule the world from the place of God's presence. Second, the temporal framework of Psalm 110:1 – 'Sit . . . *until*' – captures the already-but-not-yet tension that shapes the eschatological, soteriological and cosmological argument of Hebrews. Third, the Melchizedekian priesthood as described in Psalm 110 informs the Joshua–Jesus typology in Hebrews 4. Fourth, Christ's covenant faithfulness manifested in his *priestly* self-sacrifice qualifies him to receive the permanent priesthood of the Melchizedekian order. Fifth, the soteriological argument of Hebrews cannot be separated from the Christological fulfilment of Psalm 110:4: 'The LORD has sworn and will not change his mind, "You are a priest for ever after the order of Melchizedek."' In other words, believers receive salvation through Christ's role as the mediator (priest) of a new and better covenant. The new covenant is better than the Mosaic (old) because its priesthood is better than the Aaronic. Sixth, and related to the previous point, the significance of the Melchizedekian priesthood is found in its permanent nature and association with the Abrahamic and Davidic covenants. By becoming a priest after the order of Melchizedek, Christ receives a priesthood for ever and inaugurates the fulfilment of the promise to Abraham as David's Lord and greater son.

Hebrews 1: the enthronement of the Son of God

Hebrews 1:1–4

The epistle opens with a discussion of the supremacy of Jesus Christ over angels as the final revelation of God (1:1–14; 2:5–18). Hebrews 1:1–4 sets the stage for the remainder of the epistle by laying the groundwork for a Son-priest-king Christology rooted in the logic of Scripture. In Hebrews 1:1–3, Christ's revelatory character is a product of both his divine nature

---

(note 2 *cont.*) king, and high priest (i.e., Christ's royal priestly primogeniture) represents the restoration of an original and superior form of covenant mediation that has been lost since the institution of the Levitical priesthood in response to Israel's covenant infidelity.' I do not agree that the Levitical priesthood replaced Israel's status as a kingdom of priests after the golden calf incident. See my discussion in chapter 3 on the relationship between Israel's royal priesthood and the Aaronic priesthood.

and his human nature. He is the divine eternal Son who was the agent of creation in the beginning and even now is its providential sustainer (1:2–3). Furthermore, he shares in God's essence as the 'radiance' (*apaugasma*) of God's glory and the 'exact imprint' (*charaktēr*) of God's nature (1:3).

Christ's human nature is also apparent in the exordium. The description of the Son in these verses is reminiscent of God's design for humanity as the image of God (Gen. 1:26–28).[3] Jesus has the right to rule the cosmos, not only as its divine creator (1:2) but also because of his success as the messianic Son. He has achieved human vicegerency over creation and thus becomes the 'heir of all things' (*klēronomon pantōn* [1:2]). By alluding to Psalm 2:8 – 'heir of all things' – in Hebrews 1:2, the author situates the Son's kingship in the context of Davidic royalty.[4] A Davidic king bearing God's image and ruling from the heavenly Zion receives dominion over the world (cf. Ps. 2:6–8). The author of Hebrews clearly understood Christ's 'sonship' in terms of both his divine nature and his human kingship. To use Carson's words, 'Hebrews 1 leaps from preexistent-Godhead-as-Son-of-God christology to Davidic-king-as-Son-of-God christology.'[5]

The Davidic incarnate Son takes his seat at God's right hand only after his priestly work of purification is complete (1:3).[6] In the logic of Hebrews, royal enthronement cannot be separated from priestly purification.[7] Or,

---

[3] Beale (2011: 317–318) suggests that Heb. 1:1–4 contains 'classic Adamic language'. This language, he argues, consists in the following: '1. God's "son" (who is the first Adam) has come "in these last days," 2. As the image of God, 3. As a ruler, 4. Inheritor of the earth, and 5. As a new creation.'

[4] For the sake of simplicity, unless otherwise indicated I will refer to the English OT chapter and verse system when referring to OT citations in Hebrews. It is widely recognized that the LXX was the source text for the author of Hebrews.

[5] Carson 2012: 61–62.

[6] *katharismon tōn hamartiōn poiēsamenos* evokes the priest's work on the Day of Atonement.

[7] Much debate exists on the timing of Christ's high priesthood in the epistle to the Hebrews. Was Christ a priest on earth? Did he become a priest at the time of his self-sacrifice? Or did he only become a high priest upon his entry into the heavenly realm? I take the view that Hebrews presents Jesus' earthly ministry as a priestly ministry, but he only takes on the office of the Melchizedekian priesthood after his resurrection and ascension. Perhaps the character Aragorn from the *Lord of the Rings* trilogy is an appropriate illustration here. Aragorn is the king throughout the narrative. He is the rightful king and the heir to the throne of Gondor. But Aragorn is not appointed/enthroned over his kingdom until the enemy forces of Sauron are defeated. Similarly, Jesus is the Son of God and Messiah during his earthly career. He is the rightful Davidic king and occupies a priestly ministry (without the office) as God's Son. But he is only appointed the messianic Son of God (Heb. 1:5; cf. Rom. 1:4) – and therefore king and priest – upon his resurrection after he had conquered sin and death at the cross. On the relationship in Hebrews between Jesus' eternal, divine sonship and sonship as the office of messianic rule he enters at his enthronement, see the excellent analysis of Jamieson 2021.

to put it another way, priestly faithfulness gives rise to universal kingship. We would expect, then, that Psalm 110 – the most explicit text on the union and interplay of kingship and priesthood in the Old Testament – would play an integral role in the author's argument, and this is precisely what we find in the exordium. He describes the Son as having 'sat down at the right hand of the Majesty on high' (Heb. 1:3 ESV) – the first reference to Psalm 110 in the epistle – and suggests that this enthronement is the result of the Son's priestly work of purification. By connecting the kingly imagery of Psalm 110:1 to the priestly work of atonement, the author hints at what will become two of his primary Christological categories for the remainder of the epistle, namely priesthood and kingship.

It was these two roles (priesthood and kingship) that defined the original image-bearer's (Adam's) task at creation. Thus, from a biblical-theological perspective, Hebrews 1:1–4 situates the exaltation of the divine–human Son within the progress of redemptive history from Adam to the Davidic Melchizedekian priest-king. Just as Adam was made in the image of God to be God's son and royal priest, and just as David's Lord later embodied that role, so now Jesus brings the progress of God's revelation to its climax: he is the true image of God, the true Son of God, the Son of David and the final priest-king.

Hebrews 1:5–13

Hebrews 1:5–13 contains a catena of seven Old Testament citations. According to Joshua Jipp, the allusion to Psalm 110:1 in Hebrews 1:3 'sets the theme for the rest of Heb 1.5–14 as the catena centers upon the Son's enthronement and entrance into the Father's heavenly throne room'.[8] The catena amplifies the imagery of Psalm 110:1 in order to solidify Christ's superiority over angels as the royal Son of God who has been enthroned over the universe. A heavy emphasis on Davidic royalty surfaces from these Old Testament texts (see Table 8.1 opposite). Christ's exaltation is, for the author of Hebrews, the fulfilment of God's covenant promises to David and part of a Davidic typology.[9] Each of these Davidic passages deserves a few brief comments.

---

[8] Jipp 2010: 559.
[9] My analysis of Ps. 2:7, 2 Sam. 7:14 and Ps. 45:6–7 has been shaped by Carson 2012 and personal correspondence with Dr Carson on these texts in Heb. 1.

Table 8.1 Davidic passages referenced in Hebrews 1:5–13

Old Testament passage	Theme
Psalm 2:7 (Heb. 1:5)	The Davidic heir is begotten as the covenantal son of God (king) upon his enthronement in Zion.
2 Samuel 7:14 (Heb. 1:5)	The promise of the Davidic covenant was that David's heir would exist in a father–son relationship with God.
Psalm 89:27 (Heb. 1:6)	This Davidic passage is not cited in the catena of quotations, but it is alluded to in 1:6 through the use of *prōtotokon*. God would establish David's son as the 'firstborn' (*prōtotokon* [LXX Ps. 89:28]), the highest of the kings of the earth.
Psalm 45:6–7 (Heb. 1:8–9)	An anointed king represents God's righteous rule.
Psalm 110:1 (Heb. 1:13)	David's Lord and eschatological priest-king will rule from God's right hand.

Psalm 2:7 and 2 Samuel 7:14 appear first in the catena with reference to Jesus' heavenly enthronement. In their original contexts, both passages define the Davidic king's relationship to God as a father–son relationship. Their filial relationship in these passages is covenantal. Whenever a Davidic heir officially entered his office of kingship, he became God's 'son' – he would represent God, image God, rule as God rules with righteousness, justice and truth.[10] The author of Hebrews read these Old Testament passages as part of a Davidic typology that found its ultimate fulfilment at the resurrection of Jesus and his enthronement in heaven. Christ was 'begotten today' when he took his seat at God's right hand, that is, when he was installed as king over the cosmos as the Davidic Son (1:3; cf. Ps. 110:1).[11] Though eternally glorious as the divine Son, his exaltation as the messianic Son (Davidic king) happened only after he had successfully fulfilled his

---

[10] Carson 2012: 46.

[11] That these OT texts should be applied to Christ's resurrection is consistent with their use by other NT writers. See e.g. Acts 13:33 and Rom. 1:1–4.

mission to provide purification for sins through his own covenant-keeping faithfulness (cf. 1:3; 5:7–10; 12:2).[12] The divine eternal Son became the victorious messianic Son. He is the true expression of the image of God in humankind – an image that was intended from the beginning to convey royalty and sonship. No angel was ever given such authority or familial solidarity.

Christ's resurrection and exaltation to the right hand of God solidified him as the 'firstborn' (*prōtotokon*) of a new creation (1:6).[13] The reference to *prōtotokon* evokes Psalm 89:27 and God's promise to establish a Davidide as the *prōtotokon*, the highest of the kings of the earth (LXX Ps. 88:28). The king's status of 'firstborn' in Psalm 89 is a reference to the filial promises of the Davidic covenant (Ps. 89:3–4, 26; cf. 2 Sam. 7:14) but carries the nuance of pre-eminence as indicated by the parallel expression 'the highest of the kings of the earth'. David's heir would be without equal, possessing supreme authority because of his unique relationship to God. The Davidic typology is once again at work in Hebrews 1:6. Jesus became the firstborn, that is, the supreme king of kings and heir of all things, at his resurrection and entrance into the heavenly realm (*oikoumenē*).[14]

The language of 'firstborn' situates the Davidic typology in the Bible's narrative framework from Adam to Israel.[15] Adam and Israel were sons of God. God identified Israel as his 'firstborn' in Exodus 4:22. Israel was God's treasured possession, a nation of royal priests, and heirs of the land promise given to Abraham (Exod. 19:5–6; cf. Gen. 12:1–3). Israel's covenantal status of firstborn became embodied in its king, as Psalm 89 suggests. Psalm 89:25 indicates that the king's dominion would extend beyond the borders of Israel, stretching from seas to rivers. When Jesus entered the heavenly realm, these Adamic, Israelite and especially Davidic trajectories reached their terminus. A Davidic priest-king conquered death, ascended to heaven, entered the true tabernacle and took his seat as ruler of heaven and earth. This firstborn's inheritance is the heavenly realm (*oikoumenē*),

---

[12] To suggest that Jesus was begotten as the 'Son' upon his resurrection and ascension is not to deny that he was the divine Son of God ontologically from eternity past. The Son of God, the second person of the Trinity, has always been and always will be the Son. But in his humanity, the divine Son of God achieves an exalted status by virtue of his covenant faithfulness as a man. See esp. Jamieson 2021: 49–75, 99–121.

[13] For a discussion of the issues regarding the source of the OT quotation in Heb. 1:6, see Cockerill 1999.

[14] See my comments on Heb. 2:5 for understanding *oikoumenē* as the heavenly realm.

[15] Israel was God's *prōtotokon* in Exod. 4:22. The term *prōtotokon* is never applied to Adam, but he clearly occupied the role as the first man, image of God and covenantal son of Yahweh.

which Hebrews 2:5 defines as the 'world to come' (*oikoumenēn tēn mellousan*). His reign extends to the eschatological world, the city with foundations (Heb. 11:10), the better country (Heb. 11:16), the city which is to come (Heb. 13:14). The angels in heaven must give their worship to the God-man, the firstborn, the most high king who obtained humanity's redemption.

In Hebrews 1:8–9, the author cites Psalm 45:6–7 to contrast the exalted, divine and permanent nature of the Son and his kingdom over and against the role of angels, mentioned in 1:7 as 'servants' (*leitourgous*), and their transient depiction as 'winds' (*pneumata*) and 'flames of fire' (*pyros phloga*).[16] In its original context, Psalm 45 celebrates the marriage of the Davidic king. The psalmist praises the king as superior to the sons of men (45:2). He lives for the cause of truth, humility and righteousness (*dikaiosynēs* [LXX 44:5]). His throne will endure for ever (45:6), his name will never be forgotten and the nations will declare his praises (45:17). The psalmist so closely associates the king's righteous rule with God's rule that he addresses the king as 'God' in verse 6 (ESV): 'Your throne, O God, is for ever.' Despite attempts to provide alternative translations that remove the vocative 'O God', the text most naturally reads as a noun of direct address: 'Your throne, O God'.[17] The psalmist, however, is not addressing Yahweh; he is talking to the Davidic monarch because he says in the very next verse, 'Therefore, God, your God, has anointed you' (45:7 ESV). God has no God. God is not anointed with oil, but the king is. Neither should we conclude that the psalmist has the divinity of Jesus in mind because he says the king's marriage will result in sons who will be 'rulers in all the earth' (45:16). Jesus had no sons, and he has no successor. The vocative, 'O God', is the psalmist's way of talking about the king's representative rule. He will exercise authority as God exercises authority – with moral uprightness and righteousness (45:6). The king is God's covenantal son imaging God's dynamic reign and mediating God's blessing. When this Davidide rules over God's people, it is as if God himself is ruling in their midst. Psalm 45 is about a Davidic son, not an ontologically divine Son.

Once again, the author of Hebrews picks up on the Davidic typology in applying Psalm 45:6–7 to Christ. The author presents Jesus as the Davidic antitype – the king who represents God's rule and mediates God's

---

[16] See Jipp 2010: 563–565.
[17] Carson 2012: 57.

rule and blessing. But should we also understand the application of Psalm 45:6 to Christ ('Your throne, O God') in Hebrews 1:8 as a statement about his divinity? The answer is most certainly 'yes' because Hebrews 1:1–4 has already established the Son's divine nature as the agent of creation, the radiance of God's glory, the imprint of God's nature and the sustainer of the entire universe (Heb. 1:2–3). 'Your throne, O God' in reference to the risen Jesus captures both his divine sonship and his messianic Davidic kingship. Jesus mediates God's rule as the messianic Son, but he is and always will be the eternal Son of God. He is superior to angels because he sits on heaven's throne as the divine incarnate Son.[18]

Psalm 45:6–7 also advances the Christological argument of Hebrews 1 by grounding the Son's royal exaltation in the faithfulness of his earthly life. God anointed the Son at his right hand to reign on an eternal throne because (*dia*) the Son loved righteousness and hated lawlessness (1:9). The connection here between Christ's exaltation and his earthly righteousness anticipates the author's fuller discussion of Christ as the faithful priest after the order of Melchizedek. Melchizedek, after all, means 'king of righteousness', as the author will later make plain (7:2).

The author presents Jesus' faithful earthly career throughout Hebrews as the necessary prerequisite to his high priesthood. Jesus became a priest after the order of Melchizedek by being made perfect through obedience (5:8–10). He has been exalted to the right hand of God because he faithfully endured the cross, despising the shame (12:2). He is a high priest in heaven who sympathizes with our weaknesses because during his earthly life he experienced temptation, yet without sin (4:15). He is the high priest of our confession because he was faithful to him who appointed him (3:1–2). He learned obedience through suffering and remained faithful while knowing that he would endure his own sacrificial death (5:7–8). Thus, Hebrews 1:8–9 foreshadows the fuller development of the faithfulness of Jesus that qualifies him to become a priest-king after the order of Melchizedek.

The catena of Old Testament passages culminates in the seventh and final Old Testament citation in Hebrews 1:13. The author cites Yahweh's

---

[18] Carson (ibid. 59–61) argues that because Heb. 1:1–4 establishes the theme of divine sonship before the quotation of Ps. 45, 'it is virtually impossible not to see that when God addresses the Son with the words, "Your throne, O God, will last for ever and ever," the words, "O God" cannot be taken hyperbolically as they could with David and his immediate heirs. The Son, quite simply, is to be thought of as God.'

words to David's Lord in Psalm 110:1: 'Sit at my right hand until I make your enemies a footstool for your feet.' If it was not explicit enough already, this verse confirms Christ's superiority over angels because he is the Melchizedekian priest-king ruling from the right hand of God. The author introduces this final Old Testament citation with the same introductory formula that began the catena in Hebrews 1:5:

Hebrews 1:5a: *Tini gar eipen pote tōn angelōn*
Hebrews 1:13a: *Pros tina de tōn angelōn eirēken pote*

This literary technique forms an inclusio around the catena and establishes a conceptual link between Psalm 2 and Psalm 110. I argued earlier that these two psalms share numerous parallels and are, to some degree, mutually interpretative. The author of Hebrews appears to share the same presupposition. He employs Psalm 2 to support all three of his primary Christological categories – sonship, priesthood and kingship (1:2, 5; 5:5). He uses Psalm 110 towards the same end (1:3, 15; 5:6; 7:17, 21, etc.).[19] In the epistle's exordium, allusions to Psalm 2:8 (1:2) and Psalm 110:1 (1:4) bracketed the description of the Son as the true image of God (1:3). The allusion to Psalm 2:8 in Hebrews 1:2 emphasized Christ's royal status as the 'heir of all things', while the allusion to Psalm 110:1 in Hebrews 1:4 grounded Christ's royal enthronement in his priestly faithfulness. It is no surprise, then, that the catena immediately following the exordium begins with Psalm 2 and ends with Psalm 110. These two psalms situate the resurrection and ascension of Christ in the context of Israel's hope for a messianic king, but they also anticipate the fuller discussion of Christ as Melchizedekian high priest (Heb. 5 – 7). In Hebrews 5:5–6, the same two psalms appear again, this time in juxtaposition to defend the God-given nature of the Son's appointment to the high priesthood.

What is the function of the catena in the context of Hebrews? Jipp suggests that the Christological argument in Hebrews 1:5–14 frames the soteriological argument of the entire epistle:

At the very least, the Son's exaltation, depicted in Heb. 1:5–14, functions as the means whereby God secures his promises to humanity (2.5–18), is the basis for the argument that Jesus is humanity's

---

19 Wallace 2003: 44.

Melchizedekian high priest (5.5–6; 7.1–28), and establishes the narrative goal or pattern which God's children follow (12.1–3).[20]

Jipp's point is well taken. Inheritance language frames the catena of Old Testament citations. In Hebrews 1:4, Christ has 'inherited' (*keklēronomēken*) a name superior to angels, which, in the light of 1:3, was a name he received upon his enthronement to the right hand of God in fulfilment of Psalm 110.[21] As the one who has been made 'heir' (*klēronomon*) of all things upon his appointment to the right hand of God, Christ will bring others to share in his inheritance. According to 1:14, the inheritance given to faithful humanity is the inheritance of 'salvation' (*sōtērian*). From the outset, the author wants his readers to see Jesus as the Son-priest-king not just because that was God's ideal for humanity from the beginning but because it is as the true Son-priest-king that Christ has been able to accomplish redemption on behalf of humankind. To use the language of Hebrews, the royal priest after the order of Melchizedek has become the mediator of a new covenant because of his exalted sonship (7:21–22; 9:15). Christology cannot be separated from soteriology, and neither should be severed from the logic of Psalm 110.

Finally, it is worth highlighting that the author chose to cite *seven* Old Testament passages to authenticate the royal enthronement of the resurrected Son. The author may have settled on seven Old Testament passages to echo the creation narrative, where God creates the world in six days and rests on the seventh (Gen. 1 – 2). In Genesis 1, the image of God in humankind carries both royal and familial connotations. Adam represented the rule of God as a prince represents the authority of his father. Similarly to Genesis 1, Hebrews 1 describes the enthronement of God's true image, namely Jesus the Son of God. The author takes the reader through seven Old Testament citations culminating in the promise of the Son's universal dominion: 'Sit at my right hand until I make your enemies a footstool for your feet' (1:13; cf. Ps. 110:1).[22] Jesus is the firstborn

---

[20] Jipp 2010: 558–559.

[21] For a compelling argument that the name Christ inherited is the name 'Son', see Jamieson 2021: 99–121.

[22] If Heb. 1:5–13 is intended to evoke the Gen. 1 narrative, then perhaps the seventh OT citation – Ps. 110:1 – parallels the seventh day of creation. On the seventh day, God rested from all his works. The picture of Ps. 110:1 is that of the king who has achieved rest from his works by taking his seat at God's right hand. In the light of the Joshua typology developed later in the epistle, it would not be outside the realm of possibility to see the theme of rest in the

son who inherited the Adamic role of priest-king and has excelled even beyond Adam by accomplishing redemption in a world hostile to God (1:13). Jesus, now the exalted royal Son, reigns from his priestly position of access to God's heavenly temple. He will rule from God's right hand until his conquest over evil is complete (1:13).

Hebrews 2: Adam's dominion restored by a new and better Adam

Hebrews 1 ended with a quotation of Psalm 110:1b and a comment on the believer's future inheritance of salvation (1:13–14). Moving into Hebrews 2, Psalm 110:1 and the promise of an inheritance become the basis for understanding both the eschatological, cosmological and soteriological argument of Hebrews 2:5–9, and the author's Christological reading of Psalm 8.

After issuing an appropriate and severe warning in 2:1–4, the author continues his discussion of Christ's superiority over angels in 2:5. The *gar* of 2:5 connects the author's exposition of Psalm 8 in Hebrews 2:5–9 directly to the warning of 2:1–4. Just as God was right to punish people for rebelling against the message delivered by angels (under the old covenant), so too will he punish those who reject the message of greater salvation that he has now spoken in his Son (Heb. 2:2–3; cf. Heb. 1:2). As additional proof to what he has already given in Hebrews 1, the author continues to build his case for the Son's superiority over angels in Hebrews 2:5–9: 'For it was not to angels that he subjected the world to come' (Heb. 2:5a).

The argument of Hebrews 2:5–9 picks up themes that the author began developing in Hebrews 1. Specifically, Hebrews 2:5 builds on the author's use of Psalm 110:1 and the idea of salvation as an 'inheritance' in Hebrews 1:13–14:

Hebrews 1:13–14: And to which of the angels did he ever say,
　　　　　　　　'Sit at my right hand until I make your enemies
　　　　　　　　a footstool for your feet'? Are they not all
　　　　　　　　ministering spirits sent out to serve on behalf of
　　　　　　　　those about (*tous mellontas*) to inherit salvation?

---

heavenly session of Jesus Christ. In fact, Heb. 4:14 depicts Jesus' entry into the heavenly realm in the context of Joshua's failure to achieve rest for the people of God (4:8–10). As a great high priest, Jesus enters the state of God's rest as a forerunner for the people of God (4:14; cf. 6:20).

Hebrews 2:5:   For it was not to angels that he subjected the
world to come (*tēn mellousan*) of which we are
speaking.

The already-but-not-yet eschatological framework of Psalm 110:1 – 'Sit at my right hand [already] until I make your enemies a footstool [not yet]' – becomes the basis for the already-but-not-yet cosmological framework of Hebrews: 'For it was not to angels that he subjected [already] the *world to come* [not yet]' (2:5; emphasis mine).[23] In other words, the heavenly realm already subject to the reign of Christ will one day characterize the earthly realm (new creation) when all of Christ's enemies are made a footstool for his feet (Ps. 110:1). Hebrews intertwines eschatology and cosmology, and both on the basis of Psalm 110:1.[24]

An analysis of *oikoumenē* in 2:5 and 1:6 clarifies the relationship between eschatology, cosmology and soteriology. The *oikoumenēn tēn mellousan* ('world to come') in Hebrews 2:5 is the same *oikoumenē* that Christ, as *prōtotokos*, received as a royal inheritance in 1:6.[25] The *oikoumenē* in 1:6 and 2:5 is, therefore, the eschatological world ('world to come') already present in heaven.[26] It is not the earthly realm of humanity, which Christ enters at his incarnation,[27] or the world at the time of his parousia,[28] but the heavenly realm where he took his seat as the resurrected Christ in fulfilment of Psalm 110:1.

Yet, as Psalm 110:1 indicates, there is both an inauguration and consummation of the fulfilment of Psalm 110:1 – 'Sit [inauguration] . . . until [consummation]'. The implication is that at the time of consummation, the *oikoumenē* will come from heaven to earth when Christ puts an end to all of his enemies so that the entire cosmos will exist as God's sacred sanctuary. The future world to come is surely what the author has in mind when he refers to the inheritance of salvation (1:14) as belonging to 'those

---

[23] The participle *tēn mellousan* in 2:5 gives the *oikoumenē* an eschatological orientation.

[24] In the verses that follow (2:6–9), the author attaches the concept of redemption to Ps. 8 and the creation mandate to take dominion over the earth. By doing so, he further weds soteriology to eschatology and cosmology.

[25] Moffitt 2011: 53–142. Cockerill (1999: 63) has observed that the phrase *hotan . . . eisagagē* in Heb. 1:6 recalls similar language in the LXX used to describe Israel's entry into the Promised Land (cf. Deut. 6:10; 11:29).

[26] The *oikoumenē* is thus both a spatial (worldly) and temporal (eschatological) reality.

[27] Attridge 1989: 56.

[28] Lane 1991: 27.

about to' (*tēn mellousan*) receive it.[29] Clearly, the salvific blessings of atonement, forgiveness and the gift of the Holy Spirit are already benefits enjoyed by believers (1:3; 2:17; 6:4). But the inheritance they wait to possess in the future is the sacred space that they will enjoy in God's presence in the new heavens and new earth. This sacred realm already belongs to the royal Son who stormed heaven as the Melchizedekian priest-king, and he guarantees that 'many sons [and daughters]' (*pollous huious*) will share in his inheritance (cf. 2:10).

Wearing humanity's original crown

The reign of Christ over the heavenly realm fits within the framework of the Bible's storyline. Psalm 110:1b – 'Sit at my right hand until I make your enemies a footstool for your feet (*tōn podōn*)' – flows naturally into the author's Christological application of Psalm 8, which describes creation under the 'feet' (*tōn podōn*) of humankind (2:6–8; cf. Gen. 1:26–28; Ps. 8:4–6).

According to Psalm 8:4–6, God created human beings, not angels, to rule the earth (Heb. 2:5–8). As I argued in chapter 2, Psalm 8 is a commentary on the image of God as described in Genesis 1:26–28. Reflecting on the image of God in Adam, David describes human beings as 'crowned' (*estephanōsas*) with glory and honour and having everything in 'subjection' (*hypotassō*) under their 'feet' (*podōn* [Heb. 2:7–8; cf. Ps. 8:6]). The problem, for the author of Hebrews, is that at the present time (*nyn*) we do not see all things 'subjected' (*anypotakton*) to humanity (Heb. 2:8). But we do see Jesus who fulfilled humanity's original design. At his incarnation, he was made for a little while lower than the angels (2:9). He is now crowned (*estephanōmenon*) with 'glory' (*doxē*) and 'honour' (*timē*) because he restored to humanity the glory that Adam lost (2:10).

The author's use of Psalm 110 and Psalm 8 in tandem develops the argument of Hebrews 1.[30] Psalm 8, which describes humanity's design to

---

[29] The repetition of the participial form of *mellō* in 1:14 and 2:5 ties the believer's future inheritance of salvation to the spatial reality of the eschatological world to come. The author is not simply saying that this inheritance of salvation is the heavenly realm believers receive upon death. It is a heavenly realm that is coming. In other words, it is the realm of the new heavens and new earth that will characterize the cosmos once the earth under the curse of sin is removed (cf. Heb. 1:10–12; 12:26–27).

[30] By weaving together these two psalms, the author reveals more clearly his interpretative presuppositions with regard to the meaning of Ps. 110. In other words, Ps. 110 is to be read as

rule the world, is a natural counterpart to Psalm 110 and the Messiah's exaltation over the world to come (cf. Heb. 1:6; 2:5). In order to fulfil God's original design for human beings and simultaneously to accomplish their redemption, the Son of God had to be a human being, not an angel. In the author's logic, the pattern of creation and the pattern of redemption cannot be separated.

Jesus, the firstborn, has become the 'founder' (*archēgos*) of humanity's salvation (*sōtērias* [Heb. 2:10]). He is able to 'lead' (*agō* [2:10]) 'many sons' (*pollous huious*) 'to glory' (*eis doxan*) because God has already led (*eisagō* [1:6]) him into *oikoumenē* where he sits crowned with glory (*doxē* [2:9]). Christ had to be made like his fellow humans in every respect to become their high priest and atone for their sins (2:17). As 'flesh and blood' (2:14), Christ was made perfect through suffering to accomplish what angels could never do as 'winds' (*pneumata* [1:7, 14]) and 'flames of fire' (*pyros phloga* [1:7]), namely the salvation of humanity (2:10). For Christ did not come to help angels, but the offspring of Abraham (2:16).[31]

A faithful priest

The author's portrayal of Christ as the ideal human being in Hebrews 2:5–9 (cf. Ps. 8) may explain why he chose to move from the theme of regal dominion directly into the subject of priestly salvation (2:10–17). Concerning the 'narrative' flow of Hebrews 2:5–17, Beale suggests:

> The earlier Adamic depiction leads directly into the first discussion in the epistle of Christ as 'high priest' (2:10–17). Could this echo the pattern that we have seen in Genesis 1–2, where Adam is first portrayed as a 'king' (1:26–28) and then as a priestly figure, ruling and worshipping in a temple (Gen. 2:15)?[32]

(note 30 *cont.*) part of the story of God's creation project (Ps. 8), while simultaneously superseding God's creation project because the Melchizedekian priest-king had to 'win back' (redeem) what Adam lost. In other words, Christ had to achieve Adam's dominion and Abraham's redemption. Christ's successful ministry is even greater than Adam's because Christ had to take dominion over a world under a curse. He had to overcome sin, the flesh and the devil to restore human vicegerency to the world (Heb. 2:14–18).

[31] The identification of the recipients of Jesus' ministry as the 'seed of Abraham' (2:16) and the association of salvation with inheritance (*klēronomein* [1:14]) suggests that the realm Jesus entered is to be identified as the eschatological realization of the Promised Land. Jesus, the representative of God's people, has blazed a trail into their eternal inheritance.

[32] Beale 2004: 299.

The author has already used a similar logic in Hebrews 1:2–4, where the description of Christ as the image of God receiving a regal inheritance (1:2–3) precedes the explanation of his priestly work of purification for the sins of humanity (1:4).

The flow of thought from kingship to priesthood in both Genesis 1 – 2 and Hebrews 2 is striking. In Genesis 1 – 2, God made Adam as the royal image-bearer and then placed him in the garden-sanctuary as a priest, where he would be confronted by the serpent (Gen. 3). Similarly, after the discussion of Christ's royal authority as the new Adam in Hebrews 2:5–9, the author of Hebrews describes Christ's work of salvation in terms of his priesthood and confrontation with the devil (2:14–17). Christ's priestly work supersedes even what God designed for Adam at creation because Christ actually had to undo the curse of Adam's fall. He conquered the serpent's power over death by defeating death through his own death (2:14). He is, therefore, able to deliver those who were subjected, by fear of death, to slavery.

Jesus had to be 'made like' (*homoiōthēnai*) his fellow humans in every respect (2:17), for it was humanity that was made in the image and likeness of God and it was humanity that needed redemption. Christ did not come to help angels; he came to help the 'offspring of Abraham' (*spermatos Abraam* [2:16]). Christ's salvific work as the great high priest overturned Adam's curse by effecting the blessings of the Abrahamic covenant. The inheritance of salvation (1:14) that believers will receive is the typological fulfilment of God's promises to Abraham (cf. 6:12–20).[33]

For Jesus to mediate the promises of the Abrahamic covenant, he had to become a merciful and faithful high priest of an order even greater than the priesthoods of Adam and the Levites. His priesthood had to not only embody the creational ideal of Adam's priesthood but also effectively propitiate the sins of a fallen humanity, and that in a way that the Levitical priesthood could never do (2:16–17; cf. 7:11). What order of priesthood could capture both the creational ideal and the redemptive blessings of the Abrahamic covenant? As the author of Hebrews has already hinted from Psalm 110 and will make plain in Hebrews 5 – 7, only a priest *after the order of Melchizedek*.

---

[33] Harris 2009: iv–v.

Hebrews 3:1–6:
the Davidic priest-king over God's house

There is no allusion to Psalm 110 in Hebrews 3:1–6. However, whenever the author of Hebrews mentions the high priesthood of Christ, it is fair to assume that he has the Melchizedekian priesthood in mind. In Hebrews 3:1 (ESV), the author refers to Jesus as the 'high priest of our confession, who was faithful (*piston*) to him who appointed him'. As we have already seen, Christ's appointment to the high priesthood occurred at the time of his resurrection when God installed him as the messianic Son and a priest after the order of Melchizedek (1:5, 13; cf. 5:5–6; Ps. 110:4).

We must allow the reference to Christ's priesthood in 3:1 and the argument of Hebrews 1 – 2 to inform the purpose of comparison between Moses and Jesus. Hebrews 1 – 2 set up the epistle's soteriological argument by contrasting Christ with angels because angels were mediators of God's revelation in the old covenant (2:2), and because angels are not the objects of God's plan of salvation (2:16–17). Christ is superior to angels because he mediates full forgiveness (new-covenant blessing) to human beings – not angels – as the royal Son of David (1:5–6), the new and better Adam (2:5–9) and the faithful high priest (2:17). Like the angels, Moses is associated with the old covenant – a covenant unable to provide forgiveness for sins (cf. 8:6–13; 9:6–27). The argument of Hebrews 3:1–6, therefore, hinges on the relationship between Moses and Christ and their respective covenants. In other words, Christ is superior to Moses because Christ mediates a covenant better than the one Moses mediated. As I will argue below, this better covenant, according to Hebrews 3:1–6, is the Davidic covenant because its mediator (the Son) is superior to the mediator of the old covenant (i.e. Moses, the servant).

Numbers 12:7, 1 Samuel 2:35 and the promises of the Davidic covenant in 2 Samuel 7 and 1 Chronicles 17 make up the subtext of the author's argument in this section.[34] The mention of Christ's high priesthood in the context of his faithfulness over God's house (3:1–2, 6) echoes the promise of 1 Samuel 2:35: 'I will raise up for myself a *faithful* priest, who shall do according to what is in my heart and in my mind. And I will build for him a faithful house'. The 'faithful house' in the context of 1–2 Samuel is the dynasty promised to David in the Davidic covenant (2 Sam. 7:11).

---

[34] Hahn 2009: 288.

One of David's offspring would rule over this dynasty from an eternal throne (2 Sam. 7:13). David's heir would have God as his Father and be to God a son (2 Sam. 7:14).

Moses existed in God's house only as a 'servant' (*therapōn*) with a unique prophetic ministry to bear witness to God's better redemptive revelation still in the future (3:5). The better revelation has been fulfilled in Christ, who is not a servant but a son (3:6). His sonship here is Davidic sonship. As David's heir, Christ is the Davidic *king* of 2 Samuel 7:11–16 and the faithful (Davidic) *priest* of 1 Samuel 2:35 – offices that would be occupied by David's Lord in Psalm 110. It appears that Psalm 110 may have influenced the author's reading of 1–2 Samuel so that he understood the priestly promise of 1 Samuel 2:35 and the royal sonship promise of 2 Samuel 7 to be referring to a single Davidic figure.[35]

Jesus occupies the unique privilege of building God's house ('bringing many sons [and daughters] to glory' [2:10]). He is over God's house because he is responsible for building it as the first and only man to make propitiation for sins (2:17), ascend to the throne room of God as Davidic king (1:3) and mediate salvation (new-covenant blessings) as the

---

[35] Perhaps the author is operating on the logic that the Davidic covenant in 2 Sam. 7 (1 Chr. 17) is the means to bring the promise of 1 Sam. 2:35 to fulfilment. In this case, the author of Hebrews validates the reading of 1 Sam. 2:35 that I adopted from Karl Deenick in chapter 5 of this project. In other words, the faithful priest of 1 Sam. 2:35 is the messianic king of 2 Sam. 7. D'Angelo (1979: 84–85) similarly suggests that the priest of 1 Sam. 2:35 is to be understood as one and the same figure as the Davidic king of 2 Sam. 7. Her interpretation of 1 Sam. 2:35 is different from Deenick's, but it adds another possibility for how the 'two' figures of 1 Sam. 2:35 – priest and Messiah – might be one. She writes, 'An examination of the context of the oracle helps to clear up the difficulty of applying to a single messianic figure, the royal priest, the second half of 1 Sm. 2:35 LXX: ". . . I will raise up for him a sure house, and he will go in and out before my anointed forever" (. . . οἰκοδομήσω αὐτῷ οἶκον πιστόν, καὶ διελεύσεται ἐνώπιον χριστοῦ μου πάσας τὰς ἡμέρας). So read, the verse speaks of a second figure, the Messiah, before whom the priest will serve in the house of the Lord. However, it is also possible to read the verse: "I will build him a sure house and *it* shall go in and out before my anointed always." Such a reading might easily be either inspired by or justified from the immediate context: "Your house and your father's house will go in and out before me forever" (2.30). In both verses 30 and 35, διελεύσεται refers to the priestly service in the sanctuary. The house is the priestly line, which serves in the sanctuary before the Lord and his Christ – by our reading, his anointed priest. Such a reading would of course admirably suit the purposes of the author of Hebrews. In He. 3.7–4.16, we, who are Christ's house if we stand firm, are exhorted to hear and to enter. This exhortation is summarized by the call to draw near after the example of our great high priest, Jesus who has "traversed" (διεληλυθότα) the heavens, entering through the veil into the eternal sanctuary (4.14–16; cf. 6.19–20, 10.20–22). The other biblical meaning of the word διελθεῖν, "to lead," also comes into play here: Christ traverses the heavens as "the captain of our salvation" (2.9), making for us the way by which we "with confidence draw near to the throne of grace, that we may receive mercy and find grace to help in time of need" (4.16)'; emphasis original.

Melchizedekian priest to his people (7:20–22). The author, thus, exhorts his readers to remain faithful as God's house (3:6).

Hebrews 4:8 – 5:10: Joshua, Melchizedekian conquest and Christ our great high priest

Hebrews 4:8–16

In Hebrews 4:1–7, the author exposits Psalm 95 to encourage his readers to strive to enter the eschatological rest that awaits the people of God. As a continuation of his argument, the author draws a typological connection between Joshua and Jesus (4:8–14). He introduces Joshua in 4:8–10, transitions to a paraenetic section in 4:11–13 and then resumes his argument with the inferential conjunction *oun* in 4:14. By removing the paraenetic section, the flow of the argument and the Joshua–Jesus typology become more obvious:

> For if *Iēsous* (Joshua) had rested [the Israelites], he would not have spoken of a day after these things . . . Therefore (*oun*) having a great high priest who has passed through the heavens, *Iēsoun* (Jesus) the Son of God, let us hold fast the confession.
> (4:8, 14)

The typological connection between Joshua and Jesus is more apparent in the Greek, since 'Joshua' and 'Jesus' are both translations of the same Greek name. Joshua did not provide rest through the conquest of the land, but Jesus has provided rest through the conquest of heaven.[36] What is not so obvious is how the mention of Jesus as 'high priest' fits into the logic of the Joshua typology. In other words, on what basis does the author describe Jesus' Joshua-like conquest of heaven as a function of his priesthood (4:14)? Some scholars have tried to answer this question by appealing to Zechariah 3, where Joshua the high priest stands before the divine council and receives pure vestments and

---

[36] Concerning the Joshua typology in Hebrews, see Whitfield 2008; 2013; Ounsworth 2012.

the promise of rulership over Yahweh's house if he remains faithful (Zech. 3:1–7).[37]

A more likely basis for the connection here between Joshua and Jesus' priesthood is found in the logic of Psalm 110. After all, Jesus' priesthood in Hebrews is of the Melchizedekian order – a fact the author will make explicit for the first time in just a few verses when he quotes Psalm 110:4 (Heb. 5:6). Chapter 5 of this book presented the inner-biblical connections between the conquest imagery of Psalm 110, Joshua's defeat of the pagan kings in Joshua 10 and the Melchizedek episode in Genesis 14. The conclusion drawn there was that the Melchizedekian priest-king of Psalm 110 carries out his own Joshua-like conquest over the entire world.[38] If Psalm 110 buttresses the logic of the Joshua–Jesus typology, then it makes sense why a *priestly* (Melchizedekian) Jesus 'passes through' (*dielēlythota*) heaven to provide the rest that Joshua could not (4:14).[39] Jesus, the new Melchizedek, has begun his work of conquest – 'Sit at my right hand until I make your enemies a footstool for your feet' – by passing through the borders of the Promised Land (heavenly Zion; cf. Heb. 12:22–24) as the forerunner of the people of God (6:20).[40] Joshua gave Israel the land in fulfilment of God's promises to Abraham, but he did not provide ultimate rest (4:8). Jesus, however, has successfully obtained the fulfilment of the land promise (inheritance) given to Abraham by entering into the Promised Land's antitype – the heavenly realm – as a forerunner of the people of God and as a priest after the

---

[37] See e.g. Whitfield 2008: 83–87. This suggestion has some merit and is strengthened by the fact that Joshua is promised rule over Yahweh's 'house' if he remains faithful (Zech. 3:6–7; cf. Heb. 3:1–6).

[38] See chapter 5 for my discussion on 'until I make your enemies a footstool for your feet'.

[39] The Joshua–Jesus typology is probably the reason the author of Hebrews chose to use the verb *dierchomai* (*dielēlythota*) to describe Jesus' journey through the heavens. The same verb appears thirteen times in Joshua, almost always in contexts describing the boundaries of the Promised Land. It also appears in Ps. 66:6 [LXX 65:6], which references Israel's passage through the River Jordan before occupying the land (cf. Josh. 3). Some might argue that I am forcing the logic of conquest into the argument of Heb. 3 – 4 since Heb. 3 – 4 is about rest and lacks conquest motifs. I simply suggest that the theme of rest is related to warfare and conquest in the biblical record. Yahweh entered a state of rest after creating the world and overcoming the forces of chaos (Gen. 1:2; 2:1–4). Joshua's goal was to provide people with rest in the land only after conquering the pagan people who occupied the land. Hence Josh. 11:23b: 'And Joshua gave it for an inheritance to Israel according to their tribal allotments. And the land had rest from war' (ESV). Furthermore, 2 Sam. 7:1 also attaches the theme of rest to David's victory over his enemies.

[40] Dennis Johnson (2018: 71) says that Heb. 4:14 begins a discussion (running through 7:28) of Jesus' superior priestly office in the order of Melchizedek.

order of Melchizedek (cf. 6:20).[41] Believers should draw near to the throne of grace because Jesus, as the new Joshua, has blazed a trail into the heavenly realm and, as a priest, grants the people of God access to follow him there (4:16).

Hebrews 5:1–10

Psalm 110:4 appears twice in Hebrews 5:1–10. Hebrews 5:6 contains the first citation of Psalm 110:4 in the epistle. In the broader context of these verses, the author appeals to Psalm 110:4 to demonstrate that Christ's appointment to the high priesthood was a God-given appointment (5:5). In 5:1–4, the author reminds his readers that priests in the Levitical order were men in solidarity with sinful human beings (5:1–3). The priest stood between God and other people, mediating God's forgiveness to sinners (5:2–3). Under the Mosaic covenant, no man had the right to appoint himself to such an honourable task. Only God could establish someone as a priest, as was the case with Aaron (5:4).

The inference (*Houtōs kai*), then, is that God also appointed Christ to the high priesthood (5:5). The author has carefully selected language to describe the appointment of Aaron and Christ to the high priesthood. In 5:4, the author describes the installation of the Aaronic priest as taking on a position of 'honour' (*timēn*). Then in 5:5, the author refers to Christ's appointment to the high priesthood using the language of 'glory': 'Thus also Christ *glorified* (*edoxasen*) not himself to be made a high priest' (emphasis mine). Why the language of 'honour' and 'glory' with respect to the office of the priesthood? Perhaps *timē* and *doxazō* recall the author's exposition of Psalm 8 in Hebrews 2:5–9, which, in its broader context, is the same exposition that makes the first explicit reference to Christ's high priesthood (2:17). According to Psalm 8, God created human beings (Adam) to be his viceroys. He crowned them with *doxa* and *timē* to bring the entire world into subjection – a task in which they failed (2:7–8; cf. Ps. 8:5). Jesus, however, because of the suffering of his death, is now crowned with *doxa* and *timē* (2:9). His priestly faithfulness – sacrificial death – qualified him to receive honour and glory upon his resurrection as the royal priest who has taken dominion over the world to come (2:5; cf. 5:5). By using the language of 'honour' and 'glory' in Hebrews 5:4–5 to describe

---

[41] For a more in-depth discussion of the Joshua typology in Heb. 3 – 4, see Ounsworth 2012: 55–97.

the Aaronic and Melchizedekian priesthoods, the author establishes a logical connection between primal humanity and the priesthoods of Aaron and Melchizedek. In other words, the logic appears to work like this: in the outflow of redemptive history, both the Aaronic and Melchizedekian priesthoods are expressions of the Adamic priesthood.

Christ is a priest after the order of Melchizedek, but his priestly ministry reflects the duties of the Aaronic priesthood with respect to sacrifice and atonement (Heb. 9 – 10). Since both the Melchizedekian priesthood and the Aaronic priesthood were expressions of the creational ideal, Christ fulfils both of them without actually holding both offices. In other words, Christ is a priest after the order of Melchizedek (not Aaron) who typologically fulfils the refined priestly duties of the Aaronic order. Jesus could not hold the office of the Aaronic priesthood because he was not of the tribe of Levi, but more importantly, because the Aaronic priesthood under the Mosaic covenant could never fulfil God's promises made to Abraham (7:11–19; cf. 2:16). For Christ to achieve what the Aaronic order could never do, namely definitively deal with sin for the children of Abraham, he had to be a priest who would simultaneously fulfil the creation mandate (given to Adam) and accomplish redemption (promised to Abraham). Again, there is only one priest in the biblical narrative who is associated with the archetypal priesthood given to primal humanity at creation and the covenantal blessing of Abraham, and that priest is Melchizedek.

Perhaps now it is easier to see why the author cites Psalm 2:7 as the justification for Christ's appointment to the high priesthood in Hebrews 5:5. At first glance, the appeal to Psalm 2:7 – 'You are my Son, today I have begotten you' – appears to have nothing to do with Christ's appointment to the office of high priest. Psalm 2:7 is about the enthronement of the messianic king who rules over the world as God's son. But that's just it. Upon his resurrection and ascension to the right hand of God, Christ was crowned with glory and honour as the firstborn Son – 'Today I have begotten you' – of the new creation. He inherited the *glory* and *honour* that was meant for Adam, the first son-priest-king. Psalm 2:7 is, therefore, a logical choice for the author to make in supporting Christ's appointment to the high priesthood because it builds on the blueprint of God's creation project. The Davidic son-king of Psalm 2:7 is part of a scriptural trajectory that holds sonship, kingship and priesthood together.

It is no surprise, then, that the author ploughs forward with his argument by introducing Psalm 110:4 with an adverbial comparative conjunction *kathōs kai* – 'just as also' (Heb. 5:6). In other words, Psalm 2:7 supports the God-given nature of Christ's priesthood 'just as also' does Psalm 110:4. Psalm 2 and Psalm 110 are, in the author's mind, mutually interpretative because they grow out of the soil of Scripture's metanarrative where sonship, kingship and priesthood are inseparable roles.[42]

In Hebrews 5:7–10, we begin to learn what it is about the nature of the Melchizedekian priesthood that enables it to succeed where the Levitical priesthood failed, and why Jesus was worthy of the office. The significance of the Melchizedekian priesthood is its permanence, and Christ was awarded Melchizedek's office upon his resurrection because of his faithful obedience during his earthly career (cf. 2:17). Hebrews 4:14 – 5:2 compares Jesus' earthly career to that of the Levitical priests. Former priests were able to 'deal gently with the ignorant and wayward' because of their own 'weakness' (*astheneian* [5:2 ESV]). Similarly, 'in the days of his flesh', Christ suffered so that he might be able to sympathize with our 'weaknesses' (*astheneiais* [4:15; 5:7–8 ESV]). Although he was a son, he had to learn obedience through suffering (5:8). When facing the affliction of death, he had to put his faith in God – the only one who was able to deliver him from death (2:7).

The faithfulness of Jesus during his earthly career described in these verses may have Adam's probationary state as the subtext. Adam was the son of God who was to order his life around the priority of worship as a priest before God. As part of his commission, Adam had to obey God's command concerning the tree and its penalty of death. If Adam had been faithful, God would have spared him from the experience of death.

Jesus similarly had to learn obedience, although he was a son (5:8). Jesus, however, learned obedience by trusting God, not to spare him from death but to deliver him out of death. If Hebrews 5:7 evokes Jesus' agony in the garden of Gethsemane, then Jesus displayed his obedience by obeying God's command concerning the cross (tree) and its curse of death.[43] Jesus entered into death to conquer death (2:14), trusting that

---

[42] Of course the author's juxtaposition of Ps. 2:7 and Ps. 110:4 makes even more sense if we assume that he was reading the LXX, which is most likely the case. As noted in chapter 5 of this project, the LXX of Ps. 110:3b (LXX 109:3b) reads, 'I have begotten you' (*exegennēsa se*).

[43] Against the majority opinion, Richardson (2012: 78–89) argues that Golgotha is the subtext of Heb. 5:7–8.

God would 'save him out of death' (*sōzein auton ek thanatou* [5:7]). God 'heard' (*eisakouō*) Jesus' prayers by raising him from the dead (5:7).

Having been made 'perfect' (*teleiōtheis*) upon his resurrection and exaltation, Jesus thereby became the source of 'eternal salvation' (*sōtērias aiōniou*) to all who obey him (5:9). Peterson has shown that Christ's perfection in Hebrews is vocational; that is, Jesus became qualified for his permanent mediatorial office through his incarnation, suffering, death and resurrection.[44] Perfection warrants the office of a permanent priesthood – one named after the order of Melchizedek (5:10; cf. 7:27; Ps. 110:4).[45]

Hebrews 6:13 – 7:28: the blessing of Abraham fulfilled in the Melchizedekian priest-king

After an extended paraenesis in 5:11 – 6:12, the author resumes his argument in 6:13. The *gar* in 6:13, in the immediate context, establishes 6:13–20 as supporting argumentation to the exhortation in 6:9–12. Here, the author encourages his readers to endure as those 'who through faith and patience inherit the promises' (6:12 ESV). The language of 'faith', 'inherit' and 'promises' evokes the story of Abraham and God's covenantal promises to Abraham and his seed. The exposition of God's promise and oath to Abraham in 6:13–20 is the grounds for engendering faithfulness in the readers.

But these verses should not be divorced from the exposition of Christ's priesthood in 5:1–10 either. The argument in 5:1–10 culminates in the reality that Jesus became the source of 'eternal salvation' to all who submit to his rule as the Melchizedekian priest-king (5:9–10). Since Jesus imparts that salvation to 'the offspring of Abraham' (2:16 ESV), the author now encourages those who are about to inherit salvation to remain faithful by reminding them of the certainty of God's promise. And just as the discussion of Christ's priesthood in 5:1–10 culminates in Psalm 110:4, so also 6:13–20 culminates in Psalm 110:4 and the Melchizedekian priesthood of Jesus (6:20). Moving forward, it will become evident that, in the author's

---

[44] Peterson 1982.
[45] The citation of Ps. 110:4 in Heb. 5:10 anticipates the author's discussion of Melchizedek in Heb. 7, where permanency and eternality are the fundamental characteristics of Melchizedek's priesthood (7:3, 16–17, 24, 28).

mind, Melchizedek's significance in redemptive history lies in his association with Abraham. In the logic of Hebrews 7, the promises to Abraham come to fruition through the Melchizedekian priesthood – a fact foreshadowed in Abraham's encounter with Melchizedek in Genesis 14 and later recognized by David in Psalm 110.

Hebrews 7:1–28

Hebrews 7 is an exegetical and redemptive-historical analysis of the Melchizedek narrative in Genesis 14:18–20. The purpose of Hebrews 7 is to demonstrate the superiority of the Melchizedekian priesthood over the Aaronic and, as a result, the superiority of the new covenant over the old. In 7:1–3, the author introduces Melchizedek and his relationship to Abraham by commenting on the narrative of Genesis 14:18–20. Five primary observations surface: (1) Melchizedek is king of Salem and priest of the Most High God (7:1); (2) Melchizedek met Abraham and pronounced a blessing on him after Abraham was victorious in battle (7:1); (3) Abraham paid a tenth of his spoils to Melchizedek (7:2); (4) Melchizedek is a king of righteousness and a king of peace (7:2); and (5) Melchizedek, like the Son of God, held a permanent priesthood, for he was without father or mother, genealogy, or record of birth and death in the Genesis narrative (7:3).

In Hebrews 7:4–10, the author draws one primary conclusion based on his brief exposition of Genesis 14:18–20. The Melchizedekian priesthood is superior to the Levitical priesthood because Melchizedek blessed Abraham (the ancestor of the Levites) and received a tithe from Abraham (7:6–7, 9–10). It does not appear that Melchizedek's superiority over Abraham and the Levites is merely a by-product of redemptive-historical priority. There is something about the nature of Melchizedek's priesthood that causes it to supersede the Levitical priesthood. But what is it? The answer has to do with the quality of Melchizedek's priesthood as a permanent priesthood. Hebrews 7:3 and 7:8 provide the clue to this line of reasoning. According to Hebrews 7:3, Melchizedek is 'without father or mother or genealogy, having neither beginning of days nor end of life, but being similar to the Son of God, he remains a priest for all time'. The language of this verse does not have to mean that Melchizedek was pre-existent (without beginning of days) and that he never died (without end of life). In that case, we would assume that the author of Hebrews believed that Melchizedek was either the pre-incarnate Christ, or still alive on earth somewhere, or taken into heaven.[46] Instead, Hebrews 7:3 is simply a description of the way Melchizedek appears and disappears in the Genesis narrative.

When Melchizedek arrives in Genesis 14:18, he has no genealogical record – no record of father, mother, birth or death. His missing genealogy is an important literary feature since every significant person in Genesis always has a genealogical history. The author of Hebrews assessed Melchizedek's lack of recorded family heritage as significant. Hebrews 7:8 says, 'In the one case tithes are received by mortal men, but in the other case, it is being testified (*martyroumenos*) there that he lives.' The point is not that Melchizedek lived for ever. Instead, the author employs the passive participle *martyroumenos* to describe the manner in which the Genesis narrative bore *witness* to Melchizedek – he is simply there, existing, living, with no predecessors or successors. In other words, the only witness we have of Melchizedek in the Genesis narrative is that he lives.

In the light of these observations, the author's comment about Melchizedek's 'resembling the Son of God' (*aphōmoiōmenos de tō huiō tou theou*) in 7:3 (ESV) also makes more sense. What exactly does the phrase *aphōmoiōmenos de tō huiō tou theou* mean? These six words have caused quite a few problems in the history of interpretation.[47] If the referent of *tō huiō tou theou* is the eternal Son of God, then perhaps interpreters are right to view Melchizedek as a pre-incarnate Christ. However, the permanency of Melchizedek's priesthood is what resembles the Son of God.[48] Furthermore, the author's intent in 7:1–3 is to describe Melchizedek in the context of Genesis, which would make a passing comment to the eternal Son (Christ) seem out of place.

Perhaps, then, we should not assume that *tō huiō tou theou* is a direct reference to Jesus, but only an indirect one. In other words, the reference to *tō huiō tou theou* is not only a reference to the *Son* of God but also a reference to the *son* of God. In other words, Melchizedek resembles the son of God in Genesis and throughout the narrative of Scripture. The concept of sonship in Hebrews – and in Genesis – and its relationship to

---

[46] If this were the case, then there would be two men occupying the Melchizedekian office. Such a conclusion is contrary to the Christological argument of Hebrews.

[47] Ellingworth (1983) has summarized the difficulties in interpreting Heb. 7:3 and the various proposals.

[48] The participle *aphōmoiōmenos* modifies the matrix sentence 'He remains a priest for ever'. Thus, 'He remains a priest for ever, resembling the son of God.'

the priesthood cannot be divorced from the covenantal storyline of the Old Testament. Melchizedek embodied the Old Testament's archetypal form of covenant mediation: he was like the son of God because he mediated God's blessing to Abraham – by extension the nations – as a royal priest of God Most High (Yahweh; cf. Gen. 14:22). Similarly, Adam was not a royal priest by virtue of the law; he was a royal priest by virtue of his familial relationship to God as one made in God's image. Perhaps, when the author of Hebrews uses the expression 'resembling *tō huiō tou theou*', it is his way of saying that Melchizedek's priesthood was tied to and in succession with the stipulations of a superior covenant. Even Abraham – the recipient of the covenant promises – recognized Melchizedek as a superior kind of priest-king in succession with Adam and Noah (7:6).[49] Because of Melchizedek's resemblance '*tō huiō tou theou*', the author of Hebrews asserts that when the Lord swore an oath in Psalm 110:4 – 'The LORD has sworn and will not change his mind, "You are a priest for ever after the order of Melchizedek"' – he was not just appointing a priest; he was also appointing a *huion* (7:28).

With this logic in mind, the author advances his argument for the permanency – and thus superiority – of the Melchizedekian priesthood over and against the temporariness of the Levitical priesthood (7:11–28). The Levitical priests were many in number. They became priests by the terms of the Mosaic covenant. A multitude of priests were necessary because each of them succumbed to death (7:23). No Levitical priest could bring about perfection because they were all sinful, mortal men. The law could make nothing perfect (7:18–19) because its mediators were imperfect. The very nature of the Levitical programme was insufficient and temporal.

The nature of the Melchizedekian priesthood is different. Melchizedek's priesthood was singular. He did not belong to a tribe, and he was not replaced by any descendants in the Genesis narrative. Everything about the Melchizedekian priesthood suggests permanence and superiority. It is for this reason that a priest had to arrive in the 'likeness' (*homoiotēta*) of Melchizedek (7:15). Unlike the Levites, Jesus did not receive his priesthood through genealogical descent or legal inheritance (7:16). Instead, like Melchizedek in the literary context of Genesis, Jesus became a priest by the power of an 'indestructible life' (*zōēs akatalytou*). For it was 'testified'

---

[49] See my discussion in chapter 3 of this project for the literary connections between Melchizedek and Adam and Noah in Genesis.

(*martyroumenos*) concerning Melchizedek that he lives (7:8), and it was 'testified' (*martyreitai*) concerning Jesus upon his resurrection that he is 'a priest for ever after the *order* of Melchizedek' (7:17; emphasis mine). Unlike the Levites, whose death prevented them from 'remaining' (*paramenein*) in their office (7:23), Jesus, like Melchizedek in the literary context of Genesis, 'remains' (*menein*) a priest for ever because he lives for ever (7:24; cf. 7:3).[50]

The oath

In Hebrews 7:20–28, the author builds his case for the superiority of the Melchizedekian priesthood by highlighting God's 'oath' in Psalm 110:4: 'The LORD has sworn'. The discussion of God's oath in these verses builds on the logic of 6:13–20, where God's oath and promise were the 'two unchangeable things' (ESV) that guaranteed to Abraham that God would be faithful to his word.[51] The oath in Psalm 110:4 is another link in the chain that attaches the Melchizedekian priesthood to God's covenant with Abraham. Under the Mosaic legislation, the priests became priests without an oath (7:20). But Christ became a priest by the power of God's oath – 'The LORD has sworn and will not change his mind, "You are a priest

---

[50] The same verb *menō* is used in 7:3 to describe Melchizedek's priesthood. I am not suggesting, however, that Melchizedek lived for ever. In fact, Hahn (2009: 303) has argued that the phrase *eis to diēnekes* applied to Melchizedek in 7:3 is weaker than the phrase *eis ton aiōna* applied to Christ in 7:28. According to Hahn, 'Melchizedek was not immortal but remained a priest for the duration of his life'.

[51] The thrust of Heb. 6:13–20 is the absolute certainty of God's promise to Abraham. The specific promise in mind is God's promise made to Abraham at Mt Moriah after Abraham faithfully offered up Isaac to God (Heb. 6:14). As the author of Hebrews points out, it was at Moriah that God confirmed the certainty of his promise with an oath (Heb. 6:16–18; cf. Gen. 22:16–17). God's promise and oath to Abraham are the two 'unchangeable things' that guarantee the blessing of Abraham will come to pass in the lives of Abraham's offspring (6:18 ESV; cf. 2:16). These two unchangeable things – the promise and the oath – are the same two things that guarantee the eternal Melchizedekian priesthood: 'The LORD has sworn' (oath) and 'You are a priest for ever after the order of Melchizedek' (promise). By virtue of these two unchangeable things, believers are exhorted to lay hold of the hope (*elpidos*) set before them. This hope enters into the most holy place in the heavenly realm where Jesus has already entered as a 'forerunner' and priest after the order of Melchizedek (6:19–20). Hope, therefore, cannot be separated from the priestly work of Jesus. The discussion of hope in relation to the promise and oath in 6:13–20 anticipates the author's discussion of Ps. 110:4 in Heb. 7:18–22. Through Jesus, the Melchizedekian high priest, a 'better hope' (*kreittonos elpidos*) has been 'introduced' (*epeisagōgē* [7:19]). The verb *epeisagōgē* recalls Heb. 1:6, where God 'leads' (*eisagagē*) the firstborn Jesus into the heavenly realm. This better hope, then, is to be identified with Jesus, the priest after the order of Melchizedek who has entered into the most holy place in heaven and has therefore actually brought the blessing of Abraham to fruition (6:19–20; 7:19). Jesus is the guarantor of a covenant better than the Mosaic covenant (7:22). Why is the covenant he mediates better? Because this covenant brings to fruition the promises of the Abrahamic covenant through the programme of the Davidic covenant (i.e. Ps. 110) to inaugurate the new-covenant era.

for ever"' (7:21). The oath makes Jesus the guarantor of a better covenant (7:22). But why does the oath make Jesus the guarantor of a covenant better than the Mosaic covenant? Is it merely because the Levitical priests were made priests without an oath? It seems, rather, that in the author's logic the oath establishes Jesus as the guarantor of a better covenant not because of the oath in and of itself. Instead, the oath connects Jesus' work of priestly mediation to covenants superior to that of the Mosaic covenant and its priests, namely the Abrahamic and Davidic covenants. God's covenants with Abraham and David are the only two Old Testament covenants identified with a divine oath (Gen. 22:17; Ps. 89).[52] By fulfilling the Davidic covenant as David's Lord and the Melchizedekian priest, Jesus inaugurates the blessing of Abraham while simultaneously rendering the law-covenant obsolete (7:12, 18, 27–28; 8:13).

The old-covenant law was inferior to God's covenants with Abraham and David because the law appointed weak and sinful men as priests (7:28). The Abrahamic and Davidic covenants, however, were not identified with the weakness of the Levitical priests. Melchizedek and his permanent priesthood mediated blessing to Abraham, and the word of the oath given to David in Psalm 110:4 was that a priest after the order of Melchizedek would forever mediate the Davidic covenant. As 7:27–28 implies, the word of the oath – 'You are a priest for ever after the order of Melchizedek' – which came later than the law, was rooted in the stipulations of a superior covenant because its priesthood did not depend on a legal requirement. Instead, the priesthood associated with the oath arose from a familial bond. For the word of the oath 'appoints a Son' (7:28 ESV) – a Davidic Son holding the offices of priest and king for ever.

Hebrews 8:1 – 10:18: a better priest inaugurates a better covenant through a better sacrifice

The overarching theme of Hebrews 8:1 – 10:18 is the perfect sacrifice of Jesus, the high priest.[53] Psalm 110 appears at the beginning (8:1) and near

---

[52] See my discussion in chapter 5 on the oath of Ps. 110:4 and its relationship to the Abrahamic and Davidic covenants.

[53] Cockerill 2001.

the end of the section (10:12–13), shaping the argument as a whole.[54] Hebrews 8 – 10 contends that Christ is the mediator of a better covenant by virtue of his sacrificial death and priestly position in the heavenly tabernacle.

Hebrews 8:1–13

Hebrews 8:1–2 summarizes the essence of the author's argument thus far:

> The main point of the things which have been said is this: we have such a high priest who sat down at the right hand of the throne of the majesty in the heavens, a minister of the holy things and of the true tabernacle which the Lord pitched, not man.

His 'main point' sets up his argument for the superiority of the new-covenant sacrifice over old-covenant sacrifices (8:3–13). On the basis of Psalm 110:1 and 110:4, the author positions Jesus, the high priest, in the true and heavenly tabernacle as a result of his superior sacrifice (8:2–3). Jesus' intercessory work in the heavenly tabernacle solidifies him as the mediator of a better covenant (8:5–6). The earthly tabernacle of the old covenant was merely a replica of its archetype: the heavenly tabernacle (8:5). Thus, from its inception the earthly tabernacle and its priesthood were temporal. They were merely copies and shadows of their true substance (8:5). When Christ entered the heavenly tabernacle (Zion; cf. Ps. 110:2) in fulfilment of Psalm 110:1 and 110:4, he became the mediator of a better covenant (8:6). This 'better covenant' is the new covenant promised by Jeremiah in Jeremiah 31:31–34. The point is that even the Old Testament anticipated the abrogation of the old covenant to make way for a superior covenant (8:7). But some order of priests had to mediate the forgiveness promised in this new covenant. Certainly, the Levitical priests would not suffice because they were imperfect mediators of a transient covenant, made obvious by the fact that they 'served' (*latreuousin*) in a tabernacle that was only a 'copy' (*hypodeigmati*) and 'shadow' (*skia*) of the heavenly things (8:5).[55] A change in the priesthood was necessary – and

---

[54] According to Cockerill (ibid. 179–180), Heb. 8:1 – 10:18 is 'closely associated with the writer's interpretation of Ps 110:4 in Heb 7:1–28, in which he describes the Son as a priest according to Melchizedek's order'.

[55] The author of Hebrews may have delayed his discussion of the new covenant so that he could first establish the superiority of Christ's Melchizedekian priesthood. But why would the

thus a change in the law – to mediate the promises of this better covenant (7:12). For the author of Hebrews, the Melchizedekian priest of Psalm 110 is the mediator of the new covenant promised in Jeremiah 31:31–34 because he became a 'minister' (*leitourgos*) in the permanent heavenly tabernacle, not the transient shadow of the tabernacle on earth (8:2, 4–5, 13). But how does Christ sanction the better promises of this new and better covenant? The author answers this question in Hebrews 9 – 10.

Hebrews 9:11–27

Hebrews 9:11–27 grounds the permanency of new-covenant forgiveness in the perfect self-sacrifice of Christ. Jesus' sacrifice awarded him access to the presence of God in the heavenly tabernacle and established him as the permanent mediator of a new covenant (9:11–12, 15). Again, Psalm 110 does not appear in Hebrews 9, but the royal procession of the Messiah to the right hand of God in Psalm 110:1 and his permanent priesthood in

---

(note 55 *cont.*) development of Ps. 110 and Christ's Melchizedekian priesthood need to come first? Perhaps the answer lies in the fact that the readers may have concluded that the promises of the new covenant could have been mediated through the Levitical priesthood; hence, the author's discussion of a change in the priesthood necessitating a change in the law as well (7:12) prior to the explicit quotation of Jer. 31:31–34. After all, the broader context of Jeremiah gives the impression that the blessings of the new covenant will come through a Davidic king and the Levitical priests. Jer. 33:17–22 states, '"For thus says the Lord: David shall never lack a man to sit on the throne of the house of Israel, and the Levitical priests shall never lack a man in my presence to offer burnt offerings, to burn grain offerings, and to make sacrifices for ever." The word of the Lord came to Jeremiah: "Thus says the Lord: If you can break my covenant with the day and my covenant with the night, so that day and night will not come at their appointed time, then also my covenant with David my servant may be broken, so that he shall not have a son to reign on his throne, and my covenant with the Levitical priests my ministers. As the host of heaven cannot be numbered and the sands of the sea cannot be measured, so I will multiply the offspring of David my servant, and the Levitical priests who minister to me"' (ESV). What are we to make of this text from Jeremiah in the light of the fact that Hebrews presents the Levitical priesthood as obsolete and the Melchizedekian priesthood of Jesus as the mediatorial office of the new-covenant blessings? At the very least, Jer. 33:17–22 suggests that the blessings of the new covenant will come through Davidic kingship and a permanent priesthood. Granted the priesthood in Jer. 33 is the Levitical priesthood, but we have seen in Hebrews that Christ simultaneously fulfils both the Melchizedekian and Aaronic priesthoods even though he does not occupy both offices. As a Melchizedekian priest, Christ fulfils the duties prescribed for the Levitical priests under the Mosaic law. The Levitical priests were to minister before the Lord by making sacrifices. Jesus as the permanent Melchizedekian priest transcends their priesthood while fulfilling their sacrificial duties by offering his own body as a sacrifice for sin. In this sense, Jesus typologically fulfils the duties of the Levitical priesthood while holding the office of Melchizedek. Furthermore, it is worthy of note that Jeremiah elsewhere envisaged a king with priestly access to God as the ruler of God's new-covenant people: 'Their prince shall be one of themselves; their ruler shall come out from their midst; I will make him draw near, and he shall approach me, for who would dare of himself to approach me?' (Jer. 30:21 ESV). This statement about a royal-priestly figure is followed immediately by the covenant formula: 'And you shall be my people, and I will be your God' (Jer. 30:22 ESV).

Table 8.2 Places in Hebrews 9 where Psalms 110:1 and 110:4 inform the logic of the author's Christological argument without being explicitly referenced

Hebrews 9	Psalm 110
But when Christ appeared as a high priest of the good things that have come . . . (Heb. 9:11a ESV)	Psalm 110:4 is the basis for Christ's high priesthood.
. . . then through the greater and more perfect tent (not made with hands, that is, not of this creation) he entered once for all into the holy places, not by means of the blood of goats and calves but by means of his own blood, thus securing an eternal redemption (Heb. 9:11b–12 ESV)	Psalm 110:1 and 110:4 function as the basis for Christ's royal procession into the holy places and his priestly sacrifice.
Therefore he is the mediator of a new covenant . . . (Heb. 9:15a ESV)	Psalm 110:4 is the basis for Christ's priestly mediation.
Thus it was necessary for the copies of the heavenly things to be purified with these rites, but the heavenly things themselves with better sacrifices than these. For Christ has entered, not into holy places made with hands, which are copies of the true things, but into heaven itself, now to appear in the presence of God on our behalf. Nor was it to offer himself repeatedly, as the high priest enters the holy places every year with blood not his own, for then he would have had to suffer repeatedly since the foundation of the world. But as it is, he has appeared once for all at the end of the ages to put away sin by the sacrifice of himself (Heb. 9:23–26 ESV)	Psalm 110:1 and 110:4 inform Christ's heavenly procession and the permanency of his priesthood by virtue of his perfect self-sacrifice.

Psalm 110:4 is unquestionably the logic behind much of the argument of this chapter (see Table 8.2).

Though explicit references to Psalm 110 are lacking, Compton insists that Psalm 110 is more fundamental to the author's argument concerning the superiority of Christ's self-sacrifice than even the promise of the new covenant found in Jeremiah 31.[56] He accurately summarizes the role of Psalm 110 in the argument of Hebrews 9:

> Once more Psalm 110 is not explicitly cited, but its influence is still present, something seen, especially, in the author's interpretation of Messiah's exaltation (Ps. 110.1; cf. Heb. 8.1–2 with 9.11–12) as his consecration of the heavenly tabernacle that serves the new covenant (9.23). The author, in fact, infers from Psalm 110 that Messiah must consecrate this new sacred space with superior sacrifices, the kind that can provide the sort of perfection such heavenly access requires, which is to say, the kind that can ratify a covenant that promises full forgiveness and such access. He then explains . . . that Messiah's self-sacrifice was precisely the sort of sacrifice Ps. 110.1 and 4 required and, therefore, anticipated. After all, it was unrepeatable and, thus, unrepeated, which suggests, in light of Jesus' resurrection (also implied in Ps. 110.4; cf. Heb. 7.16), that it thoroughly perfects.[57]

Hebrews 10:1–18

In Hebrews 10:1–18, the author continues to build the case for the superiority of Christ's singular priestly self-sacrifice and entrance into the heavenly tabernacle over and against the insufficient and repetitious sacrifices of the old-covenant system performed on earth. In 10:11–14, the author appeals to Psalm 110 to make his point. The priests of the old covenant 'stand' (*hestēken*) daily in the service of God, offering the same sacrifices repeatedly because they cannot take away sins (10:11). But when Christ had offered himself as a perfect sacrifice once and for all, he 'sat down' (*ekathisen*) at the right hand of God (10:12; cf. Ps. 110:1). Sitting suggests completion, finality and sufficiency, whereas standing implies insufficiency and repetition with no end in sight.

The logic here reflects that of the exordium where Christ's royal enthronement was the result of his priestly purification for sins (Heb. 1:3). Except here, the author clarifies the nature of Christ's priestly work of atonement as a component of his own self-sacrificial death (9:12, 26; 10:10–12). Christ brought the cultic ceremonies prescribed under the old

---

[56] Compton 2015: 142.
[57] Ibid. 141.

covenant to an end by offering his own body as a sacrifice, qualifying him to take his *seat* in the heavenly tabernacle. Yet the author reminds his readers that the finality of Christ's atoning work does not mean the eschaton has arrived. Christ has finished his work – he has sat down at the right hand of God – but he now awaits the time when all of his enemies will be made a footstool for his feet (10:13; cf. Ps. 110:1). This already-but-not-yet tension apparent in Psalm 110 and in the completed work of Christ gives meaning to the Christian's present experience of the blessings of the new covenant (10:14–18). For by Christ's single sacrifice he has 'perfected' (*teteleiōken*) for all time (already) those who are 'being sanctified' (*tous hagiazomenous*) (not yet) (10:14).

Hebrews 12: the pioneer and perfecter of faith leads many sons and daughters to glory

Hebrews 12:1–2

The final explicit reference to Psalm 110 in the epistle is found in the allusion to Psalm 110:1 in Hebrews 12:2: 'he has sat down at the right hand of the throne of God.' After describing the numerous imperfect, yet admirable, expressions of faithfulness in redemptive history (11:1–40), Hebrews 12:1–2 presents Jesus as the climactic expression of faith for all of humankind.[58] By using the name 'Jesus' (*Iēsoun*), the author emphasizes Christ's humanity and what he achieved on behalf of the human race (12:2). The terms *archēgon* and *teleiōtēn* recall the author's exposition of Psalm 8 in Hebrews 2:5–11, where Christ was shown to have received royal dominion over the cosmos as humanity's representative. He leads many sons and daughters to glory because he became the *archēgon* of salvation by being made 'perfect' (*teleioō*) through suffering (2:10).

Hebrews 12:2 paints a similar picture: Christ is the 'founder' (*archēgon*) and 'perfecter' (*teleiōtēn*) of faith because he faithfully endured the suffering of the cross. He trusted that God would raise him from the dead –

---

[58] On the basis of the literary context and rhetorical form of Heb. 11, Richardson (2012: 109–166) argues that Heb. 12:1–3 functions as the rhetorical climax to the heroes of the faith in ch. 11.

'for the joy set before him' – leading ultimately to his exaltation to the right hand of God (cf. 5:7–10). Here in 12:2, we discover a pattern we have seen throughout the epistle: self-sacrificial death leads to royal exaltation. Except, here in 12:2, Christ's sacrifice is more explicitly depicted as the climactic expression of faithfulness. In other words, through his faithful cross-work, Christ has 'perfected' or 'completed' faith. As we have seen at other points in the epistle, faithfulness, perfection and self-sacrifice are all characteristics of Christ's priesthood (cf. 2:17; 5:7–10; 7:28; 9:12–15; 9:24–28). Thus, here in Hebrews 12:1–2, royalty (Ps. 110:1) and priesthood (Ps. 110:4) are the author's fundamental Christological categories. Or to put it another way, Jesus' self-sacrifice was the climactic expression of human faith that qualified him for the honour of Psalm 110:1, and by implication the permanent priesthood of Psalm 110:4.

Hebrews 12:18–29

The reference to 'Mount Zion' in Hebrews 12:22 evokes the imagery of Psalm 110:2, where the messianic priest-king rules from Zion in the midst of his enemies. Mount Zion in 12:22 is the heavenly dwelling place of Jesus, the royal priest and 'mediator of a new covenant'. Jesus' new-covenant mediation from the heavenly Zion (tabernacle; cf. 8:1–2) is, as we have seen, rooted in Psalm 110:4 and his Melchizedekian priesthood.

The broader context of 12:18–24 sets up a contrast between Mount Sinai (old covenant) and Mount Zion (new covenant). In the context of the epistle thus far, the futility of the old covenant and the success of the new covenant cannot be separated from their respective priesthoods – Levitical and Melchizedekian. Believers have already come to Mount Zion through their new-covenant high priest (12:22). Even though they remain on earth, Jesus represents them in heaven. He mediates every blessing of the new covenant from the heavenly tabernacle on their behalf (12:24).

The faithful believers who have already died now dwell with Jesus in heaven (12:23) and share in Jesus' inheritance. They are the assembly of the 'firstborn' (*prōtotokōn*), the spirits of the 'righteous made perfect' (*dikaiōn teteleiōmenōn* [12:23 ESV]). The very characteristics that defined Jesus' royal priesthood are true of them. God appointed Jesus a priest after the order of Melchizedek after Jesus was made perfect (*teleiōtheis*) through his obedient suffering (Heb. 5:9–10). Righteousness (*dikaiosynēs* [7:2; cf. 1:9]) characterizes Jesus' royal priesthood, and his status as the 'firstborn' (*prōtotokōn*) Son of God (1:6) places him at God's right hand as heir of all things (1:2). While believers do not share in Christ's Melchizedekian office, they are all made a royal priesthood as children of God in union with Christ (cf. 1 Pet. 2:9). They must offer to God acceptable 'worship' (*latreuōmen*) with 'reverence' (*eulabeias* [Heb. 12:28; cf. Heb. 5:7]). One day, they will enjoy the fullness of their inheritance in the world to come in a kingdom that cannot be shaken (12:25–28; cf. 1:14; 2:5).

In Hebrews 12:25–29, the author cites Haggai 2:6 to describe the cataclysmic shaking of heaven and earth to make way for the eternal kingdom of God. A noteworthy observation about the context of Haggai is that it describes the rebuilding of the temple (1:14 – 2:8) by a Davidic king (Zerubbabel) and a high priest (Joshua). The Lord promises to be with them and all the people according to the covenant he made with the Israelites when he brought them out of Egypt (Hag. 2:5). He assures them of his presence and promises them that he will fill his temple with a greater degree of glory than that experienced by the worshippers in the first temple (Hag. 2:9). After the first exodus, the Lord instituted his covenant at Sinai to establish a kingdom of priests. The formation of this new people coincided with the shaking of the earth at the voice and presence of the Lord. Haggai describes a second exodus in similar terminology. According to Haggai, the shaking that is going to accompany this second exodus is one that will be cosmic in scope. The cosmic nature of this shaking is an act of judgment upon the nations (Hag. 2:7, 22). Just as the Israelites plundered the Egyptians upon their exodus, so also the Lord will bring the treasures of the nations to his temple. Similarly, the Lord is going to 'overthrow the throne of kingdoms' and 'destroy the strength of the kingdoms of the nations' (Hag. 2:22 ESV). Just as the horses and chariots of Egypt were destroyed in the sea, so the Lord is going to destroy the horses, chariots and riders of the nations. All the kingdoms of the world will be destroyed so that the Lord can establish a Davidic king to rule his kingdom and establish peace on the earth (2:23; cf. 2:9).

The use of Haggai by the author of Hebrews is entirely appropriate. In Haggai, the cataclysmic shaking serves God's purpose to establish his Davidic king over the nations. The author of Hebrews has a similar end in mind. God has already put his Davidic king and high priest on the highest throne in the universe – 'Sit at my right hand' (Heb. 1:13). The final cataclysmic shaking will happen when God judges the earth and establishes the 'unshakable kingdom' of his Davidic priest-king – 'until I make your enemies a footstool' (Heb. 1:13).

Conclusion

This chapter aimed at understanding how the author of Hebrews interpreted Psalm 110. Psalm 110 is the hinge on which the argument of Hebrews turns. In Hebrews, sonship and the Melchizedekian royal priesthood are the most fundamental Christological categories. As the Melchizedekian high priest (new-covenant mediator) and Davidic king at the right hand of God in the heavenly Zion, Jesus has restored universal dominion to humankind. He has given God's people access to God's presence through his sacrificial death. He secured their present forgiveness and future inheritance in the eschatological world to come. A biblical-theological approach to Hebrews clarifies the purpose of Christ's Melchizedekian priesthood in the plan of redemptive history. God's purpose in creation (the Adamic kingdom) and his plan for redemption (the Abrahamic covenant) is coming to pass through the work of a royal priest after the order of Melchizedek.

9

Conclusion

This book has attempted to offer a biblical-theological explanation for the union of kingship and priesthood in the Messiah of Psalm 110. The impetus for this project arose from the fact that modern scholarship has given no clear consensus on how to handle David's messianic expectation of a Melchizedekian priest (Ps. 110:4). Proposals have ranged from reassigning Psalm 110 to the Maccabean period to suggesting that the psalm addresses two different people: the king in verses 1–3 and the priest in verses 4–7. By situating Psalm 110 in biblical-theological and canonical context, we saw that the union of kingship and priesthood in a single figure is part of Scripture's covenantal metanarrative. Melchizedek occupies a vital role in this story because of his place in redemptive history. His servant-kingship looks back to the kind of representational authority originally given to Adam, while his office of priesthood is closely connected to the Abrahamic covenant. David grasped the importance of Melchizedek's priesthood as he reflected on Genesis 14, the patterns of his (David's) own life, and the content of God's covenant with him (2 Sam. 7).

Summary

How could David's Lord be both a priest and a king? Much of modern scholarship tried to answer this question by reconstructing the history of Israelite kingship. Higher-critical scholarship never moved beyond historical reconstruction when trying to discern the meaning of a Melchizedekian messiah. Psalm 110 is the most-quoted Old Testament passage in the New Testament, and yet many have been content to reduce it to a piece of political propaganda attempting to unite the Jebusite cult with the Davidic monarchy. More conservative scholarship has empha-sized royal priesthood as one of Scripture's controlling themes, but often to the neglect of Psalm 110 and its Melchizedekian priesthood. This book has tried to bridge the gap by showing how David's reading of Genesis 14 (Ps. 110:4) fits into Scripture's development of royal priesthood from Adam to Christ.

The union of kingship and priesthood in a single person began with God's purpose for Adam at creation. Adam bore God's image. He was God's covenantal son, worshipping God as a priest-king in the sanctuary and commissioned to establish God's kingdom on the earth. After Adam's fall into sin, his office of priest-king found expression in key covenantal figures: Noah, Abraham, Melchizedek and Israel. Melchizedek is unique because of his connection to Abraham and the Abrahamic covenant.

Flying forward in redemptive history, God's covenant with David became the programme that would bring the Abrahamic covenant to fruition. For David's greater son to bless the nations, he needed a superior priesthood; one that could overcome the inadequacies of the Levitical order and unleash the blessing of Abraham. David himself would have realized this when reflecting on Genesis 14. Through the patterns of his own life experience and the content of the Davidic covenant, David concluded that the Messiah would be a royal priest after the order of Melchizedek. David's portrait of the Messiah in Psalm 110 is unique for its explicit mention of Melchizedek, but it shares much in common with Psalms 1 – 2, which comprise the Psalter's own messianic interpretative lens.

Before the time of the New Testament, Psalm 110 influenced some of the intertestamental literature. Surprisingly, this body of literature does not contain a single explicit quotation from Psalm 110. Nevertheless, the union of priesthood and kingship in Psalm 110 significantly influenced the *Testament of Levi*, *1 Enoch*, *2 Enoch* and *11QMelchizedek*. The combined evidence of these writings indicates that messianic expectations in intertestamental Judaism did not always divide neatly into either royal or priestly messianic hopes. *11QMelchizedek*, for example, describes an eschatological priest-king named Melchizedek who rules the nations, conquers satanic forces of evil and provides atonement for the sins of his people. The members of some Jewish circles were expecting a Melchizedekian messiah to come, but they failed to see those expectations realized in the person and work of Jesus.

Psalm 110:1 appears twice in the final chapters of Mark's Gospel (Mark 12:36; 14:62). In their narrative context – the temple setting (12:36) and before the high priest (14:62) – Jesus' self-referential use of Psalm 110 evokes the psalm's broader context to inform his identity. The application of Psalm 110 to Jesus in his final confrontational encounters functions as the climax to Jesus' earlier confrontations with religious leaders over the issue of his identity. Though Mark's Gospel never explicitly identifies Jesus as a priest (Jesus was not a Levite), he carries out a priestly ministry in the early stages of Mark's narrative. By casting out unclean spirits (Mark 1:21–28; 5:1–20), cleansing the leper (Mark 1:40–45), forgiving sins (Mark 2:1–12), ruling the sabbath (Mark 2:23 – 3:6), reconstituting sacred space (Mark 2:23 – 3:6) and redefining purity codes (Mark 7:14–23), Jesus behaves like a priest. In the temple and before the high priest, Jesus' use of Psalm 110 makes explicit what was implicit earlier in Mark's narrative: Jesus is David's Lord, the messianic king and a priest after Melchizedek's order. The kingdom Jesus proclaimed at the beginning of Mark's Gospel is the kingdom he came to establish (Mark 1:15). The irony, however, is that he inaugurates this kingdom not with political power but through his own death on a cross. Regal and priestly images seem to converge at Calvary when God's crucified Son ushers in the kingdom through his own covenant sacrifice.

Because of his faithful obedience in life and in death, Jesus is now seated at the right hand of the Majesty on high (Heb. 1:3). The author of Hebrews read Psalm 110 as part of the Bible's covenantal storyline culminating in the resurrected Christ. Jesus has dominion over the universe as the Davidic Son, priest and king of Psalm 110. He has fulfilled God's creational design for humanity to rule the world (as king) from the place of God's presence (as priest) (Heb. 2:5–9). Crowned with glory and honour, Jesus presently reigns over the world to come until all his enemies are made a footstool for his feet. Better than all the Old Testament types and shadows, Jesus mediates the blessings of a better covenant as the Melchizedekian priest (Heb. 8:6). That better covenant is the new covenant. It is better than the old covenant because Jesus' priesthood is better than the Aaronic (Heb. 7). Jesus' Melchizedekian priesthood is attached to Zion, not Sinai; the promise to Abraham, not the law given to Moses. Weak, mortal, sinful men could not mediate the better promises of the new covenant (Heb. 7:23–28). But Jesus offers full and final cleansing from sin. He rose from the dead, never to die again. He holds his priesthood permanently. His life is indestructible. He is a priest for ever after the order of Melchizedek.

Theological implications

Eschatology

Psalm 110 is one of the most disputed biblical texts among dispensational and covenant theologians, and interpreters of the various positions on the millennium. The debate between these camps tends to hinge on whether the Christological fulfilment of Psalm 110 means that Jesus presently reigns on David's throne and rules over David's kingdom. How one answers that question obviously has implications for eschatology and the nature of the millennium. A question rarely explored is how the cosmological fulfilment of Psalm 110 and its relationship to Christ's present priestly mediation from heaven should influence our understanding of the second coming.

For example, the use of Psalm 110 in Hebrews clarifies the reason for Christ's absence (ascension) during these last days of human history. Christ had to ascend to heaven to mediate salvific blessings to the nations because only a priest in the true tabernacle could accomplish effective and eternal forgiveness (Heb. 8 – 10). If Christ were on earth, he would not be a priest at all because this earth is subjected to the curse and the futility of the old-covenant administration (Heb. 8:4). He had to ascend to heaven to accomplish full and final redemption for humanity because the old-covenant tabernacle on earth was merely a copy of the heavenly reality (Heb. 8:5).

This angle on the ascension and present ministry of Christ in the heavenly tabernacle may have implications for premillennial eschatology and the concept of a millennial reign of Christ on earth. In the logic of Hebrews, how would Christ continue to exercise his new-covenant mediation if he were to return to earth without bringing heaven to bear on this earthly realm? In other words, if Christ is going to reign as the Melchizedekian priest-king on earth during a 1,000-year-long period (the millennium), must the transformation of this earth-under-curse accompany his return? Must heaven come to earth when Christ returns so that the royal priest continues to mediate his eternal salvific blessings from this final cosmic temple?[1] Based on the interpretation of Psalm 110 by the author of Hebrews, is it a step backwards in redemptive history for Christ to leave the heavenly tabernacle *in heaven* and exercise his kingly

---

[1] To this it might be added that Hebrews appears to describe Christ's second coming as the decisive and final event of salvation for his people (Heb. 9:28).

authority and priestly covenant mediation on earth while the true tabernacle and world to come remains in another realm? More work needs to be done to determine if the concept of an earthly millennial reign of Christ is at odds with the eschatological and cosmological argument of Hebrews and its use of Psalm 110.

Ecclesiology

While the people of God do not share in Christ's Melchizedekian office, they constitute a royal priesthood (1 Pet. 2:9) and exist as a kingdom and priests to God (Rev. 5:10; cf. Rev. 1:6). What does it mean for the church to hold the title of royal priesthood in the new-covenant era?[2] Adam's regal priesthood was a function of bearing the divine image. United to Christ, who is the second Adam, God's people are being renewed in God's likeness as they are conformed to the image of Jesus (Rom. 8:29; Eph. 4:24). The church is God's new humanity. Situated in the flow of redemptive history, Adam's office and Israel's identity now belongs to the church. Adam was a priest-king in the garden; Israel was a royal priesthood in the land; the church is a body of regal priests on their way to the heavenly city. True worship, doctrinal fidelity, personal holiness and love for neighbour should continue to mark out God's priestly community. Yet the church is called to exercise its institutional responsibilities in different ways in the new-covenant era. No longer walking within the boundaries of the garden, nor inhabiting the borders of a geopolitical nation, the church must embrace its distinctive calling in the time between Christ's resurrection and parousia.

Christ, the royal priest, has invested authority in his church – a new order of priest-kings. The church's authority is not exercised through the political structures of the state, but through the assembly of two or three (or thousands) gathered in the name of Christ (Matt. 18:20). Local churches fulfil their calling by representing an otherworldly kingdom: they mediate (as priests) heaven's authority (kingship) on earth.

Without a garden or national boundaries, the church's sacred space finds expression in the body of believers indwelt by the Spirit and assembled together (Matt. 18:20).[3] A temple made without hands, the

---

[2] Malone (2017: 147–178) unpacks at length what he calls 'the church's priestly commission'.
[3] I write as a Baptist, but much of this section is applicable across denominational lines. Jonathan Leeman (2016a) has presented a robust biblical-theological treatment of royal priesthood to argue for congregational polity. His views are representative of (and have influenced!) my own ecclesiological convictions.

church must exercise its priestly rule by distinguishing insiders from outsiders, holy from unholy, truth from deception, the gospel of the kingdom from the lies of the evil one (Matt. 18:15–20; 1 Cor. 5). Even in the new-covenant administration, the garden must grow, the temple must expand. The new Adam succeeds where the old failed. Crowned with glory and honour, Jesus builds his temple through the church's proclamation of the gospel. Every time an unbeliever is born again through the preaching of God's Word, the temple expands. Another blood-bought brick is added to the temple of Christ's body and the whole structure grows into a holy temple in the Lord (Eph. 2:21–22).

The work of new-covenant priest-kings no longer includes tabernacles, blood sacrifice, altars or the enforcement of civil laws in society at large. Instead, gospel proclamation, baptism, the Lord's Supper, church discipline and prayer shape the church's priestly ministry. In 1 Peter 2:9, the language of old-covenant Israel is applied to the new-covenant people of God: they are a 'chosen race', a 'royal priesthood', a 'holy nation', a 'people for his [God's] own possession' (ESV). Christ now mediates his rule and blessing through his new-covenant people. King Jesus has all authority in heaven and on earth (Matt. 28:18–20). He has given his church a commission to take the gospel to nations and summon them to repentance and faith. In Peter's words, God's people must 'proclaim the excellencies of him who called you out of darkness and into his marvellous light' (1 Pet. 2:9 ESV). Their ministry of proclamation seems to clarify Peter's earlier statement about the 'spiritual sacrifices' they offer up as a 'holy priesthood' (1 Pet. 2:5 ESV).[4]

The ordinances of baptism and the Lord's Supper delineate the church's boundaries; they distinguish insiders from outsiders. Through baptism, people once excluded from the church's membership are brought in. They are formally recognized as citizens of Christ's kingdom and tasked with responsibility as new-covenant priest-kings. Through participation in the Lord's Supper, God's people are continually set apart by a common meal (1 Cor. 10:17). Abraham's children are identifiable not by their ancestry, ethnicity or geography but by their reception of the new Melchizedek's bread and wine. Christ, the priest-king, shares his table with the members of his priestly family and authorizes them to administer the bread and wine to others in the new-covenant community.

---

4 Malone (2017: 147–153) develops this argument.

Christ mediates his authority from heaven through his priestly family on earth. He gives local churches – wherever two or three are gathered – the authority to speak on behalf of heaven's kingdom. They wield the keys of the kingdom of heaven when they render judgments on unrepentant brothers and sisters, declaring them to be like 'Gentiles and tax-collectors' (cf. Matt. 18:15–17). Through church discipline, a collective body of priest-kings guards the gospel, purifies the temple and strengthens the community's witness as a holy people.

Until Christ comes again, the church takes part in the priestly ministry of intercession for the nations. In Revelation 5:8, the golden bowls of incense around the throne of God are the prayers of his saints – a people identified as a kingdom and priests in Revelation 5:10. Paul's instructions in 1 Timothy 2:1–2 summon the church to offer intercessory prayer for all people, even rulers of nations, and people in authority. In all these ways, the church serves God and blesses the watching world. Routledge similarly applies Psalm 110 to the church today:

> More particularly, in the light of the discussion of what it means to be a priest after the order of Melchizedek, we recognize that a key part of our calling (and in 1 Pet. 2:9 we are also described as priests) is to be a channel of God's blessing to the people of God (and to the world). Read in this way, the psalm not only blesses *us*, it also challenges us to live up to our calling to be a means by which the blessing of God flows to others.[5]

Apologetics

I completed this book while serving as a pastor of a local church in the state of Utah, which is the central hub of the Church of Jesus Christ of Latter-day Saints (LDS). Many of my Mormon neighbours claim to hold the office of the Melchizedekian priesthood. Utah is one of the few places where Melchizedek is a regular topic of evangelistic conversation. Mormonism teaches that the offices of the Aaronic and Melchizedekian priesthoods are still in effect and held by worthy male members of the Mormon Church.[6] The argument of this book has proved that such teachings are in opposition to the Bible. Christ has rendered the Aaronic

---

5 Routledge 2009: 16; emphasis original.
6 Doctrine and Covenants 2013: ch. 107.

priesthood obsolete, and Christ alone qualifies for the office of the Melchizedekian priesthood on the basis of his sinless perfection and indestructible life (Heb. 7:16, 26). He holds his priesthood permanently and is, therefore, able to save to the uttermost those who draw near to God through him, since he always lives to intercede for them (Heb. 7:25). No other human being has risen from the dead to conquer death. No other human being can enter heaven on the merits of his own blood and mediate God's blessing to the nations for ever. Jesus holds this office permanently, singularly and without successors. While it is true that all believers in the new-covenant era are made royal priests like Adam and Israel (cf. 1 Pet. 2:9), no Christian, nor anyone else, can claim to represent the antitypical fulfilment of Melchizedek's priesthood. To do so is to undermine the singularity and sufficiency of Christ's redemptive work.

While some doctrines that divide Mormons and Christians may seem abstract and inconsequential to the average Mormon, priesthood and temples are part of everyday Mormon life. Christians seeking to share the gospel with Mormons would do well to understand how priesthood and temples fit into salvation history and find their fulfilment in Christ. Instead of inoculating Mormons against the gospel by wrongly mitigating the differences that divide Mormonism and Christianity, evangelicals need to know how to reason from the Scriptures to point them to the Great High Priest who saves by the gracious power of his atoning sacrifice.

Closing comments

Psalm 110 is one of the best-known passages of Scripture. By no means has this book settled all the exegetical, theological and interpretative issues associated with this psalm – nor was that the goal. I focused on one of this psalm's most difficult problems, namely, how to make sense out of the union of kingship and priesthood in a way that assumes the integrity of Scripture and its authors. My investigation began with the assumption that Psalm 110 was part of a much bigger biblical-theological trajectory than the Melchizedek episode of Genesis 14:17–24 alone. These pages have tried to prove that assumption by connecting Psalm 110 to the Bible's unfolding story.

Our job is to read the Bible the way the biblical authors did. An investigation into Psalm 110 helps us understand how to put the Bible together in a way that honours the interpretative perspectives of the biblical authors. Melchizedek, as mysterious as he may initially appear, is, as Carson stated, 'one of the most instructive figures in the Bible for helping us put our Bibles together'.[7] Jesus is our king of righteousness, our king of peace and our great high priest to whom all glory is due. He is in heaven right now holding Melchizedek's office and 'able to save to the uttermost those who draw near to God through him, since he always lives to make intercession for them' (Heb. 7:25 ESV). One day, all his enemies will be made a footstool for his feet, and all his people will reign with him as a kingdom and priests to God (Ps. 110:1; Rev. 5:10).

---

[7] Carson 2013: 147.

Bibliography

Adeyemo, T. (ed.) (2010), *Africa Bible Commentary: A One-Volume Commentary Written by 70 African Scholars*, ePub edn, Grand Rapids: Zondervan.

Alden, R. L. (1978), 'Chiastic Psalms (III): A Study in the Mechanics of Semitic Poetry in Psalms 101–150', *JETS* 21.3: 199–210.

Alexander, T. D. (2003), *The Servant King: The Bible's Portrait of the Messiah*, Vancouver: Regent College Publishing.

—— (2009), *From Eden to the New Jerusalem: An Introduction to Biblical Theology*, Grand Rapids: Kregel Academic & Professional.

—— (2012), *From Paradise to the Promised Land: An Introduction to the Pentateuch*, Grand Rapids: Baker Academic.

Allen, L. C. (2002), *Psalms 101–150*, WBC 21, 2nd rev. edn, Mexico City: Thomas Nelson.

Aloisi, J. (2005), 'Who Is David's Lord? Another Look at Psalm 110:1', *DBSJ* 10: 103–123.

Anderson, D. R. (2001), *The King-Priest of Psalm 110 in Hebrews*, New York: Peter Lang.

Andreasen, A. (1980), 'Gen 14 in Its Near Eastern Context', in C. D. Evans, W. W. Hallo and J. B. White (eds.), *Scripture in Context: Essays on the Comparative Method*, Pittsburgh: Pickwick, 59–77.

Armerding, C. E. (2004), '"Did I Ever Ask for a House of Cedar?" The Contribution of 2 Samuel and 1 Chronicles 17 to the Theology of the Temple', in T. D. Alexander and S. Gathercole (eds.), *Heaven on Earth: The Temple in Biblical Theology*, Carlisle: Paternoster, 35–47.

Arnold, B. T. (2008), *Genesis*, New Cambridge Bible Commentary, Cambridge: Cambridge University Press.

Aschim, A. (1999). 'Melchizedek and Jesus: 11Q Melchizedek and the Epistle to the Hebrews', in C. C. Newman, J. R. Davila and G. S. Lewis (eds.), *The Jewish Roots of Christological Monotheism: Papers from the St. Andrews Conference on the Historical Origins of the Worship of Jesus*, JSJSup 63, Leiden: Brill, 129–147.

Attridge, H. W. (1989), *The Epistle to the Hebrews: A Commentary on the Epistle to the Hebrews*, Hermeneia, Philadelphia: Fortress.

Averbeck, R. E. (2002), 'Sumer, the Bible, and Comparative Method: Historiography and Temple Building', in M. W. Chavalas and K. L. Younger (eds.), *Mesopotamia and the Bible: Comparative Explorations*, Grand Rapids: Baker Academic, 88–125.

Babota, V. (2014), *The Institution of the Hasmonean High Priesthood*, Boston: Brill.

Baker, D. L. (1976), 'Typology and the Christian Use of the Old Testament', *SJT* 29.2: 137–157.

Balla, P. (2000), 'Challenges to Biblical Theology', *NDBT*, 20–27.

Barber, M. P. (2001), *Singing in the Reign: The Psalms and the Liturgy of God's Kingdom*, Steubenville: Emmaus Road.

Barr, J. (1968), 'The Image of God in the Book of Genesis: A Study of Terminology', *BJRL* 51.1: 11–26.

Barrett, C. K. (1964), 'The Eschatology of the Epistle to the Hebrews', in W. D. Davies and D. Daube (eds.), *Background of the New Testament and Its Eschatology*, Cambridge: Cambridge University Press, 363–393.

Barthélemy, D. (2005), *Critique textuelle de l'Ancien Testament*, Tome 4: *Psaumes*, OBO 50.4, Fribourg: Academic Press; Göttingen: Vandenhoeck & Ruprecht.

Bartholomew, C. G. (2011), *Where Mortals Dwell: A Christian View of Place for Today*, Grand Rapids: Baker Academic.

Bateman, H. W. (1992), 'Psalm 110:1 and the New Testament', *BSac* 149.596: 438–453.

—— (1997), *Early Jewish Hermeneutics and Hebrews 1:5–13: The Impact of Early Jewish Exegesis on the Interpretation of a Significant New Testament Passage*, American University Studies 7: Theology and Religion 193, New York: Peter Lang.

—— (2001), 'Psalm 45:6–7 and Its Christological Contributions to Hebrews', *TJ* 22.1: 3–21.

Bauckham, R. (1999), 'The Throne of God and the Worship of Jesus', in C. C. Newman, J. R. Davila and G. S. Lewis (eds.), *The Jewish Roots of Christological Monotheism: Papers from the St. Andrews Conference on the Historical Origins of the Worship of Jesus*, JSJSup 63, Leiden: Brill, 43–69.

—— (2009), 'The Divinity of Jesus Christ in the Epistle to the Hebrews', in R. Bauckham, D. R. Driver, T. A. Hart and N. MacDonald (eds.), *The Epistle to the Hebrews and Christian Theology*, Grand Rapids: Eerdmans, 15–36.

Beale, G. K. (2004), *The Temple and the Church's Mission: A Biblical Theology of the Dwelling Place of God*, NSBT 17, Leicester: Apollos; Downers Grove: InterVarsity Press.

—— (2011), *A New Testament Biblical Theology: The Unfolding of the Old Testament in the New*, Grand Rapids: Baker Academic.

—— (2012), *Handbook on the New Testament Use of the Old Testament: Exegesis and Interpretation*, Grand Rapids: Baker Academic.

Becker, J. (1998), *Jesus of Nazareth*, tr. J. E. Crouch, Berlin: De Gruyter.

Beckerleg, C. L. (2009), 'The "Image of God" in Eden: The Creation of Mankind in Genesis 2:5–3:24 in Light of the Mīs Pî Pīt Pî and Wpt-R Rituals of Mesopotamia and Ancient Egypt', PhD diss., Harvard University.

Beecher, W. J. (1905), *The Prophets and the Promise*, New York: Thomas Y. Crowell & Co.

Blackburn, W. R. (2012), *The God Who Makes Himself Known: The Missionary Heart of the Book of Exodus*, NSBT 28, Nottingham; Apollos; Downers Grove: InterVarsity Press.

Block, D. I. (2003), 'My Servant David: Ancient Israel's Vision of the Messiah', in R. S. Hess and M. Daniel Carroll R. (eds.), *Israel's Messiah in the Bible and the Dead Sea Scrolls*, Grand Rapids: Baker Academic, 17–56.

—— (2013), 'Eden: A Temple? A Reassessment of the Biblical Evidence', in D. M. Gurtner and B. L. Gladd (eds.), *From Creation to New Creation: Biblical Theology and Exegesis: Essays in Honor of G. K. Beale*, Peabody: Hendrickson, 3–32.

Bowker, J. W. (1967), 'Psalm CX', *VT* 17.1: 31–41.

Briggs, C. A., and E. G. Briggs (1907), *A Critical and Exegetical Commentary on the Book of Psalms*, vol. 2, New York: Charles Scribner's Sons.

Broadhead, E. K. (1992), 'Christology as Polemic and Apologetic: The Priestly Portrait of Jesus in the Gospel of Mark', *JSNT* 47: 21–34.

Brown, W. P. (1998), 'A Royal Performance: Critical Notes on Psalm 110:3aγ–b', *JBL* 117.1: 93–96.

Brueggemann, D. A. (2005), 'The Evangelists and the Psalms',
in P. Johnston and D. G. Firth (eds.), *Interpreting the Psalms: Issues
and Approaches*, Leicester: Apollos; Downers Grove: IVP Academic,
264–278.

Brutti, M. (2006), *The Development of the High Priesthood during the
Pre-Hasmonean Period: History, Ideology, Theology*, ed. J. J. Collins,
JSJSup 108, Boston: Brill.

Buchanan, G. W. (1972), *To the Hebrews*, AB 36, Garden City: Doubleday.

Calaway, J. (2013), *The Sabbath and the Sanctuary: Access to God in the
Letter to the Hebrews and Its Priestly Context*, WUNT 2/349,
Tübingen: Mohr Siebeck.

Caneday, A. B. (2008), 'The Eschatological World Already Subjected to
the Son: The Οἰκουμένη of Hebrews 1:6 and the Son's Enthronement',
in R. Bauckham, D. Driver, T. Hart and N. MacDonald (eds.),
*A Cloud of Witnesses: The Theology of Hebrews in Its Ancient
Contexts*, LNTS 387, London: T&T Clark, 28–39.

Carmignac, J. (1970), 'Le Document de Qumran sur Melkisédeq',
Revue de Qumran 7.3: 343–378.

Carson, D. A. (2012), *Jesus the Son of God: A Christological Title Often
Overlooked, Sometimes Misunderstood, and Currently Disputed*,
Wheaton: Crossway.

—— (2013), 'Getting Excited about Melchizedek (Psalm 110)', in
D. A. Carson (ed.), *The Scriptures Testify about Me: Jesus and the
Gospel in the Old Testament*, Wheaton: Crossway, 145–174.

Charles, R. H. (1913), *Pseudepigrapha of the Old Testament*, vol. 2,
Oxford: Clarendon.

—— (2005), *Commentary on the Pseudepigrapha of the Old Testament*,
vol. 2, Bellingham: Logos Bible Software.

Charlesworth, J. H. (ed.) (2009), *The Old Testament Pseudepigrapha*,
vol. 1, Peabody: Hendrickson.

Cheung, A. T. M. (1986), 'The Priest as the Redeemed Man: A Biblical-
Theological Study of the Priesthood', *JETS* 29.3: 265–275.

Childs, B. S. (1979), *Introduction to the Old Testament as Scripture*,
Philadelphia: Fortress.

Chrysostom, J. (1998), *St. John Chrysostom Commentary on the Psalms*,
vol. 2, tr. R. C. Hill, Brookline: Holy Cross Orthodox Press.

Cockerill, G. L. (1976), 'The Melchizedek Christology in Hebrews
7:1–28', PhD diss., Union Theological Seminary.

—— (1999), 'Hebrews 1:6: Source and Significance', *BBR* 9: 51–64.

—— (2001), 'Structure and Interpretation in Hebrews 8:1–10:18: A Symphony in Three Movements', *BBR* 11.2: 179–201.

—— (2008), 'Melchizedek without Speculation: Hebrews 7.1–25 and Genesis 14.17–24', in R. Bauckham, D. Driver, T. Hart and N. MacDonald (eds.), *A Cloud of Witnesses: The Theology of Hebrews in Its Ancient Contexts*, LNTS 387, London: T&T Clark, 128–144.

Cole, G. A. (2013), *The God Who Became Human: A Biblical Theology of Incarnation*, NSBT 30, Nottingham: Apollos; Downers Grove: InterVarsity Press.

Cole, R. L. (2013), *Psalms 1–2: Gateway to the Psalter*, Hebrew Bible Monographs, Phoenix: Sheffield Phoenix.

—— (2014), 'Psalms 1 and 2: The Psalter's Introduction', in D. M. Howard and A. J. Schmutzer (eds.), *The Psalms: Language for All Seasons of the Soul*, Chicago: Moody, 183–196.

Collins, J. C. (2022), *ESV Expository Commentary: Psalms–Song of Solomon*, vol. 5, ed. I. M. Duguid, J. M. Hamilton Jr and J. Sklar, Wheaton: Crossway.

Collins, J. J. (2010), *The Scepter and the Star: Messianism in Light of the Dead Sea Scrolls*, 2nd edn, Grand Rapids: Eerdmans.

Compton, J. (2015), *Psalm 110 and the Logic of Hebrews*, LNTS 537, New York: Bloomsbury T&T Clark.

Creach, J. F. D. (2020), *Discovering the Psalms*, Content, Interpretation, Reception, London: SPCK.

Crutchfield, J. C. (2011), *Psalms in Their Context: An Interpretation of Psalms 107–118*, Paternoster Biblical Monographs, Milton Keynes: Paternoster.

Dahood, M. (1970), *Psalms III: 101–150*, AB 17A, New Haven: Yale University Press.

D'Angelo, M. R. (1979), *Moses in the Letter to the Hebrews*, Missoula: Scholars Press.

Danker, F. W., W. Bauer, W. F. Arndt and F. W. Gingrich (2000), *Greek–English Lexicon of the New Testament and Other Early Christian Literature*, 3rd edn, Chicago: University of Chicago Press.

Davidson, A. B. (1900), 'Duhm's *Die Psalmen: Erklärt*', in S. D. F. Salmond (ed.), *The Critical Review of Theological and Philosophical Literature*, vol. 10, Edinburgh: Williams & Northgate, 446–449.

Davidson, R. M. (1981), *Typology in Scripture: A Study of Hermeneutical Typos Structures*, Berrien Springs: Andrews University Press.

Davies, J. (2004), *A Royal Priesthood: Literary and Intertextual Perspectives on an Image of Israel in Exodus 19.6*, New York: T&T Clark International.

Davis, B. C. (2000), 'Is Psalm 110 a Messianic Psalm?', *BSac* 157.626: 160–173.

Day, J. (1985), *God's Conflict with the Dragon and the Sea: Echoes of a Canaanite Myth in the Old Testament*, Cambridge: Cambridge University Press.

—— (1998), 'The Canaanite Inheritance of the Israelite Monarchy', in J. Day (ed.), *King and Messiah in Israel and the Ancient Near East: Proceedings of the Oxford Old Testament Seminar*, JSOTSup 270, Sheffield: Sheffield Academic Press, 72–90.

DeClaissé-Walford, N. L. (1997), *Reading from the Beginning: The Shaping of the Hebrew Psalter*, Macon: Mercer University Press.

—— (2014), *The Shape and Shaping of the Book of Psalms: The Current State of Scholarship*, Ancient Israel and Its Literature 20, Atlanta: SBL Press.

Deenick, K. (2011), 'Priest and King or Priest-King in 1 Samuel 2:35', *WTJ* 73.2: 325–339.

Demarest, B. A. (1976), *A History of Interpretation of Hebrews 7, 1–10 from the Reformation to the Present*, Tübingen: Mohr Siebeck.

Dempster, S. G. (2003), *Dominion and Dynasty: A Biblical Theology of the Hebrew Bible*, NSBT 15, Leicester: Apollos; Downers Grove: InterVarsity Press.

DeSilva, D. A. (2000), *Perseverance in Gratitude: A Socio-Rhetorical Commentary on the Epistle to the Hebrews*, Grand Rapids: Eerdmans.

Dewey, J. (1973), 'Literary Structure of the Controversy Stories in Mark 2:1–3:6', *JBL* 92.3: 394–401.

Docherty, S. E. (2009), *The Use of the Old Testament in Hebrews: A Case Study in Early Jewish Bible Interpretation*, WUNT 2/260, Tübingen: Mohr Siebeck.

The Doctrine and Covenants of the Church of Jesus Christ of Latter-day Saints: Containing Revelations Given to Joseph Smith, the Prophet, with Some Additions by His Successors in the Presidency of the Church (2013), Salt Lake City: Church of Jesus Christ of Latter-day Saints.

Donahue, J. R. (1976), 'Temple, Trial and Royal Christology (Mark 14:53–65)', in Werner H. Kelber (ed.), *The Passion in Mark: Studies on Mark 14–16*, Philadelphia: Fortress, 61–79.

Driver, G. R. (1964), 'Psalm CX: Its Form, Meaning and Purpose', in J. M. Grintz and J. Liver (eds.), *Studies in the Bible*, Jerusalem: Kiryat Sepher, 17–31.

Duhm, B. (1899), *Die Psalmen: Erklärt*, Leipzig: Mohr Siebeck.

Dumbrell, W. J. (2002), 'Genesis 2:1–17: A Foreshadowing of the New Creation', in Scott J. Hafemann (ed.), *Biblical Theology: Retrospect and Prospect*, Leicester: Apollos; Downers Grove: InterVarsity Press, 53–65.

—— (2009), *Covenant and Creation: A Theology of Old Testament Covenants*, repr., Eugene: Wipf & Stock.

Dunnill, J. (2005), *Covenant and Sacrifice in the Letter to the Hebrews*, SNTSMS 75, Cambridge: Cambridge University Press.

Easter, M. C. (2014), *Faith and the Faithfulness of Jesus in Hebrews*, SNTSMS 160. Cambridge: Cambridge University Press.

Eaton, J. (2004), *The Psalms: A Historical and Spiritual Commentary with an Introduction and New Translation*, New York: T&T Clark.

Edelkoort, A. H. (1941), *De Christusverwachting in het Oude Testament*, Wageningen: Veenman.

Edmund, K. (1961), *Herder's Commentary on the Psalms*, tr. B. Fritz, Westminster: Newman.

Eichrodt, W. (1961), *Theology of the Old Testament*, vol. 1, tr. J. A. Baker, London: SCM Press.

Ellingworth, P. (1983), '"Like the Son of God": Form and Content in Hebrews 7,1–10', *Bib* 64.2: 255–262.

—— (1993), *The Epistle to the Hebrews: A Commentary on the Greek Text*, NIGTC, Grand Rapids: Eerdmans.

Ellison, S. D. (2021), 'Hope for a Davidic King in the Psalter's Utopian Vision', PhD diss., Queen's University Belfast.

Emerton, J. A. (1971), 'The Riddle of Genesis XIV', *VT* 21.4: 403–439.

Fairbairn, P. (1852), *The Typology of Scripture*, Philadelphia: Daniels & Smith.

Feldmeier, R., and H. Spieckermann (2021), *God Becoming Human: Incarnation in the Christian Bible*, tr. B. McNeil, Waco: Baylor University Press.

Fesko, J. V. (2007), *Last Things First: Unlocking Genesis 1–3 with the Christ of Eschatology*, Fearn: Mentor.

Fitzmyer, J. A. (2000), 'Melchizedek in the MT, LXX, and the NT', *Bib* 81.1: 63–69.

Fletcher-Louis, C. H. T. (1997), 'The High Priest as Divine Mediator in the Hebrew Bible: Dan 7.13 as a Test Case', *SBLSP* 36: 161–193.

—— (1999), 'The Worship of Divine Humanity as God's Image and the Worship of Jesus', in C. C. Newman, J. R. Davila and G. S. Lewis (eds.), *Jewish Roots of Christological Monotheism: Papers from the St. Andrews Conference on the Historical Origins of the Worship of Jesus*, JSJSup 63, Leiden: Brill, 112–128.

—— (2000), 'Jesus Inspects His Priestly War Party (Luke 14.25–35)', in S. Moyise (ed.), *Old Testament in the New Testament: Essays in Honour of J. L. North*, LNTS 189, Sheffield: Sheffield Academic Press, 126–143.

—— (2002), *All the Glory of Adam: Liturgical Anthropology in the Dead Sea Scrolls*, Leiden: Brill.

—— (2006), 'Jesus as the High Priestly Messiah: Part 1', *JSHJ* 4.2: 155–175.

—— (2007), 'Jesus as the High Priestly Messiah: Part 2', *JSHJ* 5.1: 57–79.

Gammie, J. G. (1969), 'A New Setting for Psalm 110', *ATR* 51.1: 4–17.

Garr, W. R. (2003), *In His Own Image and Likeness: Humanity, Divinity, and Monotheism*, Leiden: Brill.

Gathercole, S. (2004), 'The Son of Man in Mark's Gospel', *ExpTim* 115.11: 365–372.

Gentry, P. J., and S. J. Wellum (2012), *Kingdom through Covenant: A Biblical-Theological Understanding of the Covenants*, Wheaton: Crossway.

Gerleman, G. (1981), 'Psalm 110', *VT* 31.1: 1–19.

Gladd, B. L. (2021), *Handbook on the Gospels*, Grand Rapids: Baker Academic.

Goldsworthy, G. (2000), *The Goldsworthy Trilogy*, Exeter: Paternoster.

—— (2002), *According to Plan: The Unfolding Revelation of God in the Bible*, Downers Grove: IVP Academic.

—— (2006), *Gospel-Centered Hermeneutics: Foundations and Principles of Evangelical Biblical Interpretation*, Downers Grove: IVP Academic.

Goswell, G. (2013), 'Joshua and Kingship', *BBR* 23.1: 29–42.

Goulder, M. D. (1998), *The Psalms of the Return (Book V, Psalms 107–150)*, JSOTSup 258, Sheffield: Sheffield Academic Press.

Grabbe, L. L. (1995), *Priests, Prophets, Diviners, Sages: A Socio-Historical Study of Religious Specialists in Ancient Israel*, Valley Forge: Trinity Press International.

Granerød, G. (2010), *Abraham and Melchizedek: Scribal Activity of Second Temple Times in Genesis 14 and Psalm 110*, BZAW 406, New York: De Gruyter.

Grant, J. A. (2004), *The King as Exemplar: The Function of Deuteronomy's Kingship Law in the Shaping of the Book of Psalms*, Atlanta: SBL Press.

Grogan, G. W. (2008), *Psalms*, Two Horizons Old Testament Commentary, Grand Rapids: Eerdmans.

Grohmann, M. (2010), 'Metaphors of God, Nature and Birth in Psalm 90,2 and Psalm 110,3', in P. Van Hecke and A. Labahn (eds.), *Metaphors in the Psalms*, BETL 231, Leuven: Uitgeverij Peeters, 23–33.

Gruber, M. I. (2004), *Rashi's Commentary on Psalms*, Boston: Brill.

Gudorf, M. E. (2000), 'Through a Classical Lens: Hebrews 2:16', *JBL* 119.1: 105–108.

Guthrie, G. H. (2005), 'Hebrews', in G. K. Beale and D. A. Carson (eds.), *Commentary on the New Testament Use of the Old Testament*, Nottingham: Apollos; Grand Rapids: Baker Academic, 919–995.

Haber, S. (2005), 'From Priestly Torah to Christ Cultus: The Re-Vision of Covenant and Cult in Hebrews', *JSNT* 28.1: 105–124.

Hafemann, S. J. (2001), *The God of Promise and the Life of Faith: Understanding the Heart of the Bible*, Wheaton: Crossway.

Hagner, D. A. (2002), *Encountering the Book of Hebrews: An Exposition*, Grand Rapids: Baker Academic.

Hahn, S. (2009), *Kinship by Covenant: A Canonical Approach to the Fulfillment of God's Saving Promises*, New Haven: Yale University Press.

Hallo, W. W., and K. L. Younger (eds.) (1997), *The Context of Scripture: Canonical Compositions from the Biblical World*, Leiden: Brill.

Hamilton, J. M. (2006), 'The Skull Crushing Seed of the Woman: Inner-Biblical Interpretation of Genesis 3:15', *SBJT* 10.2: 30–54.

—— (2007), 'The Seed of the Woman and the Blessing of Abraham', *TynBul* 58.2: 253–273.

—— (2010), *God's Glory in Salvation through Judgment: A Biblical Theology*, Wheaton: Crossway.

—— (2012), 'The Typology of David's Rise to Power: Messianic Patterns in the Book of Samuel', *SBJT* 16: 4–25.

—— (2014a), *What Is Biblical Theology? A Guide to the Bible's Story, Symbolism, and Patterns*, Wheaton: Crossway.

—— (2014b), *With the Clouds of Heaven: The Book of Daniel in Biblical Theology*, NSBT 32, Nottingham: Apollos; Downers Grove: InterVarsity Press.

—— (2021), *Psalms: Volume 2*, Evangelical Biblical Theology Commentary, ed. T. D. Alexander, T. R. Schreiner, A. J. Köstenberger, Bellingham: Lexham Academic.

—— (2022), *Typology: Understanding the Bible's Promised-Shaped Patterns: How Old Testament Expectations Are Fulfilled in Christ*, Grand Rapids: Zondervan Academic.

Haney, R. G. (2002), *Text and Concept Analysis in Royal Psalms*, New York: Peter Lang.

Harris, D. M. (2009), 'The Eternal Inheritance in Hebrews: The Appropriation of the Old Testament Inheritance Motif by the Author of Hebrews', PhD diss., Trinity Evangelical Divinity School.

Hay, D. M. (1973), *Glory at the Right Hand: Psalm 110 in Early Christianity*, Atlanta: Abingdon.

Hays, J. D. (2003), 'If He Looks Like a Prophet and Talks Like a Prophet, Then He Must Be . . . ', in R. S. Hess and M. Daniel Carroll R. (eds.), *Israel's Messiah in the Bible and the Dead Sea Scrolls*, Grand Rapids: Baker Academic, 57–69.

Helck, W. (1961), *Urkunden der 18. Dynastie: Übersetzung zu den Heften 17–22*, Berlin: Akademie-Verlag.

Hengel, M. (1995), *Studies in Early Christology*, London: T&T Clark.

Hilber, J. W. (2005), *Cultic Prophecy in the Psalms*, BZAW, Berlin: De Gruyter.

Horton Jr, F. L. (1976), *The Melchizedek Tradition: A Critical Examination of the Sources to the Fifth Century A.D. and in the Epistle to the Hebrews*, SNTSMS 30, Cambridge: Cambridge University Press.

Hossfeld, F. L., and E. Zenger (2011), *Psalms 3: A Commentary on Psalms 101–150*, Hermeneia, Minneapolis: Fortress.

Ishida, T. (1977), *The Royal Dynasties in Ancient Israel: A Study on the Formation and Development of Royal-Dynastic Ideology*, Berlin: de Gruyter.

Jamieson, B. (2015), *Going Public: Why Baptism Is Required for Church Membership*, Nashville: B&H Academic.

—— (2021), *The Paradox of Sonship: Christology in the Epistle to the Hebrews*, Studies in Christian Doctrine and Scripture, Downers Grove: InterVarsity Press.

Jipp, J. W. (2010), 'The Son's Entrance into the Heavenly World: The Soteriological Necessity of the Scriptural Catena in Hebrews 1.5–14', *NTS* 56.4: 557–575.

Johnson, A. R. (1955), *Sacral Kingship in Ancient Israel*, Cardiff: University of Wales Press.

Johnson, D. E. (2018), *ESV Expository Commentary: Hebrews–Revelation*, vol. 12, ed. I. M. Duguid, J. M. Hamilton Jr and J. Sklar, Wheaton: Crossway.

Johnson, E. E. (1992), 'Hermeneutical Principles and the Interpretation of Psalm 110', *BSac* 149.596: 428–437.

Jonge, M. de, and A. S. van der Woude (1966), '11Q Melchizedek and the New Testament', *NTS* 12.4: 301–326.

Jordaan, G. J., and P. Nel (2010), 'From Priest-King to King-Priest: Psalm 110 and the Basic Structure of Hebrews', in D. J. Human and G. J. Steyn (eds.), *Psalms and Hebrews: Studies in Reception*, LHBOTS 527, New York: T&T Clark, 229–240.

Josephus, F. (1981), *The Complete Works of Josephus*, ed. W. Whiston, Grand Rapids: Kregel.

Joüon, P., and T. Muraoka (2009), *A Grammar of Biblical Hebrew*, 2nd edn, with corrections, Rome: Gregorian and Biblical Press.

Kaiser, W. C. (1974), 'The Blessing of David: The Charter for Humanity', in J. H. Skilton, M. C. Fisher and L. W. Sloat (eds.), *The Law and the Prophets: Old Testament Studies Prepared in Honor of Oswald Thompson Allis*, Philadelphia: P&R, 298–318.

Kee, H. C. (1983), 'Testaments of the Twelve Patriarchs: A New Translation and Introduction', in J. H. Charlesworth (ed.), *The Old Testament Pseudepigrapha: Apocalyptic Literature and Testaments*, vol. 1, Peabody: Hendrickson, 775–828.

Keel, O. (1978), *The Symbolism of the Biblical World: Ancient Near Eastern Iconography and the Book of Psalms*, New York: Seabury.

Keener, H. K. (2013), *A Canonical Exegesis of the Eighth Psalm: YHWH's Maintenance of the Created Order through Divine Reversal*, JTISup 9, Winona Lake: Eisenbrauns.

Bibliography

Keil, C. F. (1887), *Manual of Biblical Archaeology*, vol. 1, ed. F. Crombie, tr. P. Christie, Edinburgh: T&T Clark.

Keil, C. F., and F. Delitzsch (1996), *Commentary on the Old Testament*, vol. 5, Peabody: Hendrickson.

Kidner, D. (2008), *Psalms 73–150*, TOTC, Leicester: Inter-Varsity Press; Downers Grove: InterVarsity Press.

Kilner, J. F. (2015), *Dignity and Destiny: Humanity in the Image of God*, Grand Rapids: Eerdmans.

Kim, J. (2003), 'Psalm 110 in Its Literary and Generic Contexts: An Eschatological Interpretation', PhD diss., Westminster Theological Seminary.

Kissane, E. J. (1954), *The Book of Psalms*, vol. 2, Dublin: The Richview Press.

Kistemaker, S. (2008), 'Psalm 110 in the Epistle to the Hebrews', in R. L. Penny (ed.), *The Hope Fulfilled: Essays in Honor of O. Palmer Robertson*, Phillipsburg: P&R, 138–149.

—— (2010), *The Psalm Citations in the Epistle to the Hebrews*, Eugene: Wipf & Stock.

Kitchen, K. A. (2003), *On the Reliability of the Old Testament*, Grand Rapids: Eerdmans.

Kline, M. G. (1977), 'Investiture with the Image of God', *WTJ* 40.1: 39–62.

—— (2000), *Kingdom Prologue: Genesis Foundations for a Covenantal Worldview*, Overland Park: Two Age Press.

Klink III, E. W., and D. R. Lockett (2006), *Understanding Biblical Theology: A Comparison of Theory and Practice*, Grand Rapids: Zondervan.

Knohl, I. (2009), 'Melchizedek: A Model for the Union of Kingship and Priesthood in the Hebrew Bible, 11QMelchizedek, and the Epistle to the Hebrews', in R. A. Clements and D. R. Schwartz (eds.), *Text, Thought and Practice in Qumran and Early Christianity: Proceedings of the Ninth International Symposium of the Orion Center for the Study of the Dead Sea Scrolls and Associated Literature*, STDJ 84, Leiden: Brill, 255–266.

Kobelski, P. J. (1981), *Melchizedek and Melchiresa*, Washington, DC: Catholic Biblical Association of America.

Koester, C. R. (2001), *Hebrews: A New Translation with Commentary*, AB 36, New York: Doubleday.

Kraus, H.-J. (1978), *Psalmen 60–150*, ed. S. Herrmann and H. W. Wolff, BKAT 15, Neukirchen-Vluyn: Neukirchener Verlag.

—— (1986), *Theology of the Psalms*, tr. K. R. Crim, Minneapolis: Augsburg.

Kugler, R. A. (1996), *From Patriarch to Priest: The Levi-Priestly Tradition from Aramaic Levi to Testament of Levi*, Early Judaism and Its Literature 9, Atlanta: Scholars Press, 1996.

Kurianal, J. (2000), *Jesus Our High Priest: Ps 110,4 as the Substructure of Heb 5, 1–7, 28*, New York: Peter Lang.

Lampe, G. W. H., and K. J. Woollcombe (1957), *Essays on Typology*, vol. 22, Naperville: Alec R. Allenson.

—— (1974), *The Gospel of Mark: The English Text with Introduction, Exposition, and Notes*, NICNT, Grand Rapids: Eerdmans.

Lane, W. L. (1991), *Hebrews 1–8*, WBC 47, Dallas: Word.

Lange, A., and M. Weigold (2011), *Biblical Quotations and Allusions in Second Temple Jewish Literature*, Göttingen: Vandenhoeck & Ruprecht.

Laub, F. (1980), *Bekenntnis und Auslegung: die paränetische Funktion der Christologie im Hebräerbrief*, Regensburg: Pustet.

Leeman, J. (2010), *The Church and the Surprising Offense of God's Love: Reintroducing the Doctrines of Church Membership and Discipline*, Wheaton: Crossway.

—— (2016a), *Don't Fire Your Church Members: The Case for Congregationalism*, Nashville: B&H Academic.

—— (2016b), *Political Church: The Local Assembly as Embassy of Christ's Rule*, Studies in Christian Doctrine and Scripture, Downers Grove: IVP Academic.

Lehne, S. (1990), *The New Covenant in Hebrews*, JSNTSup 44, Sheffield: JSOT Press.

Leithart, P. J. (1999), 'Attendants of Yahweh's House: Priesthood in the Old Testament', *JSOT* 24.85: 3–24.

Letham, R. (1993), *The Work of Christ*, Contours of Christian Theology, Leicester: Inter-Varsity Press; Downers Grove: InterVarsity Press.

Levinsohn, S. H. (2011), *Self-Instruction Materials on Non-Narrative Discourse Analysis*, Dallas: SIL International, <www.sil.org/~levinsohns>, accessed 8 February 2015.

Lierman, J. (2004), *The New Testament Moses: Christian Perceptions of Moses and Israel in the Setting of Jewish Religion*, WUNT 2/173, Tübingen: Mohr Siebeck.

Lohfink, N. (1968), *The Christian Meaning of the Old Testament*, tr. R. A. Wilson, Milwaukee: Bruce.

Longman III, T. (2001), *Immanuel in Our Place: Seeing Christ in Israel's Worship*, Phillipsburg: P&R.

McCann, J. C. (1993), *The Shape and Shaping of the Psalter*, JSOTSup 159, Sheffield: JSOT Press.

McConville, J. G. (1994), 'Abraham and Melchizedek: Horizons in Genesis 14', in R. S. Hess, G. J. Wenham and P. E. Satterthwaite (eds.), *He Swore an Oath: Biblical Themes from Genesis 12–50*, Eugene: Wipf & Stock, 93–118.

McKelvey, R. J. (2013), *Pioneer and Priest: Jesus Christ in the Epistle to the Hebrews*, Eugene: Wipf & Stock.

Mackie, S. D. (2007), *Eschatology and Exhortation in the Epistle to the Hebrews*, WUNT 2/223, Tübingen: Mohr Siebeck.

Malone, A. S. (2017), *God's Mediators: A Biblical Theology of Priesthood*, NSBT 43, London; Apollos; Downers Grove: InterVarsity Press.

Mann, T. W. (1977), *Divine Presence and Guidance in Israelite Traditions: The Typology of Exaltation*, Baltimore: Johns Hopkins University Press.

Manzi, F. (1997), *Melchisedek e l'angelologia nell'Epistola agli Ebrei e a Qumran*, AnBib 136, Rome: Pontificio Istituto Biblico.

Marcus, J. (1992), *The Way of the Lord: Christological Exegesis of the Old Testament in the Gospel of Mark*, Louisville: Westminster John Knox.

—— (2000), *Mark 1–8: A New Translation with Introduction and Commentary*, New York: Doubleday.

Martínez, F. G. (1996), *The Dead Sea Scrolls Translated: The Qumran Texts in English*, 2nd edn, Grand Rapids: Eerdmans.

Mason, E. (2008), *'You Are a Priest Forever': Second Temple Jewish Messianism and the Priestly Christology of the Epistle to the Hebrews*, Leiden: Brill.

Mathews, D. (2012), *Royal Motifs in the Pentateuchal Portrayal of Moses*, LHBOTS 571, New York: T&T Clark.

Mathews, J. G. (2013), *Melchizedek's Alternative Priestly Order: A Compositional Analysis of Genesis 14:18–20 and Its Echoes throughout the Tanak*, BBRSup 8, Winona Lake: Eisenbrauns.

Mathews, K. A. (1996), *Genesis 1–11:26*, NAC 1A, Nashville: Broadman & Holman.

Meade, J. (2008), 'The Meaning of Circumcision in Israel: A Proposal for a Transfer of Rite from Egypt to Israel', *Adorare Mente* 1: 14–29.

Meier, J. P. (1985a), 'Structure and Theology in Heb 1:1–14', *Bib* 66.2: 168–189.

—— (1985b), 'Symmetry and Theology in the Old Testament Citations of Heb 1:5–14', *Bib* 66.4: 504–533.

Merrill, E. H. (1993), 'Royal Priesthood: An Old Testament Messianic Motif', *BSac* 150: 50–61.

—— (2008), *Kingdom of Priests: A History of Old Testament Israel*, Grand Rapids: Baker Academic.

Mettinger, T. N. D. (1976), *King and Messiah: The Civil and Sacral Legitimation of the Israelite Kings*, Lund: CWK Gleerup.

Middleton, J. R. (2005), *The Liberating Image: The Imago Dei in Genesis 1*, Grand Rapids: Brazos.

Mitchell, D. C. (1997), *The Message of the Psalter: An Eschatological Programme in the Book of Psalms*, JSOTSup 252, Sheffield: Sheffield Academic Press.

Moffitt, D. M. (2008), '"If Another Priest Arises": Jesus' Resurrection and the High Priestly Christology of Hebrews', in R. Bauckham, D. Driver, T. Hart and N. MacDonald (eds.), *A Cloud of Witnesses: The Theology of Hebrews in Its Ancient Contexts*, LNTS 387, London: T&T Clark, 68–79.

—— (2011), *Atonement and the Logic of Resurrection in the Epistle to the Hebrews*, NovTSup 141, Leiden: Brill.

Moore, N. J. (2014), 'Jesus as "The One Who Entered His Rest": The Christological Reading of Hebrews 4.10', *JSNT* 36.4: 383–400.

Morales, M. L. (2015), *Who Shall Ascend the Mountain of the Lord? A Biblical Theology of the Book of Leviticus*, NSBT 37, Nottingham: Apollos; Downers Grove: InterVarsity Press.

Mowinckel, S. (2004), *The Psalms in Israel's Worship*, tr. D. R. Ap-Thomas, Grand Rapids: Eerdmans.

Muir, Steven (2008), 'The Anti-Imperial Rhetoric of Hebrews 1.3: χαρακτὴρ as a "Double-Edged Sword"', in R. Bauckham, D. Driver, T. Hart and N. MacDonald (eds.), *A Cloud of Witnesses: The Theology of Hebrews in Its Ancient Contexts*, LNTS 387, London: T&T Clark, 170–186.

Nel, P. J. (1996), 'Psalm 110 and the Melchizedek Tradition', *JNSL* 22.1: 1–14.

Nelson, R. D. (1981), 'Josiah in the Book of Joshua', *JBL* 100.4: 531–540.

—— (1993), *Raising Up a Faithful Priest: Community and Priesthood in Biblical Theology*, Louisville: John Knox.

Nickelsburg, G. W. E. (1981), *Jewish Literature between the Bible and the Mishnah: A Historical and Literary Introduction*, Philadelphia: Fortress.

O'Brien, P. T. (2010), *The Letter to the Hebrews*, Pillar New Testament Commentary, Grand Rapids: Eerdmans.

—— (2011), 'God as the Speaking God: "Theology" in the Letter to the Hebrews', in A. J. Köstenberger and R. W. Yarbrough (eds.), *Understanding the Times: New Testament Studies in the 21st Century: Essays in Honor of D. A. Carson on the Occasion of His 65th Birthday*, Wheaton: Crossway, 196–216.

Orlov, A. A. (2007), 'The Heir of Righteousness and the King of Righteousness: The Priestly Noachic Polemics in 2 Enoch and the Epistle to the Hebrews', *JTS* 58.1: 45–65.

Ounsworth, R. (2012), *Joshua Typology in the New Testament*, WUNT 328, Tübingen: Mohr Siebeck.

Owens, D. C. (2013), 'The Concept of Canon in Psalms Interpretation', *TJ* 34.2: 155–69.

Park, S. J. (2011), 'Melchizedek as a Covenantal Figure: The Biblical Theology of the Eschatological Royal Priesthood', *Bible.org*, <https://bible.org/article/melchizedek-covenantal-figure-biblical-theology-eschatological-royal-priesthood>, accessed 3 March 2014.

Paul, M. J. (1987), 'The Order of Melchizedek (Ps 110:4 and Heb 7:3)', *WTJ* 49.1: 195–211.

Payne, J. B. (1962), *The Theology of the Older Testament*, Grand Rapids: Zondervan.

Peeler, A. L. B. (2014), *You Are My Son: The Family of God in the Epistle to the Hebrews*, LNTS 486, New York: Bloomsbury T&T Clark.

Pennington, J. T. (2007), *Heaven and Earth in the Gospel of Matthew*, NovTSup 126, Leiden: Brill.

Perrin, N. (2010), *Jesus the Temple*, Grand Rapids: Baker Academic.

—— (2013), 'The Temple, a Davidic Messiah, and a Case of Mistaken Priestly Identity (Mark 2:26)', in D. M. Gurtner and B. L. Gladd (eds.), *From Creation to New Creation: Biblical Theology and Exegesis*, Peabody: Hendrickson, 163–177.

—— (2019), *Jesus the Priest*, Grand Rapids: Baker Academic.

Peterson, D. (1982), *Hebrews and Perfection: An Examination of the Concept of Perfection in the 'Epistle to the Hebrews'*, New York: Cambridge University Press.

—— (2020), *Hebrews: An Introduction and Commentary*, vol. 15, ed. E. J. Schnabel, TNTC, London: Inter-Varsity Press; Downers Grove: IVP Academic.

Philo (1993a), 'De Specialibus Legibus', in *The Works of Philo*, tr. C. D. Yonge, Peabody: Hendrickson.

—— (1993b), 'De Vita Mosis', in *The Works of Philo*, tr. C. D. Yonge, Peabody: Hendrickson.

Porter, J. R. (2000), 'The Succession of Joshua', in G. N. Knoppers and J. G. McConville (eds.), *Reconsidering Israel and Judah: Recent Studies on the Deuteronomistic History*, Sources for Biblical and Theological Study, Winona Lake: Eisenbrauns, 139–162.

Rad, G. von (1962), *Old Testament Theology: The Theology of Israel's Historical Traditions*, vol. 1, tr. D. M. Stalker, New York: Harper & Row.

Rainbow, P. A. (1997), 'Melchizedek as a Messiah at Qumran', *BBR* 7: 179–194.

Rendsberg, G. A. (1999), 'Psalm CX 3B', *VT* 49.4: 548–553.

Rendtorff, R. (1986), *The Old Testament: An Introduction*, Philadelphia: Fortress.

Ribbens, B. J. (2011), 'Typology and Types: Typology in Dialogue', *JTI* 5.1: 81–96.

Richardson, C. A. (2012), *Pioneer and Perfecter of Faith: Jesus' Faith as the Climax of Israel's History in the Epistle to the Hebrews*, WUNT 338, Tübingen: Mohr Siebeck.

Robertson, O. P. (1981), *The Christ of the Covenants*, Grand Rapids: P&R.

Rooke, D. W. (1998), 'Kingship as Priesthood: The Relationship between the High Priesthood and the Monarchy', in J. Day (ed.), *King and Messiah in Israel and the Ancient Near East*, JSOTSup 270, Sheffield: Sheffield Academic Press, 187–208.

—— (2000), 'Jesus as Royal Priest: Reflections on the Interpretation of the Melchizedek Tradition in Heb 7', *Bib* 81.1: 81–94.

Rosner, B. S. (2000), 'Biblical Theology', *NDBT*, 3–11.

Routledge, R. L. (2009), 'Psalm 110, Melchizedek and David: Blessing (the Descendants of) Abraham', *Baptistic Theologies* 1.2: 1–16.

Rowe, R. D. (2002), *God's Kingdom and God's Son: The Background in Mark's Christology from Concepts of Kingship in the Psalms*, Boston: Brill.

Rowley, H. H. (1950), 'Melchizedek and Zadok (Gen 14 and Ps 110)', in W. Baumgartner (ed.), *Festschrift: Alfred Bertholet zum 80. Geburtstag*, Tübingen: Mohr Siebeck, 461–472.

Sailhamer, J. H. (2009), *The Meaning of the Pentateuch: Revelation, Composition and Interpretation*, Downers Grove: IVP Academic.

Schachter, L. (2013), 'The Garden of Eden as God's First Sanctuary', *JBQ* 41.2: 73–77.

Schenck, K. L. (2010), *Cosmology and Eschatology in Hebrews: The Settings of the Sacrifice*, Cambridge: Cambridge University Press.

Schmidt, W. H. (1983), *The Faith of the Old Testament: A History*, tr. J. Sturdy, Philadelphia: Westminster.

—— (2015), *Commentary on Hebrews*, Biblical Theology for Christian Proclamation, Nashville: B&H.

Schreiner, T. R. (2013), *The King in His Beauty: A Biblical Theology of the Old and New Testaments*, Grand Rapids: Baker Academic.

Schrock, D. S. (2013), 'A Biblical-Theological Investigation of Christ's Priesthood and Covenant Mediation with Respect to the Extent of the Atonement', PhD diss., Southern Baptist Theological Seminary.

—— (2022), *The Royal Priesthood and the Glory of God*, Wheaton: Crossway.

Scobie, C. H. H. (2000), 'History of Biblical Theology', *NDBT*, 11–20.

Seow, C. L. (1989), *Myth, Drama, and the Politics of David's Dance*, Atlanta: Scholars Press.

Sequeira, A. (2014), 'Atonement and the Logic of Resurrection in the Epistle to the Hebrews (Review)', *Credo Magazine*, <www.credomag.com/2014/01/16/atonement-and-the-logic-of-resurrection-in-the-epistle-to-the-hebrews-review>, accessed 5 January 2016.

Sherman, R. (2004), *King, Priest, and Prophet: A Trinitarian Theology of Atonement*, New York: T&T Clark International.

Silva, M. (1976), 'Perfection and Eschatology in Hebrews', *WTJ* 39.1: 60–71.

Smith, G. V. (1977), 'Structure and Purpose in Genesis 1–11', *JETS* 20.4: 307–319.

Smith, R. A. (2011), 'The Royal Priesthood in Exodus 19:6: A Festschrift in Honor of James B. Jordan', in P. J. Leithart and J. Barach (eds.), *The Glory of Kings: A Festschrift in Honor of James B. Jordan*, Eugene: Pickwick, 93–111.

Stanley, S. (1994), 'The Structure of Hebrews from Three Perspectives', *TynBul* 45.2: 245–271.

Steinmetz, D. (1991), *From Father to Son: Kinship, Conflict, and Continuity in Genesis*, Louisville: Westminster John Knox.

Stek, J. H. (1970), 'Biblical Typology: Yesterday and Today', *CTJ* 5.2: 133–162.

Stewart, A. (2010), 'Cosmology, Eschatology, and Soteriology in Hebrews: A Synthetic Analysis', *BBR* 20.4: 545–560.

Treat, J. R. (2014), *The Crucified King: Atonement and Kingdom in Biblical and Systematic Theology*, Grand Rapids: Zondervan.

Treves, M. (1965), 'Two Acrostic Psalms', *VT* 15.1: 81–90.

VanGemeren, W. A. (2008), *Psalms*, EBC 5, ed. T. Longman III and D. E. Garland, rev. edn, Grand Rapids: Zondervan.

Vannoy, R. J. (2007), 'Kingship and Covenant in 1 and 2 Samuel', in H. Griffith and J. R. Muether (eds.), *Creator, Redeemer, Consummator: A Festschrift for Meredith G. Kline*, Eugene: Wipf & Stock, 65–75.

Vickers, B. (2004), 'Mark's Good News of the Kingdom of God', *SBJT* 8.3: 12–35.

Wallace, D. (2003), 'The Use of Psalms in the Shaping of a Text: Psalm 2:7 and Psalm 110:1 in Hebrews 1', *ResQ* 45.1–2: 41–50.

Wallace, R. (2014), 'Gerald Wilson and the Characterization of David in Book 5 of the Psalter', in Nancy L. DeClaissé-Walford (ed.), *The Shape and Shaping of the Book of Psalms: The Current State of Scholarship*, Ancient Israel and Its Literature 20, Atlanta: SBL Press, 193–208.

Waltke, B. K. (2008), 'Psalm 110: An Exegetical and Canonical Approach', in L. G. Tipton and J. C. Waddington (eds.), *Resurrection and Eschatology: Theology in Service of the Church: Essays in Honor of Richard B. Gaffin, Jr.*, Phillipsburg: P&R, 60–85.

Waltke, B. K., and C. J. Fredricks (2001), *Genesis: A Commentary*, Grand Rapids: Zondervan.

Waltke, B. K., and M. O'Connor (1990), *An Introduction to Biblical Hebrew Syntax*, Winona Lake: Eisenbrauns.

Walton, J. H. (2001), *Genesis*, NIVAC, Grand Rapids: Zondervan.

—— (2003), 'Eden, Garden of', in T. D. Alexander and D. W. Baker (eds.), *DOTP*, Leicester: Inter-Varsity Press; Downers Grove: InterVarsity Press, 202–207.

Watts, R. E. (2000), *Isaiah's New Exodus in Mark*, Grand Rapids: Baker.

—— (2004), 'The Psalms in Mark's Gospel', in S. Moyise and M. J. J. Menken (eds.), *The Psalms in the New Testament*, London: T&T Clark International, 25–45.

—— (2007), 'The Lord's House and David's Lord: The Psalms and Mark's Perspective on Jesus and the Temple', *BibInt* 15.3: 307–322.

Weinfeld, M. (1981), 'Sabbath, Temple, and the Enthronement of the Lord: The Problem of the "Sitz im Leben" of Genesis 1:1–2:3', in A. Caquot and M. Delcor (eds.), *Mélanges bibliques et orientaux en l'honneur de M. Henri Cazelles*, Kevelaer: Butzon & Bercker, 501–512.

—— (1983), 'Zion and Jerusalem as Religious and Political Capital: Ideology and Utopia', in R. E. Friedman (ed.), *The Poet and the Historian: Essays in Literary and Historical Biblical Criticism*, Chico: Scholars Press, 75–115.

Wellum, S. J. (2013), 'The New Covenant Work of Christ: Priesthood, Atonement, and Intercession', in D. Gibson and J. Gibson (eds.), *From Heaven He Came and Sought Her: Definite Atonement in Historical, Biblical, Theological, and Pastoral Perspective*, Wheaton: Crossway, 517–540.

—— (2016), *God the Son Incarnate: The Doctrine of Christ*, Foundations of Evangelical Theology, Wheaton: Crossway.

Wenham, G. J. (1987), *Genesis 1–15*, WBC 1, Waco: Thomas Nelson.

—— (1994), 'Sanctuary Symbolism in the Garden of Eden Story', in R. S. Hess and D. T. Tsumura (eds.), *I Studied Inscriptions from Before the Flood: Ancient Near Eastern, Literary, and Linguistic Approaches to Genesis 1–11*, Winona Lake: Eisenbrauns, 399–404.

—— (1995), 'The Theology of Old Testament Sacrifice', in R. T. Beckwith and M. J. Selman (eds.), *Sacrifice in the Bible*, Grand Rapids: Baker, 75–87.

—— (1997), 'Flood', *NIDOTTE*, vol. 4, 460–462.

Whitfield, B. J. (2008), 'Pioneer and Perfecter: Joshua Traditions and the Christology of Hebrews', in R. Bauckham, D. Driver, T. Hart and N. MacDonald (eds.), *A Cloud of Witnesses: The Theology of Hebrews in Its Ancient Contexts*, LNTS 387, London: T&T Clark, 80–87.

—— (2013), *Joshua Traditions and the Argument of Hebrews 3 and 4*, Boston: De Gruyter.

Whybray, N. (1996), *Reading the Psalms as a Book*, JSOTSup 222, Sheffield: Sheffield Academic Press.

Widengren, G. (1957), 'King and Covenant', *JSS* 2.1: 1–32.

Wildberger, H. (1997), 'צֶלֶם *ṣelem* Image', in E. Jenni and C. Westermann (eds.), *Theological Lexicon of the Old Testament*, tr. M. E. Biddle, Peabody: Hendrickson, 1080–1085.

Williamson, H. G. M. (1976), 'The Accession of Solomon in the Books of Chronicles', *VT* 26.3: 351–361.

Williamson, P. R. (2007), *Sealed with an Oath: Covenant in God's Unfolding Purpose*, NSBT 23, Nottingham: Apollos; Downers Grove: InterVarsity Press.

Woude, A. S. van der (1965), 'Melchisedek als himmlische Erlösergestalt in den neugefundenen eschatologischen Midraschim aus Qumran Höhle XI', *Oudtestamentlich Werkgezelschap in Nederland* 25: 354–373.

Wright, N. T. (1993), *The Climax of the Covenant: Christ and the Law in Pauline Theology*, Minneapolis: Fortress.

—— (1995), *Following Jesus: Biblical Reflections on Discipleship*, Grand Rapids: Eerdmans.

—— (1997), *Jesus and the Victory of God*, Christian Origins and the Question of God 2, Minneapolis: Fortress.

Zenger, E. (ed.), (2010), *Composition of the Book of Psalms*, BETL 238, Leuven: Uitgeverij Peeters.

Index of authors

Index of Scripture references

Index of ancient sources

Titles in this series:

An index of Scripture references for all the volumes may be found at http://www.thegospelcoalition.org/resources/nsbt.